BLOCK PARTIES

Block Parties examines young children's spatial development through the lens of emergent STEAM thinking. This book explores the physical and psychological tools that children use when they engage in constructive free play, and how these tools contribute to and shape the constructions they produce. Providing readers with the tools and understanding necessary to develop children's spatial sense through the domains of mapping and architecture, this cutting-edge volume lays the groundwork for both cognitive development and early childhood specialists and educators to develop more robust models of STEAM-related curriculum that span the early years through to adolescence.

Daniel Ness is Professor of Curriculum and Instruction at St. John's University, USA.

BLOCK PARTIES

Identifying Emergent STEAM Thinking Through Play

Daniel Ness

Routledge
Taylor & Francis Group
NEW YORK AND LONDON

First published 2022
by Routledge
605 Third Avenue, New York, NY 10158

and by Routledge
2 Park Square, Milton Park, Abingdon, Oxon OX14 4RN

Routledge is an imprint of the Taylor & Francis Group, an informa business

© 2022 Daniel Ness

The right of Daniel Ness to be identified as author of this work has been asserted by him in accordance with sections 77 and 78 of the Copyright, Designs and Patents Act 1988.

All rights reserved. No part of this book may be reprinted or reproduced or utilised in any form or by any electronic, mechanical, or other means, now known or hereafter invented, including photocopying and recording, or in any information storage or retrieval system, without permission in writing from the publishers.

Trademark notice: Product or corporate names may be trademarks or registered trademarks, and are used only for identification and explanation without intent to infringe.

Library of Congress Cataloging-in-Publication Data
A catalog record for this title has been requested

ISBN: 9780367564452 (hbk)
ISBN: 9780367562557 (pbk)
ISBN: 9781003097815 (ebk)

DOI: 10.4324/9781003097815

Typeset in Bembo
by Taylor & Francis Books

To my son, Eric—STEAM player par excellence!

CONTENTS

List of illustrations		*viii*
Acknowledgments		*x*
	Introduction	1
1	Discovering STEAM in the Early Years	6
2	Play Matters	35
3	Blocks, Bricks, and Planks: Visuospatial Constructive Play Objects	54
4	Simple VCPOs Are Best	96
5	Young Children Think Like Scientists and Mathematicians	114
6	Young Children Think Like Architects and Engineers	135
7	Coding STEAM during Constructive Free Play	169
8	Promoting STEAM Play with VCPOs: What Children Can Tell Us	184
	Appendix A: Inquiry Indicators for Early Childhood STEAM	*199*
	Appendix B: Constructive Materials Play Attitude Scale—CoMPAS	*204*
	Appendix C: Constructive Play Materials Inventory—Parents (CPMI-P)	*208*
	Index	*217*

ILLUSTRATIONS

Figures

1.1	Wooden pieces of "track," support blocks, and landscape blocks in Nate's roller coaster structure	7
1.2	Sequence of events relating to Nat's removal of a piece of "landscape" (dashed lines indicate chronological sequence)	9
1.3	Nate's roller coaster structure and platform	11
1.4	Kathryn's architectural structure	16
1.5	Cross-section of a bent sponge	23
4.1	Representation of empirical, pseudo-empirical, and reflective abstractions	99
5.1	Proto-STEAM experience model	125
6.1	Progression of the young child's development of VCPO constructions schematic	145
6.2	Kathryn's structure	147
6.3	Kathryn's foundation	147
6.4	An engineer's raft foundation	148
6.5	Image of Gabe's structure	148
6.6	Instability of a structure due to wind	149
6.7	Simply supported beam with pressure being exerted downward	152
6.8	The deflection of the loaded tip of the cantilevered ruler	153
6.9	Alejandro's structural base	154
6.10	The second level to Alejandro's structure	154

6.11	The post-and-lintel foundation system: the "simplest framed system"	155
6.12	Alejandro and Karl's structure with a second floor construction	158
6.13	Lintels are supported by vertical columns	158
6.14	Anna's plank foundation	161
6.15	Border construction using planks	162
6.16	Anna's use of planks to construct cantilevers	163
6.17	Anna's cantilevered structure in progress	163
6.18	Anna's nearly completed structure	164
7.1	Spatial Architectural Coding (SPARC) system (formerly, the Spatial-Geometric-Architectural (SPAGAR) Categories)	180

Tables

1.1	Evidence of engineering thinking by Jamie, Pat, and Tyler using factors, evidence, and examples	21
5.1	Concepts and process skills learned through kite building	120
7.1	The SPAGAR and SPARC coding systems	172
8.1	Alignment of protobehaviors with basic process skills and basic process skills with complex process skills	191

ACKNOWLEDGMENTS

In many ways, acknowledgments sections of books and related publications serve as the bedrock of any literary production because without certain people in the author's life, none of the book's success would come to fruition. In this regard, I would like to thank several individuals whose presence in my life has served as my rock—ο πέτρα μου—which has supported me through thick and thin and in my thirst for knowledge.

To begin, I wish to thank the editors at Routledge who have made the production process of this book—from initial conception to the final product—a seemingly effortless undertaking. In particular, I thank Misha Kydd, who took time out of her busy, demanding schedule to listen to my ideas for a book on young children's STEAM cognition through the use of constructive play objects. I am also grateful to Olivia Powers, who took the mantle in shepherding the book through the editing process. I also thank Sue Cope for all her efforts in copyediting the manuscript. Our numerous across-the-pond communications were essential in producing a more concise and fluid manuscript.

My colleagues at St. John's University have been most accommodating in all my research endeavors. Thanks go to David Bell, the Dean of the School of Education. He has always found the time in his extraordinarily full calendar to champion my efforts and collaborate in a number of projects that are aimed to increase student success. I am utmost thankful to my chairperson, Xiaojun Chen, and my other colleagues in the Department of Curriculum and Instruction (in alphabetical order)—Sandra Schamroth Abrams, Liz Chase, Mike Downton, Smita Guha, Aliya Holmes, Bonnie Johnson, Elena Jurasaite O'Keefe, Em Maslak, Don McClure, Regina Mistretta, Nancy Montgomery, Nancy Morabito, Barbara Peltzman, Jannette Pincay, Mary Beth Schaefer, and Bernadette Zacharuk—for their unwavering support. My gratitude goes to Judy Mangione, Linda Miller, and Edwin Tjoe, and also to Mary Jane Krebbs, a former Associate

Dean of the School of Education and Executive Director of the Institute for Catholic Schools, an individual for whom I hold the highest admiration.

I am grateful to Joseph, my eldest brother, and Carmen Ness for always having the time to communicate with me on both high- and low-spirited occasions. They have been unrelenting in their persistence in checking up on me and encouraging me to change course whenever I have been feeling crestfallen during periods of toil, and instead, focus on positive, forward-looking, and constructive thinking.

I could not have completed this book without the resolute guidance of my great friend and colleague, Stephen Farenga. Ever since I was a greenhorn in academe and professional life in general, Steve has served as both my research- and practitioner-based mentor as well as a beacon in all my intellectual endeavors—always inspiring me to think of the glass half-full. Without our esprit de corps, I would have never become a successful university professor or gained expertise in STEAM teaching and learning.

Lastly, there are few, if any, words that express my indebtedness to my family for their immense love and support. My wife, Chia-ling Lin, and I met in graduate school. I will never forget the day that she suggested we enroll in a cognition course in developmental psychology. Her suggestion prompted me to pursue the topic of the development of mathematical thinking as a life-long interest. Her mom, Helen, is extremely special to me—her presence is always one of endless adoration and generosity. Chia-ling and Helen have always gone exceedingly out of their way to contend with others' needs, like mine, at the expense of their own essentials and pursuits. I cannot repay them enough for their ineffable and altruistic qualities. And last but not least, none of my inspiration would have been possible without the company and companionship of my son, Eric—my everlasting light.

INTRODUCTION

Block Parties: Identifying Emergent STEAM Thinking through Play has to do with finding approaches that enable researchers and practitioners in education and developmental psychology to identify, recognize, and appreciate emergent science, technology, engineering, arts (and architecture!), and mathematics (STEAM) in children's constructive free play when they manipulate visuospatial constructive play objects (VCPOs), which include play blocks, bricks, and planks. Why the title *Block Parties*? When children—and adults—build structures out of blocks (which we will see in Chapter 3 are part of the umbrella term—visuospatial constructive play objects, or VCPOs), they do so with two intentions, as recent neuroscientific research explains to us: they construct objects with the purpose of location also in mind. That is, they construct objects—architectural thinking—with an intention of placement of that object—mapping development. A wonderful example of this phenomenon is summed up in the following scenario involving two four-and-a-half-year-old children and their preschool teacher Ms. Kirby. The children have constructed a large, complex, and intricate block structure and Ms. Kirby asks the following question:

MS. KIRBY: What are you building?
KARL: It's a garage house.
MS. KIRBY: A garage is a house, but it's a house for cars.
KARL: Okay ….

Our instinct as adults—those who might work as researchers or educational practitioners as well as parents—is to ask the child what the structure is that has been constructed. Perhaps a better question should be multipartite: 1) What are you building? 2) How did you construct it? 3) Why did you build it in its current

DOI: 10.4324/9781003097815-1

location? This sentiment makes me think of the well-known, Nobel prize-winning physicist and professor at the California Institute of Technology, Richard Feynman, who reflected and commented on his early childhood and the types of questions that his parents would ask him as they walked in their neighborhood. As we shall encounter in Chapter 5, Feynman emphasized the importance of cognizing the ontological and epistemological underpinnings of specific phenomena and not merely acquiring lower-order knowledge, such as labeling or identifying, that can be learned by rote. Unfortunately, all too often, schooling throughout the world, from preschool through college, has emphasized the latter—to the point that students become jaded when a topic or concept in STEAM is even mentioned. So, our goal in this book is to recognize and appreciate emergent STEAM concepts that we, as adults, can identify as we observe young children in constructive free play environments. The idea of *Block Parties,* then, can take on multiple meanings: fun with blocks or block-like pieces, constructions that are defined by their location with respect to other objects that were either constructed or are present in the room (a chair, table, desk, and the like). In short, when we develop our architectural ideas, we do so with place, or topos, in mind.

To begin, I discuss the unique and relatively lacking topic of the mutual and synergistic development of architectural thinking and the development of mapping concepts in Chapter 1. To this end, we learn about *cartotecture,* which is a portmanteau of the words "cartography" and "architecture." While both cartography, mapping, and mapmaking, and architecture, structural design, and considerations have found their cognitive home in the realms of spatial thinking and spatial perception, the two domains are not necessarily mutually exclusive areas of inquiry. Moreover, in terms of child development, emergent mapping (Liben & Downs, 1989; Yuan, Uttal & Gentner, 2017) and architectural concepts (Ness, 2001; Ness & Farenga, 2007; Ness, Farenga & Garofalo, 2017) develop simultaneously and along the same lines. In this regard, few, if any, studies, let alone monographs, have considered the intertwined developmental roles of these cognitive processes in the course of human development. In Chapter 2, I delineate a brief history of play, focusing on constructive free play—the environment that best suits our purpose of studying the development of STEAM cognition. We will also examine contemporary play models, such as Playworlds, so that we can consider a wider array of play settings.

Chapter 3 is all about what we use to construct objects or models of larger things in the real world. Just about any internet search using "block" or "brick" as a keyword will yield a cacophony of search results: Common results include, but are not limited to, topics in masonry, economics, educational programs, building materials, and, yes, play. The only problem with the "play" search findings is the plethora of LEGO brand books or those whose authors suggest, or even worse, prescribe what adults should do as children engage with blocks or bricks in the constructive free-play environment or what this environment should look like. Seldom will one interested in the historical, cognitive, and sociological implications of blocks, bricks, planks, and related VCPOs find what they are looking for. This is unfortunate for a number of reasons. First, and perhaps foremost, the lack of a critical examination of VCPOs leads one to tacitly and putatively believe that all constructive free-play objects serve as a windfall for developing cognitive and social interactive skills. It is important to note that, for reasons discussed in this book, this is by no means always the case. Second, emphasis solely on blocks and bricks has the potential to have us detract from our knowledge of the diversity of VCPOs. More specifically, we need to consider planks and their possible connection with young children's intellectual development. Third, the lack of focus on critical examination of VCPOs fosters corporate interests that emphasize market success, which undermines the cognitive, social, and emotional development and success of the child.

Chapter 4 examines VCPOs from the standpoint of object affordance. The basic premise, then, is this: Not all bricks are helpful in stimulating inquiry or increasing levels of cognitive development. Chapters 5 and 6 examine young children's emergent STEAM concepts through engagement in constructive free play. Chapter 5 focuses on the development of scientific, mathematical, and technological thinking, while Chapter 6 addresses the development of architectural and engineering thinking. What do young children do with VCPOs? And how do their constructions reflect the processes and products of professional architects and STEAM professionals? We will answer these and other important questions. More specifically, Chapters 5 and 6 reconsider children's developmental stages from the perspective of changes that occur during spontaneous constructive free play. In Chapter 7, I introduce readers to and consider and examine the Spatial Architectural Coding (SPARC) System (formerly SPAGAR) (Ness & Farenga, 2016). The goal of this chapter is to provide a means by which the practitioner or researcher can code young children's spatial behaviors as they relate to their developing STEAM thinking. Both researchers and practitioners will find SPARC useful. Researchers will be able to use SPARC as a means of developing knowledge concerning young children's spatial development in particular domains. Practitioners will have the opportunity to implement SPARC as a means of understanding their young students' propensities in emergent STEAM subjects. In Chapter 8, I stress the importance of teamwork. As adults, we can garner a lot of knowledge of young children's spatial thinking skills in STEAM during solitary free play. But just think of how much more we can learn by observing children in collaborative constructive free play. In this regard, I present the analogy of STEAM professionals working together to pursue a common end that is intended to improve societal needs. I end the chapter by providing the reader with two additional tools that I created and developed for the purpose of further research and exploration in emergent STEAM thinking.

Before we embark on our adventure, it is essential to define certain terms that are indispensable to the study of constructive play materials and how they intersect with spatial development and emergent STEAM concepts.

Cognitive ability: One's reasoning about knowledge and tacit or explicit levels of knowing about something (Hofer & Pintrich, 1997).

Creativity: A dynamic process that involves motivation for the purpose of synthesizing or engineering a material thing (e.g., suspension bridge, motor vehicle, log cabin, screw) or a work that involves semiotic constructs (e.g., poem, musical composition, novel, essay) (Amabile & Pillemer, 2012).

Spatial thinking: One's ability to perceive, recognize, or conceptualize physical or intellectual constructs in terms of their position or location in both static and dynamic systems (Ness et al., 2017).

STEAM: An acronym that stands for science, technology, engineering, arts (architecture included), and mathematics. This acronym is a modification of the original acronym STEM, which left out the "A," namely, the arts and architectural component. The addition of Arts in the original STEM seems to have emerged during the onset of the Obama administration and its push to make STEM more interconnected by including a domain that emphasizes creativity and imagination—two areas that STEM and the arts have in common.

Visuospatial constructive play object (VCPO): Any object that can be stacked, connected, or juxtaposed with another similar object for the purpose of developing or creating a larger structure. These objects are most often used during the individual's times of initiative, motivation, perseverance, and self-expression (Ness & Farenga, 2016).

So, I welcome you, the reader, on this most important voyage that encourages you to consider the ever-increasing research-based evidence that suggests how precocious young children actually are in emergent STEAM concepts if they are provided with environments that are conducive to spontaneous constructive free play with the most beneficial VCPOs. I look forward to this journey as I hope you will too.

Daniel Ness
New York, NY

References

Amabile, T. M., & Pillemer, J. (2012). Perspectives on the social psychology of creativity. *The Journal of Creative Behavior*, 46(1), 3–15.

Hofer, B. K., & Pintrich, P. R. (1997). The development of epistemological theories: Beliefs about knowledge and knowing and their relation to learning. *Review of Educational Research*, 67(1), 88–140.

Liben, L. S., & Downs, R. M. (1989). Understanding maps as symbols: The development of map concepts in children. In H. W. Reese (Ed.), *Advances in child development and behavior* (pp. 145–201). New York: Academic Press.

Ness, D. (2001). The development of spatial thinking, emergent geometric concepts and architectural principles in the everyday context. Doctoral dissertation, Columbia University, New York.

Ness, D., & Farenga, S. J. (2007). *Knowledge under construction: The importance of play in developing children's spatial and geometric thinking.* Lanham, MD: Rowman & Littlefield Publishers.

Ness, D., & Farenga, S. J. (2016). Blocks, bricks, and planks: Relationships between affordance and visuospatial constructive play objects. *American Journal of Play*, 8(2), 201–227.

Ness, D., Farenga, S. J., & Garofalo, S. G. (2017). *Spatial intelligence: Why it matters from birth through the lifespan.* New York: Routledge.

Yuan, L., Uttal, D., & Gentner, D. (2017). Analogical processes in children's understanding of spatial representations. *Developmental Psychology*, 53(6), 1098–1114.

1
DISCOVERING STEAM IN THE EARLY YEARS

> The true poem is the poet's mind; the true ship is the shipbuilder. In the [person] we should see the reason for the last flourish and tendril of [her/his] work.
>
> Ralph Waldo Emerson

YOUNG CHILDREN AS ACTIVE AGENTS OF STEAM

Nate, 5 years and 1 month of age, attends a preschool in an urban community for both low-income and middle-income families. He thus has the opportunity to interact with a diverse group of children and benefit from the many resources afforded by the preschool. On the surface, Nate certainly has his share of confidantes on the one hand and adversaries on the other. But what makes Nate unique is that he is able to express his spatial and cartographic ability and architectural prowess with minimal interaction with peers.

While looking for more logs in the bins, Nate stumbles upon two wooden pieces of railroad track. Although these pieces are attachable, Nate does not connect the pieces immediately. Through trial and error, Nate finally attaches the two pieces of track (Track 1 and Track 2). He places this track on a section of the classroom floor where he can work.

After placing the initial connected pieces of track on the floor, Nate returns to the block cabinets. He is stationary for approximately 30 seconds. He appears to be in deep thought. Instead of taking more pieces of track, Nate takes two cylinder blocks and two indented arch blocks, and brings the four pieces to the floor area where he is about to work. Nate then picks up an undulated, as opposed to flat, track piece (Track 3) that is lying on the floor near his work area, and attaches it to the two initial pieces. The piece is undulating in that it curves in a vertical

DOI: 10.4324/9781003097815-2

Discovering STEAM in the Early Years   7

fashion—like in the form of a hill—and not as a flat, non-bending curve. Subsequently, he takes a small flat, curvilinear piece of track, which curves in a horizontal manner, and attempts to attach it to the undulated track piece. Nate says "Hi" to José, one of the teachers' aides. Given that one end of the unfinished track system is left suspended in mid-air, Nate takes a unit block that had been also lying nearby, and places it under the suspended track, and uses the unit block as a support, or foundation, for the suspended part of the track system. Initially, he is unsuccessful in supporting the track, because the positioning of the unit block (large face down) left a gap so that the track remained suspended. Nate turns the unit block (medium face down), and at this point, he successfully supports the track with the block. To get a better idea of the types of visuospatial constructive play objects (VCPOs) (Ness & Farenga, 2016) Nate uses for his make-believe roller coaster, see Figure 1.1. (See Chapter 3 for a more complete definition of VCPOs.)

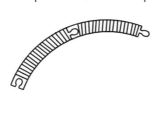

a)

b) Cylinder Block   c) Arched Unit Block   d) Unilaterally Curved Block

e) Half Unit Block

f) Single Unit Block

g) Double Unit Block

h) Quadruple Unit Block

FIGURE 1.1 Wooden pieces of "track," support blocks, and landscape blocks in Nate's roller coaster structure

> Nate returns to the block cabinets and bins to search for more track. He pauses, again in deep thought, for approximately 30 seconds. Finally, he finds a fifth piece of track—flat track. Before he connects this flat track, he knows that he needs another support. Nate reaches into a nearby cabinet, and does not find a block to his liking. He then finds a unit block nearby on the floor, which seems to work as a support. There is a problem however: The space underneath the track does not allow the supporting block to be positioned in the direction he had intended—i.e., in the same direction as the track. So, Nate turns the supporting unit block approximately 45 degrees so that it fits in the narrow space. In doing so, Nate attempts to support the joint between Track 1 and Track 2 using the unit block placed in a 45-degree position. He realizes however that the weight of Track 2 will not be fully supported. Nate then pulls the unit block out. But this is only temporary, because the real obstacle for Nate is the first of 13 quadruple blocks that are touching and placed parallel to each other. The quadruple block is the longest piece in the standard block set. Other blocks include double unit blocks (half the size of quadruple unit blocks), unit blocks (quarter the size of the quadruple), and half unit blocks, which are one-eighth the size of quadruple blocks (see Kathryn's case study below and Figure 1.4 for a more elaborate description of block sizes). This group of quadruple blocks is referred to here as the "landscape," for it serves as one part of the structure's ground setting—the other being the floor. So, Nate removes the first quadruple block, so that the supporting unit block could be positioned in the direction that he initially planned. The supporting unit block is placed in the original position and Track 2 is now attached and partially supported. Track 2 is not fully supported because part of it is suspended over the "landscape"—the remaining parallel, and touching, quadruple blocks. To support the suspended track, Nate takes a unit block, and initially places it on the supporting unit block, but then realizes that this would prevent the continuation of track. He then removes it and places this small one-quarter unit block in the correct location—on the landscape as a means of supporting the suspended part of Track 2. At this point, Track 2 is successfully in place. Nate carefully inspects all the joints to ensure that they are secure. The episode ends as Nate tells one of the teachers that he is making a roller coaster: "Latucia, look [at] what I'm making! I'm making a roller coaster!"

The above episode of Nate's construction of his roller coaster structure represents a telling example of a preschool aged child who exhibits a propensity to construct like an engineer, design like an architect, and map like a navigator. But all his successes as an emergent engineer, architect, and cartographer come at the price of trial and error, perseverance, and the ability to learn from miscalculations in the construction process.

Discovering STEAM in the Early Years

One major element of Nate's episode has to do with the way in which the boy grapples with physical obstacles that seem to frustrate the continuation of the roller coaster system. The obstacle issue arises as Nate takes a unit block on the floor and attempts to use it as a means of supporting "overhead" track, particularly the joint that connects two pieces. He deals with this situation in two ways. In the first way, Nate deals with the oncoming wooden block "landscape" (which is approximately 2 or 3 inches above the floor landscape) by turning his "material"—namely the unit block support, so that overhead track can continue onto the wooden block "landscape." This method of support could have been successful; however, Nate was still dissatisfied. He seemed wary about the positioning of the support. He then deals with the situation in a second way, one which involves the altering of the "landscape." Nate's decision to alter the landscape for the continuation of the roller coaster system is one of the several unique aspects of this videotaped segment, one that clearly demonstrates the child's knowledge of architectural principles. (See Figure 1.2 for sequence of events regarding the removal of a piece of "landscape.")

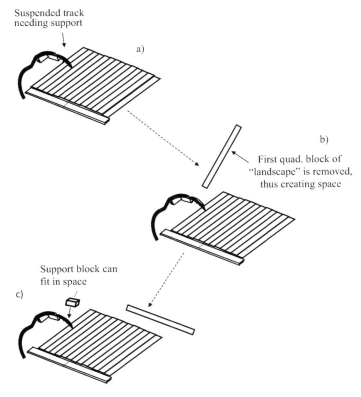

FIGURE 1.2 Sequence of events relating to Nat's removal of a piece of "landscape" (dashed lines indicate chronological sequence)

It should be noted that analysis of Nate's cognitive behaviors and his experiences with model wooden train track and wooden play blocks are based on the method of naturalistic observation. Cultivated, developed, and advanced by Lincoln and Guba (1985) and innovated by Ginsburg and his colleagues (Ginsburg, Inoue, & Seo, 1999, Ginsburg, Pappas, & Seo, 2001, Ginsburg, Lin, Ness, & Seo, 2003), naturalistic observation methodology provides the researcher and practitioner with a panoramic vista that accentuates the everyday, spontaneous emergent thinking that is made evident as the child is engaged in free play.

In one respect, naturalistic observation can be used as a means of collecting data on some aspect of cognitive or social development that is of interest to the researcher. For example, Ginsburg and colleagues (Ginsburg et al., 1999, Ginsburg et al., 2001, Ginsburg et al., 2003) were interested in identifying mathematically related activities that children have the potential to engage in during free play. They investigated the extent to which specific, individual four- and five-year-old children engaged (or did not engage) in an emergent, mathematically related activity by examining minute-by-minute segments that were part of 15-minute excerpts for each child. Moreover, they were able to study possible socioeconomic status (SES) differences in terms of time spent on one or more of six different types of emergent mathematical areas (i.e., enumeration, classification, pattern and shape, dynamics, magnitude/comparison, and spatial relations).

In addition to conducting naturalistic observation methodology for the purpose of quantitative analysis, naturalistic observation can also be extremely useful in studying spontaneous science, technology, engineering, arts/architecture, mathematics (STEAM) related activity, particularly exhibited by children who spend more than one-third of their free-play time with VCPOs. Such investigations offer what Geertz (1973) would refer to as a thick description of the goings on in the environment of the individual—in the present case, a four-and-one-half-year-old child. They can offer rich insight as to how a particular child constructs her model structure and to what extent that particular child's model structure resonates with the architect's blueprint or the cartographer's map.

Getting back to the case of Nate, we ask: How does Nate deal with the landscape? Within the context of the preschool classroom, Nate's "landscape" is the floor area of the classroom that is surrounded by the area's block cabinets. This "landscape" includes the floor itself, as well as 13 parallel, touching quadruple unit blocks whose ends are leveled by two quadruple blocks on one of the two sides (Figure 1.3).

Two types of architectural principles are evident here. First, Nate clearly shows his understanding of support, that is, the notion that overhead constructions need a form of support in order to remain standing and not fall down. He creates support (through the use of unit blocks) in the form of posting (see Chapter 6), similar to the posts or towers that support different types of bridges. Second, Nate's ability to employ techniques of engineering (another architectural principle described in Chapter 6) is exhibited in this part of the episode. This is evident

Discovering STEAM in the Early Years 11

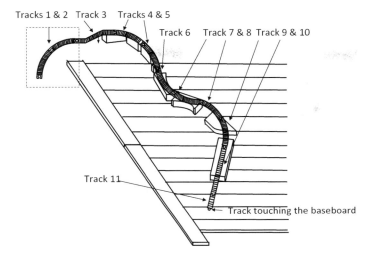

FIGURE 1.3 Nate's roller coaster structure and platform

through his seemingly skillful manipulation of the "landscape," and his method of determining whether the support block will fit between another support block and the "landscape" as a means of sustaining overhead track (informal measurement).

Although Nate has removed a piece of the "landscape," his problem of supporting the overhead track is not completely solved. This is due to the fact that the support for Track 5 on the floor is taller than the distance from the floor to the surface of the wooden block "landscape." Thus, Track 5 remains partly suspended over the "landscape." Nate seems to have learnt from past experience that a large unit block would be too large to support track suspended over the "landscape"; clearly, the suspended distance is less at this position than the suspended distance of overhead track on the floor. Accordingly, as a means of rectifying this situation, Nate takes a quarter unit block (approximately one-quarter the height of a unit block) and places it on the "landscape" for successful support.

Nate's episode should clearly demonstrate to the reader that children are active agents in their environments. Nate is actively engaged in constructive free play to the extent that—without adult interference—he can construct a large roller coaster structure that consists of track, columns that suspend the track, and a landscape that allows the track to have a starting and ending point. Moreover, the fact that Nate is engaged in free play demonstrates all the more that children possess agentive roles as they put blocks or bricks together, test and retest materials (i.e., VCPOs) to ensure strength or durability of materials, and spend long periods of time constructing their structures not solely for the ends—the products or complete constructions—in and of themselves, but also for the means—the process of construction—that lead to the ends.

In addition to being actively engaged in his constructive free play environment, Nate is engaged in STEAM. STEAM is increasingly becoming an important part of the 21st century workforce. For years, STEM learning was believed—rightly so—to help students prepare for new professional opportunities. As the editors of AllEducationSchools.com posit, the "Art" in STEAM is essential for providing students with a holistic understanding of the STEM disciplines and allows students to think critically about the sciences and engineering. It is important to note that the "A" in STEAM refers not solely to art in and of itself; it also includes the liberal arts, language arts, social studies, physical arts, fine arts, and performing arts. In terms of the main theme of this book, I would argue that "A" can also stand for architecture as one of the fundamental constructs of this discipline is aesthetics (in addition to strength and function). As is clearly pointed out in the above episode, Nate uses architecture as the thrust of what holds together his understanding of scientific laws, technological advancements, engineering principles, and mathematical ideas. STEAM can also promote children's diverse levels of creativity (Kim & Park, 2012). That the 21st century is characterized as a knowledge-based era grounded in the essentials of digitalization is even more reason why STEAM is central to what we provide for children in school.

Makerspaces are increasing dramatically with intensity as places that encourage or promote making, learning, exploring, and sharing in which the individual uses tools of various levels of technology—from no technology to the application of high-tech environments. On the website, makerspaces.com (2020), makerspaces can be places that include schools, libraries, or separate public or private facilities like museums or summer camp settings. Are makerspaces, then, places that can promote STEAM? And if so, might we include preschool children's VCPO (e.g., LEGO and block) centers in the preschool environment? The definition of makerspace clearly indicates that STEAM is an essential component of any makerspace setting (Ramey, Stevens & Uttal, 2018; Ramey & Uttal, 2017). It is also important to note that makerspaces have the potential to increase meta-disciplinary skill learning and also increase the possibilities of promoting interest and equity in STEAM (Hilton, 2010; Martin, 2015; Sheridan, et al., 2014; Vossoughi & Bevan, 2014). Moreover, VCPO centers at preschools can indeed be makerspace environments as a makerspace does not need to include elaborate technologies like 3D printers, laser cutters, cnc machines, soldering irons, sewing machines, and related equipment; clearly, makerspaces can include LEGO, blocks, planks, and other types of VCPOs that children can make, learn, explore, and share. If anything at all, the VCPO centers at preschools can serve as makerspace places for children to gather together their ideas that are represented in their VCPO models of buildings, towers, bridges, houses, dams, garages, and the like. Therefore, we can make the analogy that a young child's VCPO constructions—which are founded on STEAM principles—are like the architect's or engineer's blueprint.

Given the role of STEAM in contemporary society, it is important that we reconsider how adults construe children—not as empty vessels but as individuals who can think and be creative and can do research just like adults do. In this regard, as a way to help understand the role of children for the purpose of research, I look to Christensen and Prout's (2002) definitions that pertain to the extent to which children are positioned in research. More specifically, Christensen and Prout posit that children have been perceived in four ways in research: as objects; as subjects; as social actors; and "as participants and co-researchers" (Christensen & Prout, 2002, p. 480). The first two positions—as object and as subject—have been common threads in research since the early days of scientific research. In experimental studies throughout most of the twentieth century, children were seen and treated as objects to study in the course of which the researcher would fail to see the child as a human being with individual qualities and cognitive propensities. Instead, they were treated as beings to be acted upon.

I embrace the third and fourth positions taken up by Christensen and Prout (2002)—namely, children as social actors and "as participants and co-researchers." In the third position—children as social actors—children are represented as active and social beings who both alter and are altered by their social and cultural environments. This third perspective is one that is taken up by researchers who examine children's behaviors and actions with the premise that they are agentive beings who make their own decisions and engage in activities in an active, willful manner. The fourth perspective, children as "participants and co-researchers," also embraces the idea that children are social beings, but in this case, they are on equal terms with the researcher and should be considered as active participants in the research process. The research that is presented in this book is based on the third and fourth positions presented by Christensen and Prout.

Terms in Construction and Navigation

The above episode of Nate playing in the block area of his preschool demonstrates a young child who is engaging, through trial and error, in the process of the development of architectural and cartographic thinking. In other words, he is mapping and structuring—that is, designing the sections of his roller coaster—at the same time! Nate's scenario demonstrates a clear-cut example of what is meant by the unfolding of spatial thinking in terms of architectural development and mapping development.

Unfortunately, the research literature seems to have overlooked the simultaneousness and symbiotic relationship of the development of architectural and cartographic thinking. Prior to discussion and analysis of this important relationship that occurs as an emergent spatial thinking skill in the early years, we will need to define specific terms as they are associated with architectural thinking and mapping. In short, the purpose of defining terms in construction and navigation is to show the intrinsic connections between what professional architects and engineers do when they are engaged in the process of construction and what young children do when they engage with VCPOs as they construct their model structures. As we define these terms from an architectural or engineering perspective, we will need to consider whether or not these definitions align with, or fit within the context of, the child's experiences with the building materials that they use when constructing larger objects from VCPOs—which, once again, refer to all types of toys in the form of small pieces (i.e., in the form of blocks, bricks, planks, or non-brick related connective devices) that are used to construct larger configurations (e.g., buildings, bridges, robots, etc.). We will use Nate's roller coaster example above, along with examples from three additional free play episodes of four- and five-year-old children, to determine the alignment of architectural terms with young children's constructions.

Structure

To begin, let us consider the term "structure." As a noun, it is used by professional architects and engineers and is a common term in everyday vernacular—used by children and adults. From an engineering standpoint, "structure," according to Gordon (2009), is any of the load-carrying elements of a building, bridge, or tower. One thing that we might wish to ask is the following: Are children's VCPO constructions structures? In other words, can their VCPO constructions be considered load-carrying structures that serve as models of buildings, bridges, or towers? The answer is—it depends on the construction. In Nate's case, we are safe to say that it is a structure. Based on Figure 1.3, Nate takes a small toy car and imagines that he himself is riding a roller coaster car on his track construction. With the combination of the toy car and his hand, which he uses to ensure that the car does not derail, Nate is placing pressure onto the suspended track pieces thereby placing stress on the pieces of his construction.

We can argue, then, that Nate's construction *is* a structure. The tracks, cuboidal (i.e., rectilinear) blocks that serve as posts or columns, and the platform made from contiguous quadruple blocks (i.e., wooden play blocks that are four times the size of the standard cuboidal block) all serve as load-carrying elements—another term that we will need to define. A follow-up question, however, would be: Are all children's constructions with VCPOs considered structures? And, if not, what are they? Or we can ask—if not, should another definition of *structure* be considered in order to accommodate how children engage with VCPOs for the purpose of development and learning?

Let us take the following dialogue between Fernando and Gabe who are both building what seem to be tall constructions out of bricks. Fernando, four years, seven months, walks over to the LEGO box and takes two square LEGOs, one red and one yellow. As he returns to his construction, Gabe, another child, four years, five months, drops a tower of blocks onto his construction and says, "It broke my structure?" Fernando adds the two LEGOs and says, "Look! Look at mine. Look it, Gabe." As Fernando says this, he hits down on one end of the piece of wood and flips the LEGOs and the piece of wood off the top of his construction, accompanying this action with some kind of noise. The LEGOs fall to the floor and he mumbles something to Gabe as he picks them back up.

GABE: Can I do that?
FERNANDO: Yeah.
GABE: "Let me try [doing that] on my structure ...." [Gabe then accidentally knocks over his construction]
FERNANDO: See? Look at mine! My ... my ... mine's not breaking. You see mine? Mine's not breaking!
GABE: I broke my structure!

Based on the dialogue, is it fair to call these vertical constructions *structures*? In this short dialogue, it is not entirely clear whether Gabe and Fernando's constructions are structures according to the scientific definition of the term. That is, they were not built necessarily to accommodate load-carrying elements. Fernando uses his construction—a vertical tower-like brick figure in a dynamic manner. As indicated in the dialogue description, Fernando takes two wooden planks and places them on top of his construction. He then taps the two wooden planks to see how they flip from the top of the construction. Similarly, Gabe's construction has no load-carrying elements—his construction keeps falling over because he keeps building LEGO brick towers with a cantilever (defined below) construction, and thus lacks a gravitational center and stability.

Load and Load-Carrying Elements

An element that is load carrying is one that is under stress as a result of an external force—that is, a load—acting on it. In Nate's case above, the load-carrying elements include, but are not necessarily limited to, Tracks 1 through 11, the blocks that serve as columns that make the tracks of the make-believe roller coaster suspended over air spaces, and the platform made up of the quadruple blocks. Examples of load that are evident in Nate's case include the toy car that is placed on the track, Nate's hand, which both serves as a guide for the toy car and presses down (i.e., downward pressure) onto the toy car to ensure both lateral and up-down movement on the track, and there are even minor wind or light breezes that might be present in Nate's classroom environment. These breezes might be the result of an open window which could allow wind to enter or a breeze produced when another child runs by Nate's construction.

Structuring

Structuring is a term that we will use to define a child who is actively engaged in the construction process. In this case, we will use "structure" as a verb, that is, to build. Based on Nate's roller coaster episode, then, we would argue that Nate is

16 Discovering STEAM in the Early Years

structuring as he is constructing his model roller coaster with wooden track pieces and standard play blocks. As for Gabe and Fernando, while their constructions are not necessarily structures—given the lack of load or load-carrying elements (with the possible exception of the two plank pieces set on the top of the LEGO tower ready to be flipped)—the two children are, in fact, engaged in the structuring process. We shall see below that Kathryn, four-and-one-half years of age, also is engaged in structuring as she builds a wooden play block structure.

Beam

From a professional architect's, engineer's, or cartographer's perspective, a beam is a structural element that is subjected to transverse loading and carries load in bending. Similarly, from the perspective of the young child as architect and engineer, a beam, usually in the form of a single unit block, double unit block, or quadruple unit block, generally behaves in the same way. To illustrate beams in action as a child is structuring, we refer to Kathryn's structure (see Figure 1.4). As seen in Figure 1.4, Kathryn's structure consists of four beams—one quadruple unit block suspended above the two anchoring columns and three blocks suspended at a higher height and placed on the tops of both single and double blocks serving as columns. Her beams are subjected to loads by bending, thereby producing tension. It is hard to see actual bending or tension in a play block that serves as a beam, but it is in fact present as this serves as a principle in physics

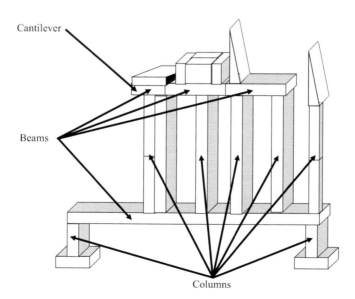

FIGURE 1.4 Kathryn's architectural structure

whether one refers to actual beams in real-world skyscrapers or other large buildings or children's play models.

Cantilever

From the point of view of the professional architect or engineer, a cantilever is a structural element that serves as a beam, which is supported at one end but not the other. Moreover, the single support must prevent the supported end of the beam from rotating. Similar to beams discussed above, cantilevers can be found in children's constructions. I have indicated above that Gabe's tower structure keeps falling down because it is built out of cantilevers in the form of LEGO bricks; he builds his construction by repeatedly having LEGO pieces jutting out in one direction thereby disregarding the construction's center of gravity. In another example, there is a cantilever built as part of Kathryn's structure; one of her beams—a double block—is supported on one end by a column below and a wooden wedge-shaped block set with its bottom flat surface on top. The other end is totally unsupported, thus serving as a cantilever. In the professional world, cantilever constructions can often be seen in the form of building balconies or terraces of large, high-rise buildings. The so-called Jenga Building at 56 Leonard Street in New York City is an exaggerated—yet perfectly stable—example of cantilever construction. We can see, then, that young children as architects and engineers are doing similar things that professional architects and engineers do in their everyday work.

Column

Again, going on the perspective of the professional architect and engineer, a column is a structural element that carries load, primarily in compression—also called a compression member. Once again, we refer to Kathryn's fascinating structure, which consists of eight columns. Two of the columns are supporting the structure at the base. Five of the columns are supporting the three beams on the highest level, and one column is a stand-alone which is supported by the quadruple unit block beam and compressed by a wedge-shaped block. Beams cannot be supported without columns. We sometimes refer to columns and beams as a post-and-lintel construction, or what I refer to as a trabeated construction when examining young children's post-and-beam constructions. Professional architects and engineers engage in this type of construction when building homes, commercial buildings, industrial complexes, and skyscrapers.

Compression and Tension

Beams, columns, and cantilevers are structural elements. But tension and compression are physical properties. Structures cannot remain standing without the dynamic processes of compression and tension. Compression is an internal force that causes a structural element to shorten. This is precisely what beams do to columns—they shorten them. This might not be able to be seen with our eyes when viewing the inner workings of a building or bridge in the process of construction. Nor can it be seen in the block constructions of children. But compression is present; architects and engineers can tell you that buildings, bridges, and towers undergo compression-tension subtleties; without them, these structures would not remain standing due to brittleness, or the lack of ductility—the tendency of a material to fail suddenly and catastrophically, without plastic (i.e., stretching) deformation. Problems arise, however, when beams become too heavy and columns too thin or unsteady, in which case the column will buckle. Both professional architects and engineers and emergent architects and engineers as young children engage in behaviors that involve structural elements being in a state of compression, as seen in the examples above.

Tension, in contrast to compression, is an internal force that causes a structural element to elongate or stretch. Tension is what happens to beams, which are supported at two ends by columns or other elements that keep beams from falling. In addition, live loads add additional stress or tension to the tension member, which could be a beam, deck, or cable. Tension members undergo elasticity that prevents them from snapping or breaking—assuming there is no strain on the members. Similar to compression, it is important to note that tension is a process that may not necessarily be seen, but is present. Again, we see tension in action in both examples of professional architects and engineers and those of emergent architects and engineers as young children.

Engineering

Engineering is the thinking, planning, and devising that goes into the act of construction. On a more formal level, engineering can be defined as the application of mathematics, science, and technology in order to create a system, component, or process that meets a human need. But if we examine this second definition a little bit more deeply and from the perspective of comparison between the young child and the professional engineer, we may notice that young four- and five-year-old children do informal, spontaneous mathematics, science, and technology when they are engaged in building their constructions.

To illustrate, we refer to Jamie, Pat, and Tyler's dialogue. Jamie, Pat, and Tyler are three four-and-one-half-year-old children from Taipei, Taiwan, who are engaged in the collaborative effort of constructing a model garage made of snap bricks which they created in order to put their toy cars in—also made from snap bricks, and with the addition of snap wheels. As we read the children's dialogue, notice the various terms that the children use in their discourse that are connected with emergent mathematical, scientific, and technological thinking.

This excerpt illustrates Jamie, Pat, and Tyler's strategy in collaborating to construct an ideal parking unit in which all three cars fit without bumping into each other. From a vernacular architectural vantage point, this scenario makes a good deal of sense since parking spaces in a large city like Taipei are a desirable commodity in a city that accommodates primarily mopeds and motorcycles as a form of city and regional travel. At the beginning of the excerpt, most of the garage is already constructed. However, during the excerpt, the children alter the structure to accommodate each of the three cars. Pat is the primary engineer who is actively engaged in the construction process, Jamie does most of the directing—similar to a lead engineer in a group— and Tyler is also involved in the engineering process. The children are engaged in constructive play with free, non-themed bricks; this feature affords the children greater flexibility with regard to creativity and imagination of construction. The following excerpt (cf. Ness et al., 2017) has been translated from Mandarin Chinese by Chia-ling Lin.

JAMIE: The rain will get in here. The rain will get in here. The rain will get in here. [Referring to the LEGO garage (with openings in the top) that is being built by Pat and Tyler]
PAT: I am making a big fat car! So, I hope it fits.
JAMIE: Will I [my car] get wet? Here is a car that can be used [by me]. This car is mine. I don't want to park outside.
PAT: Fire the cannon!
JAMIE: [Loud sound] Going in! The car is going in. The car is in there. The car is in there.
PAT: Oh! I'm going to tell the teacher.
JAMIE: [Imitating car sound]
PAT: This is my parking lot.
JAMIE: [Imitating car sound] You have to go further in so I can have a [parking] space!
PAT: Tyler's car is in front of it [my car]. I can't hit him [Tyler's car].
JAMIE: I feel [if we do it your way] I won't have a space. [Either] I'm going to tell the teacher [or] move in a little more [so I can park my car].
PAT: Wait! Wait! Wait! Wait! I'm going to park in there first.
JAMIE: Tyler won't get hit. He [his car] is far away [from yours]. Ah ha! The car can't go it. What are you doing? Can I …? I feel that I can remember it. Oh! Right! I remember it. Oh-oh. I do [loud sound].
PAT: Wait! Wait!
JAMIE: [Makes a loud sound].
PAT: Jamie, make some nicer sound!
JAMIE: Okay. [Makes another loud sound]
TYLER: Ay!
JAMIE: [Laughter]
PAT: [Uses hand to drive his car into the garage]

JAMIE: [sound] I can't get in! I can't get in! But ... But ... This way I don't have a space. It [Pat's car] is too long. Very long. I [my car] can't get in! It's really very long. I [my car] can't get in. You have to take it apart so I [my car] can get in. Oh! It's still very long. I [my car] can't get in. I don't want to play!
PAT: Wait! Wait! [working on changing the size of his car]
JAMIE: Very far.
PAT: Then is this Okay? [showing Jamie his car]
JAMIE: Ha! Okay!
PAT: Wait! Wait! [working on changing the size of his car]
JAMIE: [loud sounds]
TYLER: Ay! This way, will the rain get in there? [Points at the roof of the garage]. I just made a little more.
JAMIE: Ah! A little is fine. Ah! There is no space. Yours [your garage] can't cover it [my car]. There is no space. It [my car] will get wet [by the rain].
PAT: [Laughter]
TYLER: [Repetitive sound]
JAMIE: Ah! It's broken [looking at the top of the garage structure]
PAT: [I am] ... working on the top level. This way, I [my car] won't get wet [by the rain]. [Tyler and Pat are fixing the garage]
JAMIE: [Loud sound]
PAT: This way, I [my car] won't get wet [by the rain]. [Tyler and Pat are fixing the garage. Shortly after, the garage breaks to a degree]
JAMIE: [Screams]
TYLER: It fell again!
JAMIE: Wow! It broke! The top [of the garage structure] broke.
PAT: That's Okay. Right? [Asks for Tyler's confirmation]
TYLER: Yes. Even though my car is under yours ...
JAMIE: It broke! [Jamie begins to sing a number song in English] one, two, three, four, five, six, eight, nine, ten ... [While Jamie is singing, Tyler and Pat are still working on fixing the garage structure. When they finish the structure, Jamie then laughs and then drives his car into the garage]
TYLER: [Says to Jamie] Don't mess it [the garage] up ...
JAMIE: [Laughter] Climb up!

This passage makes it clear that engineering thinking involves numerous scientific, technological, and mathematical factors. These factors include, but are not limited to, size, measurement, distance, surface, volume, location, and topological constructs. As illustrated in the following table (Table 1.1), these factors reflect how Jamie, Pat, and Tyler's language reflects their everyday engineering activities as represented by their brick-constructed garage structure and brick-constructed cars. The factors, evidence of these factors, and their examples clearly demonstrate that the children are engaged in engineering thinking as they are constructing their garage structure.

TABLE 1.1 Evidence of engineering thinking by Jamie, Pat, and Tyler using factors, evidence, and examples

Factors	Evidence	Example
Size	Large and small	Pat says, "I am making a big fat car! So, I hope it fits."
Measurement	Close v. far; short v. long	Jamie says, "He [his car] is far away [from yours]." Jamie also says, "It [Pat's car] is too long. Very long."
Distance	Length	Jamie says, "You have to go further in so I can have a [parking] space." Pat says, "I can't hit him [Tyler's car]."
Surface	Two-dimensional space	Jamie says, "I feel [if we do it your way] I won't have a space."
Volume	Three-dimensional space	Pat says, "[I am] … working on the top level."
Location	The placement of a brick	Jamie says, "The car is in there." Pat says, "Tyler's car is in front of it [my car]." Tyler says, "Even though my car is under yours."
Topological constructs	Proximity, separation, enclosure, order, continuity, and openness	Jamie says, "Rain will get in here!" and "Yours [your garage] can't cover it [my car]" Tyler asks, "This way, will the rain get in there?"

The Development of Architectural Thinking

Place the search words "architecture" and "education" in a Google Scholar search, and you will undoubtedly come up with publications having to do with the sustainable design of learning environments (Taylor, 2009), or possibly, the education of home design or landscape architecture (Lenzholzer & Brown, 2013). No publications, to my knowledge, examine the psychological, developmental, and cognitive ramifications of architecture and its connection with spatial orientation—more specifically, mapping. Plugging in "architecture" and "thinking," or, "architectural thinking," also falls short in yielding results of publication listings that examine architectural development or emergent architectural thinking and how it relates to subsequent learning in the formal school environment. When plugging one of these terms into Google Scholar, one will find areas of inquiry having to do with the following domains: information technology (IT), cyber security, or information systems engineering (Van der Raadt, Soetendal, Perdeck, & van Vliet, 2004); architectural thinking purely from the level of the professional architect, that is, non-emergent thinking (Krier & Vorreiter, 1988); mathematical thinking—as in architectural geometry (Pottmann, Asperl, Hofer,

Kilian & Bentley, 2007), organizational and industrial psychology (Duffy & Hutton, 2004), and arts and aesthetics (Burdett, Kipnis & Whiteman, 1992).

In her discussion on architectural thinking and art-based research, Dyrssen (2010) defines architectural thinking as "a field that revolves around a creative practice on space and matter/materiality," and is "rooted at the crossing point between art, technology, and socio-cultural aspects of space" (p. 224). This definition is heavily rooted in the practice-based or professional environment of the artist and architect—but not in the *development* of architectural thinking (henceforth DAT). DAT is the cognitive unfolding of ideas that represents the everyday goings on of an individual's approach to the complex or cautiously and sensitively designed structure of a thing—whether it be a building, a model of a building, a toy car, a real car, and the like.

In order to distinguish between the increasingly standardized notion of architectural thinking in the current research literature and the views that are proposed in this book, I will refer to what is discussed here as emergent architectural thinking. But what literature is available that directly, remotely, or even tangentially connects with emergent architectural thinking or DAT? We can hark back to an earlier era, that of the 1980s, to find a publication that just tangentially connects architecture with the educational realm as it has to do with emergent thinking and cognitive development. That book, *Architecture in Education: A Resource of Imaginative Ideas and Tested Activities*, edited by Abhau, Copeland, and Greenberger (1986), is a reference, which consists of numerous approaches to learning environments that promote architectural thinking in schools. The curriculum in the book is in the form of lesson activities that accommodate students from Kindergarten through to grade 12. According to the editors, the content of the program, which has served as a partnership between the Foundation for Architecture and Philadelphia, Pennsylvania, regional public schools, is founded on the outline of basic concepts about architecture and the built environment.[1] The editors point out that the activities, which focus on architecture and the built environment, reflect three general areas: the perceptual environment, the social environment, and the technological environment. What is fascinating about this text is that it presents everyday architectural activities—the kind of activities that young children would do on their own during VCPO free play—that pertain to the everyday built environment.

Take, for example, one activity involving the basic vocabulary of structural principles. After defining eight vocabulary terms having to do with principles of structure—gravity, weight, load, span, thrust, stress, tension, and compression—the editors ask teachers—who then ask their students—to draw a horizontal line along the edge of a sponge and divide the edge into equal sections (see Figure 1.5). They add that when the sponge is bent, one side will always be stretched and the divisions will have a larger spread. This part of the sponge will be in a state of tension. The other side will be smashed together—as an accordion looks when pressed together; the divisions get smaller. This part of the sponge will be in a state of

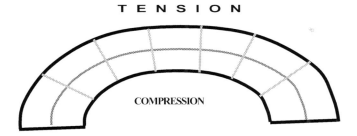

FIGURE 1.5 Cross-section of a bent sponge

compression. The editors go on to connect these concepts with the tools and materials with which architects work. As they state, some materials are strong in tension as a steel-based cable for a suspension bridge, while some are strong in compression, like the tower of a suspension bridge or the bricks of a building. In the same way that architects must select different materials according to whether the weight is pushing or pulling that part of the structure, so too does the young child need to consider which block, or system of blocks (bricks or planks), is best for sustaining a structure and ensuring that it does not collapse.

The Development of Cartographic Thinking

While this book emphasizes the need and role of emergent architectural thinking and the development of cartographic thinking (DCT), it equally stresses the importance of action—modifying the static curriculum to serve the needs not only of a changing and diverse society but also the needs of a progressively transforming workforce. To this end, spatial thinking is often connected with mapping, also referred to here as DCT. It is much easier to find research on mapping and DCT by plugging these two terms in to a standard Google Scholar search. What comes up, in fact, is a polysemous, kaleidoscopic inventory of ways in which young children develop their mapping skills. Perhaps the closest we will get in tapping research that examines children's DCT is to run a search with the term "children's mapping." When running this search, we come up with two overarching themes: children's cognitive mappings from one domain to another and the more literal idea of children's mapping ability or skills related to one's location and placement of objects or environments—the theme that pertains to our interests in this book.

Mapping, in one way or another, has always been a commonplace domain in children's development. The mapping concept stems from infancy and early childhood and emanates from an infant's or young child's experiences with objects in space. Children as young as three years of age are capable of producing maps when given miniature toys or play blocks (Blaut & Stea, 1974; Downs & Liben, 1987; Ness, Farenga & Garofalo, 2017; Yuan, Uttal & Gentner, 2017). It can be somewhat challenging, however, to identify the specific techniques and strategies that children use when demonstrating their abilities in mapping and navigation. Although they are capable of having some knowledge of maps, young children will make errors if maps lack specific landmarks or cognitive indicators such as make-believe post offices, food stores, or fire stations (Ness & Farenga, 2007).

Research on spatial cognition has also addressed issues relating to young children's understanding of maps and their local environments. Most young children are able to learn the relative distances between landmarks once they are familiarized with certain roads and pathways. They may even possess the ability to measure scaled routes as soon as they are familiar with them. Older children and adolescents are able to learn from consulting maps. Those who consult maps in order to learn a route through a six-room house learn the route more quickly than those who use navigation—searching by walking or traveling—alone.

Maps and mapping as they relate to DCT are of great importance for early childhood education for a number of reasons. First mapping concepts are linked to the development of young children's thinking and cognitive structures. Researchers have argued that the ability to orient oneself through maps and mapping contributes to the improvement of spatial and geometric concepts (Clements, 1999). Second, mapping concepts in connection with DCT are developmental, and are based on young children's experiences and learning. Further, cognitive psychologists have suggested that strong content knowledge of mapping developed in the early years will help children learn concepts in geography. Spatial analysis is a fundamental component of understanding geography (Bednarz & Lee, 2019; Fan, Zipf, Fu, & Neis, 2014; Rogers, 2008).

Research studies seem to corroborate that the inclusion of maps in children's books would greatly enhance the development of DCT in general (Goga & Kümmerling-Meibauer, 2017). However, although children begin to master their native language between the ages of four and five years, they are much slower when it comes to deciphering the meaning of maps and their symbols when maps are embedded in picture books (Liben, 2009; Liben & Myers, 2007; Liben & Yekel, 1996; MacEachern, 1995). Maps often appear in children's books, but they focus, for the most part, on the overall narrative and the nature of the plot from a literary perspective (Charleton et al., 2014; Druker, 2012; Honeyman, 2001; Pavlik, 2010; Rogers, 2008). In other words, they tend not to emphasize children's conceptions of maps and mapping. The goal of map inclusion in early childhood picture books, then, is to engage young children so that they develop map sense and possibly develop their own representations of maps (Kümmerling-Meibauer & Meibauer, 2015). Thus, given early experiences with maps, young children's map-making development can commence during the early childhood years as they become emerging cartographers.

In the first episode that began this chapter, Nate engages in mapping. His episode presents a model example of DAT and DCT—a child who is engaged in architectural thinking as he changes the landscape of his model roller coaster as well as cartographic thinking in that his model roller coaster structure spans several feet in distance. The very idea and initiative in constructing his roller coaster structure is by its nature a mapping activity. Roller coaster structures go somewhere; they don't stay in one location, but instead transition from one location to another as the child has a structure in mind that is under construction.

What Is Cartotecture?

This brings us to cartotecture, which, as mentioned in the Introduction, is a portmanteau of the words "cartography" and "architecture." When we consider human development, it is important to note that these two constructs do not develop as mutually exclusive entities; rather, they are part of the cognitive domain that sees these two seemingly disparate entities as one in which two concepts overlap and enmesh with one another. In fact, recent neuroscientific research from the University of Chicago has concluded that the area of the brain responsible for planning movements and spatial awareness is the posterior parietal cortex (PPC), which is located in the posterior (back) region of the brain, and, equally as important, the PPC also plays a major role in decision-making, that is, it is the brain region that decides what images should be in the field of view (Zhou & Freedman, 2019). This new finding makes the synergistic and interdependent nature of mapping and architectural thinking and development all the more plausible.

This brings us back to Nate, who engages in the decision-making process that enables him to determine where specific blocks are to be laid for the "roller coaster" structure to come to fruition. Nate's construction is a perfect example of cartotecture: He constructs his configuration based on mapping concepts of space as location and direction and uses the blocks as means of constructing an actual model or representation of an architectural achievement.

Connecting Playful Learning with STEAM

In their seminal publication, *A Mandate for Playful Learning in Preschool*, Kathy Hirsh-Pasek, Roberta Michnick Golinkoff, Laura Berk, and Dorothy Singer (2009) call for our educational system to "turn the tide back" to when play was considered a sine qua non of the educational process—particularly during preschool (if children attended it) and Kindergarten. Nothing can be more important than this call to action to bring play back into school. All too often, skill and drill and rote worksheets are the name of the day when it comes to early childhood education. But it does not seem as if we have turned the tide back yet. Unfortunately, school teachers, administrators, and parents rely overwhelmingly on how well children and even preschool children perform on worksheets and flashcards, which they believe will help our youngest of students succeed in their academic life.

Actually, as research has confirmed, nothing could be further from the truth. Heavy reliance on worksheets that lead to drilling factual knowledge and eventually high-stakes testing environments is highly detrimental to children's active engagement and wonder when they pursue STEM related subjects in school or in their everyday life. Such a heavy dependence on skill and drill at the expense of free play and playful learning have led to deleterious effects in children's social and emotional development, which impacts intellectual outcomes as well. That is, social skills can improve cognitive development because they both serve to reinforce each other (Ladd, Herald & Kochel, 2006).

Parents also have conflicting beliefs about what it means for their children to engage in play. More often than not, they think of play as being a trivial endeavor that is seen as meaningless—that is, "just play …." They don't see play as a source of imagination, which serves as the touchstone for deepening children's social skills and intellectual propensities. While play research is conflicting with regard to the extent to which play and playful learning contributes to cognitive dividends as outcomes, longitudinal studies have shown some consistency that indicates that children's free play positively influences their intellectual development with regard to spatial skills, especially free play with blocks and bricks (Jirout & Newcombe, 2015; Ness & Farenga, 2016; Ness, et al., 2017).

Hirsh-Pasek and colleagues' (2009) position on playful learning is one based on the premise that a false dichotomy exists between play and learning. This false dichotomy has been in existence from time immemorial. That is, it is not the case that playful learning served as a foundational component of the curriculum—not even the early childhood curriculum. While it is true that indoor and outdoor play assumed a central role in the life of the child in decades past, play and learning were mutually exclusive as were teaching and learning—the two never really did coalesce at any point in our educational history.

Cartotecture, while not the only academic learning area, can serve as an excellent way to connect play with learning and teaching. It has been shown that young children's constructive free play is very closely related to the methods that STEAM professionals use when they are engaged in the act of science-in-the-making. A relatively little known yet classic set of studies of eminent scientists by Anne Roe (1951a, 1951b, 1952) set the stage that led to the inextricably linked process that connects the imaginative powers of young children during constructive free play with the imagination and intuition that professional scientists, engineers, architects, cartographers, and mathematicians use when they develop hypotheses, laws, and theories that are used in both practical and theoretical applications. In her investigation of eminent scientists, Roe suggested links between early childhood science and engineering related experiences and physical science related careers. Her examination of the lives of eminent scientists has indicated noticeable group differences between life scientists (e.g., biologists) and physical scientists (e.g., geologists and physicists) and between natural scientists and social scientists (e.g., sociologists and psychologists). What emerged from

Roe's work was a pattern of psychosocial characteristics and basic common experiences that may be compared to personality formation. According to Roe (1952), the scientists who she interviewed were persistent in their work and put in long hours. This factor is consistent with children engaged in cartotecture—they are persistent, and, with food and rest aside, they, too, could put in long periods of time in developing and creating their structures and model environments.

Roe (1952) also discusses the experiences of scientists that may have fostered personality characteristics that are consonant with greater independence. She found subtle differences in adjustment patterns for physical scientists, biological scientists, and social scientists. Among these three groups of scientists in her study, by far the most consistency was found between the physicists and biologists—the natural scientists. For example, the physicists reported greater time spent on early extra-curricular interests during childhood—interests that closely related to their later career interests. As young children (mostly boys), they enjoyed playing with physical devices and Meccano sets, dabbled with electric gadgets, and loved spending time experimenting and tinkering with objects. The biologists, as young children were fond of being in the presence of living or non-living organisms and studying their behaviors and the ways in which they searched for food and reproduced. In terms of non-living organisms, the biologists as children would engage in dissection and learn about the different systems that allow organisms to survive. As with young physicists, the biologists as children enjoyed dabbling with physical gadgets and experimenting with various physical objects. Roe (1981) suggested that the most important trait mentioned in each of her studies of eminent scientists was independence. As she states:

> The most important single factor in the making of a scientists [is] the need and ability to develop personal independence to a high degree. The independence factor is emphasized by many findings: the subjects' preference for teachers [who] let them alone, their attitude toward religion, their attitude toward personal relations, their satisfaction in a career in which, for the most part, they follow their own interest without direction or interference.
>
> *(Roe, 1981, p. 109)*

Roe's studies integrate well with theories of psychosocial development and thus provide a plausible explanation for propensities toward STEAM related fields in the course of human development. The importance of personality development as it is affected by common experiences in early childhood is directly expressed by object relations theory. On a social level, Roe's work exposes how conflictual events and sense of self develop during childhood and how they play a role in the internal and external experiences of adulthood.

Roe's investigations into the early childhood experiences of well-known scientists makes one think of how VCPOs played a role in the lives of STEAM professionals and luminaries. One of the most vivid examples of a recollection of early childhood experiences by a famous STEAM personality is that of Frank Lloyd Wright, who we shall discuss at greater length in Chapter 3, and his indebtedness to Friedrich Froebel's Gifts—particularly the wooden sphere, the three-dimensional wooden polyhedrons, and related construction blocks. Attributable to his career in architecture, Wright's most notable recollection was the time shortly after his mother, Anna Lloyd Jones, returned to Wisconsin from the 1876 Centennial Exposition in Philadelphia's Fairmount Park where she had seen a display of toys and learning tools that were created and developed by Friedrich Froebel—a late 18th- and 19th-century German pedagogue and educational reformer who developed the concept and practice of Kindergarten, in which the child can grow and develop intellectually and experiment through engagement in activities that promote creativity and logical thinking. Froebel believed that his toys and Gifts, which were representations of the real world, can be excellent tools for the teaching and learning of geometry. Anna noticed that the Froebelian toys could be stacked, placed side by side, folded, and handled in multiple ways in both two- and three-dimensional forms. These toys could be manipulated in ways that can represent three-dimensional constructions, such as buildings and entire city models. Wright remembered the time when his mother, a school teacher by profession, purchased the Froebel toys and Gifts in Boston for her own classroom. Wright recalled the way he and his sister, Mary Jane, spent hours on end playing with Froebel toys and experiencing the diversity of patterns of shape, color, and spatial relationships that can be constructed (Johnson, 2017; Rubin, 1989; Twombly, 1987). This undoubtedly contributed in part to Wright's success as a world-renowned architect.

More recently, the well-known geoscientist Ellen Kooijman, explained how her early childhood and general upbringing was filled with experiences that included constructive play toys and materials. Kooijman is an expert in the fields of geochemistry, metamorphic petrology, and tectonics. She was absorbed in the natural sciences as a young child, and was particularly interested in astronomy. In school, her favorite subjects were mathematics and physics. Her enthusiasm for combining physics, mathematics, and chemistry influenced her to study geoscience.

In an editorial in which she was interviewed (Kooijman, 2018), Kooijman elaborated on how she became involved with LEGO bricks by stating that she had been a toy brick builder her entire life and has been using toy bricks as an adult to model various concepts in geoscience. Moreover, she attributes her success as a geoscientist to her LEGO brick play as a child. She even went as far as to develop a LEGO idea that she submitted to the LEGO Ideas website. Kooijman explained that she became inspired by changing the ways in which toy construction bricks and blocks would favor males over females—as can be seen in most LEGO sets that include an overwhelming number of male minifigures. This factor, along with her desire to make LEGO more diverse, was a key reason why she developed the LEGO Research Institute. Kooijman explained that her rationale for developing the LEGO Research Institute was to emphasize the need to include more girls and women in STEAM and engage them in building with construction bricks. Consequently, she hoped to inspire young girls to engage in brick play as a way to get them to consider possible careers in science and technology. Kooijman developed new designs for minifigures that depict females engaged in STEAM-based initiatives. As a result of her designs, LEGO decided to base the chemist minifigures on Kooijman herself.

Wolfgang Ketterle is another major figure in STEAM whose early childhood was filled with constructive play materials. In 2001, Ketterle, along with Eric Allin Cornell and Carl Wieman, was awarded the Nobel Prize in Physics for his work on Bose-Einstein condensation. In an autobiographical sketch, Ketterle reminisced about his early childhood experiences and his parental upbringing, and within that recollection, he elaborated on how play bricks contributed to his interest in science.

> My parents supported all our interests in music, sports and sciences. As they hadn't been exposed to many of these activities themselves, they did not steer us in certain directions, but rather observed our interests and then reinforced and supported them. That may be one of the reasons why my brother and sister are successful in quite different areas: finance and education. My explorations of the technical world started with LEGOs, with which I was quite creative in constructing moving objects with the basic building blocks that were then available. (LEGOs have become much fancier since then!)
>
> (Ketterle, 2001)

This passage should resonate with educational practitioners, researchers, and parents in that while Ketterle was influenced by LEGO bricks, he makes it quite clear that toy brick manufacturing has become much more elaborate with popular themes. This is evidenced by his statement about LEGO "becoming much more fancy" in more recent times. As we shall see in later chapters, LEGO and the many clone brick companies all include step-by-step instructions to complete brick models, which may detract from the creativity and levels of complexity of construction. But Ketterle makes the point that original (i.e., generic) LEGO bricks led to his interest in technology and science. He goes on to say:

> I remember playing with electricity kits, doing repairs of household appliances, and using my father's power tools for woodworking projects. Explorations into chemistry were done in our basement .... Other projects included taking old radios and a TV set apart and combining a portable radio and a vacuum tube audio amplifier to create stereo sound. I was interested in learning more about electronics, but I was disappointed that the electronic kits explained only how to put the parts together, not how they really worked.
>
> (Ketterle, 2001)

In this passage, Ketterle is explicit about how consumerism with regard to science and technology education kits diminishes a genuine understanding of how electronic devices actually operate. This is evident when he states that these kits explain mechanical assembly but not function. What is most important, however, is that Ketterle explicitly remembers the positive role constructive play objects had on his emergent scientific and technological knowledge.

A few decades after Roe's seminal studies, Choderow (1978) argued that a child's early socialization is a determining factor in psychological growth and personality formation. More recently, Hirsh-Pasek and colleagues have posited that social skills can improve cognitive development if educator practitioners and researchers embrace the notion of playful learning. They state:

> Characterizing content areas as cognitive or social masks the fundamental relationships between these areas that emerge in the whole-child view. Importantly, not only do cognitive and social skills reinforce one another, but social skills can actually lead to better cognitive skills, especially for children with average cognitive abilities.
>
> *(Hirsh-Pasek et al., 2009, p. 22)*

Roe's research—as early as the 1950s—in tandem with object relation theory, informs us of the importance of preschool children's early experiences. The quality of the experience, the availability of certain materials and objects, and the support and encouragement of adults and peers provide young children with an additional option in their cognitive portfolio—they have more of a chance to increase their potential in STEAM subjects at school as they get older and are more inclined to demonstrate intrinsic motivation in these areas.

The main idea here is to show that intrinsic motivation at the level of professional scientists, architects, engineers, and mathematicians is equated with persistence—a trait that can be developed if a child has an ideal environment for cartotectural learning, the equivalent to Hirsh-Pasek et al.'s (2009) playful learning. A concrete behavior that represents persistence, in my investigations, is time on task with VCPOs. An example of persistence can be seen in children who spend more than one-third of their free play time actively engaged in cartotecturally related activities. Thus, an environment that is rich in VCPO materials—LEGO-like objects and wooden play blocks as well as planks—is one that is conducive to the development of spatial abilities, geometric skills, physical science knowledge, and architectural design.

I would take Hirsh-Pasek, Golinkoff, Berk, and Singer's clarion call for both playful learning in early childhood and childhood settings and to make cartotecture a bedrock component of playful learning. Cartotecture is all about emergent architectural and cartographic, or mapping, thinking—the type of thinking that engages the young child, allows her to explore and try novel ways to make something work, keep a structure from tipping over and falling, or arrange the most optimal model environment for continual free play to take shape.

In the next chapter, we will review the research literature on play, specifically play that is associated with VCPOs and their importance in the development of STEAM. Doing so will prepare us for Chapter 3, which provides an overview of the different types of VCPOs on the market.

Note

1 The built environment has to do with everything we encounter when we are inside our homes and when we walk outside our homes, into our neighborhoods, and into other neighborhoods, the inner city, and surrounding areas.

References

Abhau, M., Copeland, R., Greenberger, G. (1986). *Architecture in education: A resource of imaginative ideas and tested activities*. Philadelphia. Foundation for Architecture.

Bednarz, R., & Lee, J. (2019). What improves spatial thinking? Evidence from the spatial thinking abilities test. *International Research in Geographical and Environmental Education*, 28 (4), 262–280.

Blaut, J. M., & Stea, D. (1974). Mapping at the age of three. *Journal of Geography*, 73(7), 5–9.

Burdett, R., Kipnis, J., Whiteman, J. E. M. (1992). *Strategies in architectural thinking*. Chicago: Chicago Institute for Architecture and Urbanism.

Charleton, E., Cliff Hodges, G., Pointon, P., Nikolajeva, M., Spring, E., Taylor, L., & Wyse, D. (2014). My place: Exploring children's place-related identities through reading and writing. *Education 3–13*, 42(2), 154–170.

Choderow, N. J. (1978). *The reproduction of mothering*. Los Angeles: University of California Press.

Christensen, P., & Prout, A. (2002). Working with ethical symmetry in social research with children. *Childhood*, 9(4), 477–497.

Clements, D. H. (1999). Geometric and spatial thinking in young children. In J. Copley (ed.), *Mathematics in the early years* (pp. 66–79). Reston, VA: NCTM Press.

Downs, R. M., & Liben, L. S. (1987). Children's understanding of maps. In P. Ellen & C. Thinus-Blanc (Eds.). *Cognitive knowledge and developmental aspects* (202–219). Dordrecht: Martinius Nijhoff.

Druker, E. (2012). Mapping absence: Maps as meta-artistic discourse in literature. In L. Dahlberg (Ed.), *Visualizing law and authority: Essays on legal aesthetics* (pp. 114–125). New York: De Gruyter.

Duffy, F., & Hutton, L. (2004). *Architectural knowledge: The idea of a profession*. New York: Taylor & Francis.

Dyrssen, C. (2010). Navigating in heterogeneity: Architectural thinking and art-based research. In M. Biggs & H. Karlsson (Eds.), *The Routledge companion to research in the arts* (pp. 223–239). New York: Routledge.

Fan, H., Zipf, A., Fu, Q., & Neis, P. (2014). Quality assessment for building footprints data on OpenStreetMap. *International Journal of Geographical Information Science*, 28(4), 700–719.

Geertz, C. (1973). *The interpretation of cultures*. New York: Basic Books.

Ginsburg, H. P., Inoue, N., & Seo, K. H. (1999). Young children doing mathematics: Observations of everyday activities. In J. V. Copley (Ed.), *Mathematics in the early years* (pp. 88–99). Reston, VA: National Council of Teachers of Mathematics.

Ginsburg, H. P., Lin, C. L., Ness, D., & Seo, K. H. (2003). Young American and Chinese children's everyday mathematical activity. *Mathematical Thinking and Learning*, 5(4), 235–258.

Ginsburg, H. P., Pappas, S., & Seo, K. H. (2001). Everyday mathematical knowledge: Asking young children what is developmentally appropriate. In S. L. Golbeck (Ed.), *Psychological perspectives on early childhood education: Reframing dilemmas in research and practice* (pp. 181–219). Mahwah, NJ: Lawrence Erlbaum Associates.

Goga, N., & Kümmerling-Meibauer, B. (2017). Introduction: Maps and mapping in children's literature. In N. Goga & B. Kümmerling-Meibauer (Eds.), *Maps and mapping in children's literature: Landscapes, seascapes, and cityscapes* (pp. 1–13). Amsterdam, The Netherlands: John Benjamins Publishing Company.

Gordon, J. E. (2009). *Structures: Or why things don't fall down*. Cambridge, MA: Da Capo Press.

Hilton, M. (2010). *Exploring the intersection of science education and 21st century skills: A workshop summary*. National Research Council. Washington, DC: National Academies Press.

Hirsh-Pasek, K., Golinkoff, R. M., Berk, L. E., & Singer, D. (2009). *A mandate for playful learning in preschool: Presenting the evidence*. Oxford: Oxford University Press.

Honeyman, S. (2001). Childhood bound: In gardens, maps, and pictures. *Mosaic: A Journal for the Interdisciplinary Study of Literature*, 34(2), 117–132.

Jirout, J. J., & Newcombe, N. S. (2015). Building blocks for developing spatial skills: Evidence from a large, representative US sample. *Psychological Science*, 26(3), 302–310.

Johnson, D. L. (2017). *Frank Lloyd Wright: The early years, progressivism, aesthetics, cities*. New York: Routledge.

Ketterle, W. (2001). Wolfgang Ketterle – biographical. NobelPrize.org. Nobel Media AB 2020. Wed. Dec 16, 2020. Retrieved from: https://www.nobelprize.org/prizes/physics/2001/ketterle/biographical.

Kim, Y., & Park, N. (2012). The effect of STEAM education on elementary school student's creativity improvement. In T. H. Kim, A. Stoica, W. C. Fang, T. Vasilakos, J. Garcia Villaba, K. P. Arnett, M. K. Khan, & B. H. Kang (Eds.), *Computer applications for security, control and system engineering* (pp. 115–121). Berlin: Springer.

Kooijman, E. (2018) Women in geoscience: An interview with Ellen Kooijman. *Cogent Geoscience*, 4(1). doi:10.1080/23312041.2018.1432282.

Krier, R., & Vorreiter, G. (1988). *Architectural composition*. New York: Rizzoli.

Kümmerling-Meibauer, B., & Meibauer, J. (2015). Maps in picture books: Cognitive status and narrative functions. *BLFT-Nordic Journal of ChildLit Aesthetics*, 6, 1–10.

Ladd, G. W., Herald, S. L., & Kochel K. P. (2006). School readiness: Are there social prerequisites? *Early Education and Development*, 17, 115–150.

Lenzholzer, S., & Brown, R. D. (2013). Climate-responsive landscape architecture design education. *Journal of Cleaner Production*, 61, 89–99.

Liben, L. S. (2009). The road to understanding maps. *Current Directions in Psychology Science*, 18, 310–315.

Liben, L. S., & Downs, R. M. (1989). Understanding maps as symbols: The development of map concepts in children. In H. W. Reese (Ed.), *Advances in child development and behavior* (pp. 145–201). New York: Academic Press.

Liben, L. S., & Myers, L. J. (2007). Developmental changes in children's understanding of maps. What, when, and how? In J. M. Lumert & J. P. Spencer (Eds.), *The emerging spatial mind* (pp. 193–218). New York, NY: Oxford University Press.

Liben, L. S., & Yekel, C. A. (1996). Preschoolers' understanding of plan and oblique maps: The role of geometric and representational correspondence. *Child Development*, 67, 2780–2796.

Lincoln, Y. S., & Guba, E. G. (1985). *Naturalistic inquiry*. Beverly Hills, CA: Sage.

MacEachern, A. (1995). *How maps work: Representation, visualization, and design*. New York: Guilford Press.

Makerspaces.com (2020). *What is a makerspace?* Retrieved from: https://www.makerspaces.com/what-is-a-makerspace.

Martin, L. (2015). The promise of the Maker Movement for education. *Journal of Pre-College Engineering Education Research*, 5(1), 30–39.

Ness, D. (2001). The development of spatial thinking, emergent geometric concepts, and architectural principles in the everyday context. Doctoral dissertation, Columbia University, New York.

Ness, D., & Farenga, S. J. (2007). *Knowledge under construction: The importance of play in developing children's spatial and geometric thinking*. Lanham, MD: Rowman & Littlefield Publishers.

Ness, D., & Farenga, S. J. (2016). Blocks, bricks, & planks: Relationships between affordance and visuo-spatial constructive play objects. *American Journal of Play*, 8(2), 201–227.

Ness, D., Farenga, S. J., & Garofalo, S. G. (2017). *Spatial intelligence: Why it matters from birth through the lifespan*. New York: Routledge.

Pavlik, A. (2010). A special kind of reading game: Maps in children's literature. *International Research in Children's Literature*, 3(1): 28–43.

Pottmann, H., Asperl, A., Hofer, M., Kilian, A., & Bentley, D. (2007). *Architectural geometry* (Vol. 724). Exton, PA: Bentley Institute Press.

Ramey, K. E., Stevens, R., & Uttal, D. H. (2018, January). STEAM learning in an in-school makerspace: The role of distributed spatial sense making. In *Proceedings of the 13th International Conference of the Learning Sciences* (pp. 168–175). London: International Conference of the Learning Sciences.

Ramey, K. E., & Uttal, D. H. (2017). Making sense of space: Distributed spatial sense making in a middle school summer engineering camp. *Journal of the Learning Sciences*, 26(2), 277–319.

Roe, A. (1951a). A psychological study of eminent biologists. *Psychological Monographs*, 65 (serial no. 331), 459–470.

Roe, A. (1951b). A psychological study of eminent physical scientists. *Genetic Psychology Monographs*, 43, 121–235.

Roe, A. (1952). A psychologist examines 64 eminent scientists. *Scientific American*, 187(5), 21–25.

Roe, A. (1981). A psychologist examines 64 eminent scientists. In W. B. Barbe & J. Renzulli (Eds.), *Psychology and education of the gifted* (pp. 103–110). New York: Irving Publishers.

Rogers, L. (2008). *Shaped by the standards: Geographic literacy through children's literature*. Westport, CT: Teacher Ideas Press.

Rubin, J. S. (1989). The Froebel-Wright Kindergarten connection: A new perspective. *The Journal of the Society of Architectural Historians*, 48(1), 24–37.

Sheridan, K., Halverson, E., Litts, B., Brahms, L., Jacobs-Priebe, L., & Owens, T. (2014). Learning in the making: A comparative case study of three makerspaces. *Harvard Educational Review*, 84(4), 505–531.

Taylor, A. (2009). *Linking architecture and education: Sustainable design for learning environments*. Albuquerque, NM: University of New Mexico Press.

Twombly, R. C. (1987). *Frank Lloyd Wright: His life and his architecture*. New York: John Wiley & Sons.

Van der Raadt, B., Soetendal, J., Perdeck, M., & van Vliet, H. (2004). Polyphony in architecture. In *Proceedings of the 26th International Conference on Software Engineering* (pp. 533–542). Los Alamitos, CA: IEEE Computer Society.

Vossoughi, S., & Bevan, B. (2014). *Making and tinkering: A review of the literature*. Washington, DC: National Research Council: National Research Council.

Yuan, L., Uttal, D., & Gentner, D. (2017). Analogical processes in children's understanding of spatial representations. *Developmental Psychology*, 53(6), 1098–1114.

Zhou, Y., & Freedman, D. J. (2019). Posterior parietal cortex plays a causal role in perceptual and categorical decisions. *Science*, 365(6449), 180–185.

2
PLAY MATTERS

In order to understand young children's cognitive propensities in STEAM subjects, even prior to the time they enter formal schooling, it is necessary for teachers, researchers, administrators, and parents to acquire and develop a more robust understanding of the environment in which young children engage in emergent STEAM activities—namely, play. For our purposes, we will focus on constructive free play as a backdrop for studying young children's development of STEAM concepts.

Early and Modern Conceptions of Constructive Play

Attempts to define play as it relates to humans, and even non-humans, have been time-honored efforts, not only among experts in play, but also among developmental and social psychologists, philosophers, evolutionary biologists, and specialists in medicine and kinesiology. Moreover, as experts in the field of play would affirm, play is one of the thorniest terms to define because discourses on the subject are prolix when it comes to exactitude in meaning. Moreover, play is unpredictable in that it can be at once organized—that is, with rules, regulations, records, and arbiters who officiate the extent to which a particular game or activity is being adhered to—and unsystematic to the extent that it can be ephemeral, whimsical, and tenuous—in other words, without rules, instructions, or guidelines. It should also be noted that there are different characteristics of people at play. Some are consistent in their play in terms of diligent practice, preparation, training; they are resolute in their performance and engage in play with élan. Others, however, reflect, laugh, dawdle, and forget that they have engaged in play shortly after the play event has started. What is more, while our focus is on young children's play, it is imperative to note that play is an activity that all people can do at any age level.

DOI: 10.4324/9781003097815-3

From a Western historical perspective, play has been interpreted through two essential, yet seemingly diametrically-opposed, belief systems. In one system, as alluded to above, play is interpreted as a whimsical or frivolous behavior, which minimizes the role of play as a factor in intellectual and social development. In the other system, play is understood to be a serious, contemplative activity that involves learning, intuition, imagination, and progress (Sutton-Smith, 2009). In this regard, anecdotal evidence of play exists from antiquity to the present. Play was a central component in Aristotle's treatise entitled *Nicomachean Ethics*, in which he referred to *eudaimonia* as the notion of an individual excelling and flourishing in a particular skill (Barnes, 2014). For Aristotle, then, play leads to contentment and fulfillment in an activity that is participated in for the sake of the activity itself. In other words, *eudaimonia*, as it relates to play, refers to the self-actualization of a practicing activity. *Eudaimonia* is connected with realization and accomplishment in that it counters the motives associated with *hedonia* (or hedonism)—the idea that our actions lead to happiness and the seeking of pleasure (Huta, 2013). For Aristotle, as well as more recent thinkers, play was an action that occurred throughout the lifespan and not solely in childhood.

The same can also be said about key literary figures and aesthetes of the Enlightenment. In *Letters on the Aesthetic Education of Man* of 1794, Friedrich Schiller stated that the authenticity of character and temperament is most evident when the individual is at play. More specifically, in "Letter 12," Schiller outlines human nature as being set apart by two fundamental drives—the sense drive and the form drive (Deligiorgi, 2011; Roehr, 2003). The sense drive takes shape from our physical existence. It positions the individual within a time and change in which we are concerned solely with self-preservation. In contrast, the form drive asserts the individual as a constant being throughout change and insists on truth over deception. It is concerned with dignity. Abstract principles comprise the outcome of the form drive while chaos and disorder comprise the outcome of the sense drive. In "Letter 14," Schiller proposes that when an individual experiences both these drives in equilibrium, a new drive is roused and developed—the play drive. In the play drive, Schiller postulates, the sense drive and form drive work harmoniously, and are "directed toward annulling time within time, reconciling becoming with absolute being and change with identity" (1943 [1794], p. 353). By contributing to their harmony, the play drive liberates the individual from the domination of the sense drive and the form drive, thereby allowing the individual to flourish and be unshackled. For Schiller, the fundamental basis of play is freedom and, like Aristotle, the participation in play for its own sake.

Definitions of play in the modern period of the late 19th and early 20th centuries tended to be more deterministic and utilitarian in nature (Gordon, 2008). For Freud, play is functional; it repeats events or the child's experiences with objects as a form of secondary symbolism that the child uses as a means of making sense of reality. Freud regards the child's compulsion to repeat as the primary dynamism in play. When visiting the physician, for instance, the child is generally passive in terms of disposition; however, during play, the child will pretend to be the physician and repeat the procedures carried out by the physician in a spirited, enthusiastic manner with a friend or younger sibling. In fact, as Courtney (1989) has asserted, the child will be extremely active, so much so, that the friend or younger sibling is helpless in the same way that the child was in the physician's consulting room. Freud argues that this repetition of a difficult experience assumes a major role in the child's play.

As a follower of Darwin's evolutionary theory, the German philosopher and psychologist Karl Groos ascribed a functional importance to play in that the animal's or human's participation in play provided exercise and the necessary future skills for survival. Play, for Groos, is essential in that it prepares the individual for important future events. His two most cited writings on play, *The Play of Animals* (1898) and *The Play of Man* (1901), outlined his position on the purposeful foundations of play. In general, the purpose of play for the animal and for the child is essentially the same: to prepare the young for what will be necessary for survival during adulthood (see Bruner, Jolly, & Sylva, 1976). Just as a puppy engages in play with a plastic bone in imitation of the older dog for the purpose of stalking for food for survival in adult life, so, too, does the young child play "house" for the possible future role of managing a household (Hughes, 2010).

Groos also examined pretense, the act of pretending in animals and children during play. He in essence reasoned that pretense in play refers to activities that are the gratifying acting out of instincts that occur prior to their functionality in adult life. The young animal or young child simulates the actions of the adult, who is unaware that simulation of these actions is taking place. Further, Groos took Darwin's stance in that when animal or children players experience the real action that was imitated during play, they begin to become sensitive to the relationships between the play activity and the real action that the play has simulated (Mitchell, 2002). From the perspective of the playing child, Groos believed that pretense seems to have originated from the child acknowledging that current actions are based on previously acted upon events. In addition, Groos took an extreme position on play in that childhood existed so that play could occur (Smith, 2006).

In 1938, the Dutch anthropologist, Johan Huizinga, introduced a profoundly novel conception of play—namely, that play is an activity in which one engages for its own sake. For Huizinga, an activity is considered to be play if it completely engrosses the individual, if there are hints of uncertainty, if it encompasses a sense of fantasy or exaggeration, and, perhaps most significantly, if it takes place outside the realm of everyday life. This is to say that individuals engaged in play are always aware that the play they encounter is not real and that it does not affect them in their lives when they are not engaged in play.

Jean Piaget's (1951) interpretation of play is defined in structuralist terms (i.e., definable components that can then be aggregated to analyze a larger structure). He based almost all conceptualizations and meanings of play on two of his essential constructs that define his theory of intellectual development—assimilation and accommodation. From both an ontological and epistemological standpoint, Piaget's answer to when play begins is unambiguous: It begins during infancy when the infant is adapting to changes in reflexes through repetition. Piaget suggests that a nascent form of play happens when the infant engages in primary and secondary circular reactions. This is because the infant is repeating actions that connect sensorimotor activities that follow primary schemata, such as finger sucking, gazing, and grasping. He argues that the infant's practice of sucking is a form of emergent play in that the infant engages in it apart from meals. Piaget then discusses play in terms of the second sub-stage—primary circular reactions (when the infant engages in actions relative to the self)—by positing that the identification of when post-reflex emergent play ends and play based on adaptive behaviors begins is hard to determine. He goes on to compare the infant's actions during the reflex sub-stage and primary circular reactions and the more advanced motor skills in sub-stage two, and argues that little difference exists in the autotelic responses of the infant in terms of sub-stage one and sub-stage two. Although circular reactions in which infants engage do not necessarily possess a ludic quality (i.e., evidence of spontaneous play), Piaget argues that these repeated acts of assimilation leading to accommodation eventually end up as play and games. From a thoroughly theoretical perspective, Piaget noticed in primary circular reactions that play stems from what he calls "pure assimilation,"—not necessarily assimilation that is based on actions that lead to adaptation, but those that allow for functional assimilation, that is, the infant's engagement in the pleasure of the activity for its own sake. Piaget continues to point out that play continues into the third sub-stage of the sensori-motor stage—secondary circular reactions; only this time, the infant is involved in more advanced intellectual assimilation in that external objects are involved instead of the infant's own body (e.g., hand movements, finger sucking, etc.). Thus, Piaget states:

> The action of things, which begins with each new secondary reaction, in a context of objective interest and intentional accommodation, often even of anxiety (as when the child sways new hanging objects or shapes new toys which produce sound) will thus unfailingly become a game as soon as the new phenomenon is grasped by the child and offers no further scope for investigation properly so called.
>
> *(1951, p. 91)*

Piaget identified two new elements related to play in the fourth sub-stage—coordination of secondary reactions. First, he refers to the finding that behaviors, in which previously acquired schemas are applied to new situations, are now developed to the point that they continue to arise as ludic manifestations—that is, they come about for the pleasure of the activity alone, and not necessarily for the adaptation to achieve a definite end. Second, given greater mobility on the part of the infant, Piaget noticed that greater mobility of the infant's schemas allows for the development of ludic combinations in which the child is engaging in one schema and then going on to the next, not in any particular order, for the sake of the pleasurable moments, and not for the process of adaptation. In the fifth sub-stage, tertiary circular reactions, the schema now show the young child beginning to encounter some phenomenon in order to see the result. Piaget posits that the young child in this sub-stage engages in combining unrelated actions without necessarily attempting to experiment. The young child, now motivated, repeats the action to the point that it becomes game-like. According to Piaget, this is the point when play, as we know it from the young child's perspective, begins to emerge. In the sixth, and final, sub-stage of the sensori-motor period, the young child begins to move from engagement with physical objects to interpretation of phenomena in terms of representation, namely, the semiotic function or the ability to create representations of objects or events outside the realm of sight. During this sub-stage, the ludic symbol—spontaneous play—detaches from the young child's ritual tendencies, which involve repetition of bodily functions or external objects that result in pleasurable tasks, and attaches itself to symbolic schemas. At this point in the young child's life, according to Piaget, empirical intelligence (i.e., the young child's new knowledge resulting from pleasurable tasks) is now a mental construct and external imitation becomes internalized.

Due to its spontaneous, unstructured nature, play has been perhaps most suited to study through naturalistic observation of individuals in their everyday settings. Piaget, who utilized observation as a central research method to study infants' and children's play, argued that play serves an important cognitive function and supplies the child with numerous opportunities and materials to explore the environment, allowing greater opportunities to assimilate and accommodate new knowledge schemata. Piaget's theory and interpretation of play has garnered a great deal of criticism since the 1980s in that his findings are the results of a structuralist model that does not take socio-cultural implications of play into account (Nicolopoulou, 1993; Sutton-Smith, 1966).

The Soviet psychologist Lev Vygotsky (1993 [1922]), who also engaged in observation as a possible method within his research agenda, differed from other epistemologists in that he argued that play is dependent on one's socially interactive engagement in a particular pursuit. Moreover, he recognized variation in play from one society to another; namely from play as an individualistic enterprise to one that emphasizes the collective roles of all participants. In order to understand and appreciate play in the context of vernacular architecture and other STEAM related disciplines, it is important to consider Vygotsky's notion of play as an activity that enables the direction of a child's future behavior. Vygotsky is one of the most prominent philosophical and psychological theorists to propose a relational argument between play and tool use.

In addition to the influence of Karl Marx with regard to tool use and the historical origins of language and labor, Vygotsky was also greatly indebted to the work of the philosopher Georg Hegel, who introduced the concept of dialectic as a way of interpreting interaction in various forms: art, science, music, aesthetics as a whole, and play. For Vygotsky (1966 [1933]), play would not exist if a child did not experience unrealizable tendencies during preschool. He argues that when the child desires something that cannot be immediately gratified, she exhibits a latent form of this gratification through play later on in life. That is, after an ungratified event, the child will enter an imaginary, invented period in which an unrealizable event becomes realized. Vygotsky, then, defines this period as play. Vygotsky does so in support of Groos's contention that play serves a significant purpose in order for the individual to successfully function in future endeavors. Vygotsky writes:

> Only in light of Groos's theory of play and the new theory of exercise can one really understand and appraise the significance of a child's movement and its educational sense .... A child's movement (in certain components) must be analyzed as an experience in the rationalization and organization of group play among children on an international scale. That is, play in a revolutionary era, which, like any game, prepares the child for the future, implants the fundamental lines of his future behavior.
>
> *(1993 [1928], p. 161)*

From the standpoint of objects, Vygotsky states that when the child is very young, she constructs meaning on what she sees, that is, whatever is in her visual field. Vygotsky says that it is impossible for the very young child to separate meaning from what she sees because the two are inextricably entwined. Moreover, the very young child will not refer to something that she sees as an untrue condition. Only later, when the child experiences the lack of immediate gratification from a parent or another person will she begin to separate meaning from the physical object or event. In terms of play and objects, Vygotsky says that the development of the individual to be able to make deliberate choices occurs when she attributes meaning to actions. In the same manner, Vygotsky claims, the development of the child to be able to attribute meaning to things— that is, objects—leads to abstract thought. His point is akin to Piaget's contention that things or events can and will eventually become representations in the child's mind, especially after the sixth sub-stage in the sensori-motor stage, when the semiotic function emerges and is thus available to the child. While some play researchers interpret Vygotsky's discussion about play as one that avoids examination about object manipulations (Bodrova & Leong, 2015), I maintain that Vygotsky alludes to object manipulation in the broad sense to the extent that tools of play can fit within the concept of physical movement and placement of objects. In other words, the child who manipulates a particular VCPO does so because it represents a real-life activity that is beyond the child's reach.

Contemporary Interpretations of Constructive Play

Perhaps one of the most outspoken play theorists of the late 20th century and early part of the current century was Brian Sutton-Smith, whose book, *The Ambiguity of Play* (2009), charted new territory in play research. Sutton-Smith was one of the initiators of what we now know as play from a cross-cultural perspective, as well as play for individuals of all ages. In his quest to come to terms with the definition of play, Sutton-Smith investigates the role of play and its many interpretations in the fields of biology, psychology, paleontology, education, metaphysics, mathematics, and sociology. From an evolutionary perspective, he observes that the underlying forces of play and therefore a definition of play that can account for the variability of play must be based on biological processes that bring about the same class of situation that is akin to variability in nature. In searching for connections with environmental variability, Sutton-Smith refers to the research of the paleontologist and evolutionary biologist, Stephen Jay Gould. It was Gould who argued that evolution is governed by adaptive variability exemplified by "sloppiness, broad potential, quirkiness, unpredictability, and, above all, massive redundancy. The key is flexibility, not admirable precision" (Gould, 1996; quoted in Sutton-Smith, 2009, p. 221). Sutton-Smith identified with Gould's interpretation of evolution by stating that "if quirkiness, redundancy, and flexibility are keys to evolution, then finding play to be itself quirky, redundant, and flexible certainly suggests that play may have a similar biological base" (Sutton-Smith, 2009, p. 222). Sutton-Smith identifies with the field of biology in connecting play with the development of the brain. In doing so, he attempts to define play: "I define play as a facsimilization of the struggle for survival as this is broadly rendered by Darwin. Biologically, its function is to reinforce the organism's variability in the face of rigidifications of successful adaptation ..." (2009, p. 231). We can interpret Sutton-Smith's position here as contemplating play as a form of psychological feedback, in that it lessens or cancels out altogether the rigidity that takes place after the adaptation of a phenomenon, which, in turn, reinforces variability.

Sutton-Smith considers constructive play, along with sociodramatic play, a modern play form. He writes that of all the play types, constructive play and sociodramatic play are the only two that can be considered to have been subject to play deprivation in human culture (Sutton-Smith, 1975). Sutton-Smith goes on to say that children of lower socio-economic status and of certain cultures tend to do well in what he calls self-testing play, which refers to the time spent on activities that test physical skills with objects in the natural environment—a requirement for survival. Individuals in these environments tend to do well in contesting—self-testing play in groups—situations that require players to engage in competitive activities, such as racing, defending, and capturing. Contesting, as opposed to constructive and sociodramatic play, according to Sutton-Smith, demonstrates a good deal of variety in play levels and playfulness.

Largely inspired by Sutton-Smith's theory of play, Scott Eberle (2014) defines play in a manner that includes at least six attributes of the mind: anticipation, surprise, pleasure, understanding, strength, and poise. Therefore, play in this context is a vital component of human development and interaction with other people and the objects that exist within one's environment. Thomas Henricks (2020) refers to play as one of several "pathways of experience"—others being ritual, work, bonding, and collective celebration—all of which comprise what he calls *communitas*. Henricks concentrates on five perspectives on play, namely, the psyche, the body, the environment, society, and culture. In doing so, Henricks recognizes conditions that initiate play, and suggests possible outcomes with regard to these settings. Henricks proposed a general theory that places experience front and center as a critical element of play.

While little consensus exists on a pithy definition of play, most researchers seem to agree that play is a catalytic process whereby certain organisms remain engaged in activities involving anticipatory behaviors for a certain period of time. With regard to humans, play can serve as a vehicle in which individuals experiment, demonstrate, and test the boundaries of knowledge and everyday behaviors. In addition, play can be categorized into at least four common social interaction types: solitary play, parallel play, competitive play, and cooperative play. Play exists in a variety of forms. Within the context of vernacular architecture, constructive play, which necessitates the use of VCPOs (e.g., blocks, bricks, planks, or natural objects like tree branches, roots, logs, or woodchips), is an indispensable pursuit that leads to the development of structure (Ness & Farenga, 2016). In this sense, play is associated with a variety of traditions, which are dependent on culturally specific norms for determining patterns, conventions, or rules.

Constructive free play involves one's imagination as a means of constructing an environment with VCPOs that emulates real, workaday systems, such as homes, roads, bridges, tunnels, and parks. Thus, play is also intertwined with architecture and engineering. The development of three-dimensional solids known as "Gifts" by Friedrich Froebel in the early 19th century, which will be discussed at greater length in the next chapter, has had a major influence on architects throughout the world since the 1850s (Ness, Farenga & Garofalo, 2017; Tovey, 2016). More recent research has shown that play is dependent on the individual's spatial contexts and the resources available within those environments (Ward, 1994).

While some play researchers consider the role of play to be the work of children (Hirsh-Pasek & Golinkoff, 2008; Ness & Farenga, 2007), the position that play is work does not seem to be held in high regard as a central tenet in the Western conceptions of play—even though it should be. For example, Scarlett, Naudeau, Salonius-Pasternak, and Ponte (2004) suggest that when children are engaged in constructive free play, they often appear to be going "in and out" of play. They support this notion by referring to Forman's (1998) position that when a child engages in constructive play by asking "What if?" questions, they are participating in constructive play, but once they begin to ask "Why won't it do that?"—a question that indicates a mistake took place—Forman claims that, in this case, the child is working and not playing. Scarlett and colleagues include Forman's own words: "the playful child is content to change what he or she does, just to see what it yields. The task-oriented child is determined to achieve a particular goal" (Scarlett et al., 2004, p. 394).

But, I argue that questions like "Why won't it do that?," that is, when the child makes a mistake, represent the very essence of what play actually is! Play frequently involves making errors and finding solutions. In current and future STEAM professions and initiatives, it is, and will be, essential for the individual to not only problem solve, but problem pose as well. Unlike its cousin problem solving, problem posing is a relatively novel cross-cutting concept in science, engineering, technology, and mathematics that requires the individual to think of possibilities that may arise in future STEAM related problems. And that's the point: Problems indicate that something not quite right—a mistake is evident and therefore needs to be corrected or resolved. Boaler (2016) argues that the making of mistakes is at the heart of succeeding in mathematics. Students of all STEM fields tend to succeed in their subject if they come across obstacles and find ways to solve them (Kricorian, Seu, Lopez, Ureta, & Equils, 2020). Clearly, when we problem pose (and problem solve), we are not only asking "What if?" questions; we are also asking "Why won't it do that?" questions because doing so encourages children to develop a growth mindset (Boaler, 2016; Dweck, 2008). Moreover, I would add that not only is there an intrinsic relationship between making mistakes and play, there is also an intrinsic relationship between play and work—in other words, play is work, especially for the young child. In Chapter 5, I discuss the life and times of the world-renowned physicist Richard Feynman, who, in his own words, described his childhood as one filled with imagination and the bringing of fantasy to real-life concepts. In this regard, Feynman clearly set the example that work and play, along with the making and fixing of mistakes, are inextricably connected.

Research on cross-cultural play has been making inroads in the last few decades with regard to establishing theories that are consistent with culturally-bound characteristics of play (Gaskins & Göncü, 1992). Gaskins, Haight, and Lancy (2007), for example, argue that while it is common to think of play as a universal behavior of children and qualitatively comparable in all cultural settings, it is important to challenge that perspective and consider the numerous traits of play that differ from one culture to another.

In non-Western societies, however, play as work often assumes a central role. For example, for children of the Gabbra of northern Kenya and the uplands of southern Ethiopia, play involves, in part, the acts of emulating and repeating the tent building procedures of adults. In Gabbra culture, children frequently play house by emulating adults in their environment who are engaged in physical labor as they participate in the tent building process and in reconstructing camel loads, which include materials for tent construction (Prussin, 1995). As a collective and not individualistic society, the Gabbra ensure that everyone is given sufficient food, animals for transport, shelter, and assistance. Work as a collective endeavor is of the highest priority and serves as a hallmark of Gabbra identity. Thus, play in Gabbra society is one in which children engage together in both imagination and work, and not solely play for its own sake.

Play as work is also an important factor in numerous societies in East Asia. As an example, while children in Taipei, Taiwan, often play with manufactured VCPOs, as do children in Western countries, they do so, often collaboratively, with the intention of emulating adults at work. In doing so, they involve themselves in play activities that demonstrate not only the construction of buildings or garages for their own sake, but also for the purpose of functionality. Children in Taipei often plan structures based on practical necessity, such as the construction of a toy garage for toy cars. In this instance, children decide to construct a garage collaboratively out of plastic snap bricks so that each car has a space available. Like residents in most of the world's large cities, residents in Taipei have their share of difficulties in accessing parking spaces for their vehicles. In grappling with this issue, the city manages to accommodate parking on streets and in both detached garages and those underneath city dwellings. The frequency of collaborative constructive play in this environment exemplifies a strategy to construct the ideal parking unit for all toy brick cars to fit. In this example, children modify the garage structure on a frequent basis as a means of accommodating each of the toy cars (Ness et al., 2017). Spatial language connected with vernacular architecture in this example involves numerous STEAM concepts, such as size (large and small), measurement (close and far or short and long), distance, surface area, volume location, and topological constructs (such as proximity, separation, enclosure, order, continuity, and openness) (Weisberg, Zosh, Hirsh-Pasek & Golinkoff, 2013).

Despite the paucity of research literature on the intersection of play and STEAM, the two subjects are intrinsically related in terms of content and process. Just as a large group of linguists has hypothesized that emerging pidgins spoken by children can evolve into creoles and further into greater language formalization (Crystal, 2010), so too is it conceivable that children's everyday constructive play is intertwined in and may possibly influence the architectural values and norms of a specific culture. Thus, more exploration and analysis regarding the ontological and epistemological relationships between play and vernacular architecture would be welcome additions to the research corpus.

Playworlds

The imaginative Playworld is another context in which young children can devote their time to thinking like a scientist, technologist, engineer, architect or artist, and mathematician. The original idea of Playworlds was conceived by Gunilla Lindqvist (1995), a play researcher from Sweden, who was inspired by the work of Lev Vygotsky and also by the theories and research of a number of other psychologists and educational practitioners and by the practice of Playworlds in various school settings. In particular, Lindqvist based Playworlds on Vygotsky's theories of imagination, creativity, and the psychology of art and the theoretical positions of Daniil B. Elkonin, a protégé and assistant of Vygotsky, who emerged in Soviet society as a key figure in education and psychology. Playworlds, as Lindqvist defines them, are a type of child-adult joint play in which children and adults enter into a mutually-shared imaginary play period that is intended to support the development of both children and adults. Playworlds obfuscate traditional dichotomies between such important psychological areas as cognition and emotion, imagination, and creativity.

Elkonin's chief contention was that Soviet psychology followed in the footsteps of other early Western psychologists' theories of play whereby play is interpreted as an activity in which the child engages that represents the child's interaction with the external world and with the immediate social reality. Elkonin based his argument on Vygotsky's position, which is a refutation of early 20th-century theories of play that situate imagination and realistic thinking in conflict. More specifically, Elkonin rejected theories of play emanating from Groos (1901) because he took the qualities of animal play as the foundation for understanding human play. Elkonin (2005) countered earlier play theorists, such as Groos and Bühler (1927), in that he believed play was not based solely on instinct and survival. Unlike educationists and psychologists before him, most of whom engaged in either naturalistic or psychoanalytical investigations of play activities, Elkonin argued that the problem with play theories, including those of Piaget and Freud, is that they pit the adult against the child; in other words, adult and child are dualistic entities. Moreover, earlier theories tended to place imagination and reality in diametric opposition. Strongly influenced by the ideas of his mentor, Vygotsky, Elkonin countered his predecessors in arguing that imagination and realism act in harmony through the processes of invention and creativity, thus overcoming the naturalistic and psychoanalytic theories of children's play.

He also criticized the positions of other theorists of play for situating play in terms of the exaggeration of qualities often associated with play—such as the separation of child from reality, the notion of liveliness, and the predisposition to illusion. In either case, these theorists tended to dissociate the child from social realities as well as child from parent. Moreover, these theories tend to detach children from the communities and the larger society in which they live and ignore the idea that "children learn to manipulate objects only when the action of manipulation is included in a system of interpersonal relations" (Ferholt, 2007, p. 20). Ferholt (2007) points out that the alternative to early and mid-20th-century theories of play is the Vygotskyan cultural-historical method as a means of defining how play contributes to child development.

So, Playworlds, then, allow children and adults to participate in unity in worlds of fantasy in such a way that both the child and adult learn from one another as they engage in activities that bring the fantasy to real-life activities. Unlike earlier play theories that emphasized an evolutionary approach to understanding human behavior, Playworlds account for the ontogenetic development of the individual, whereby the objective is to create activities that bring the actions and characters in both fiction and non-fiction texts to life through drama. It is the interactive space in which both children and adults are creatively engaged.

The implementation of Playworlds has been a growing phenomenon on an international level. The Laboratory of Comparative Human Cognition (LCHC, 2020) provides full descriptions of Playworld projects throughout the world. For example, there are two Playworld projects in Japan: the Ibi Kindergarten near the city of Gifu (west of Tokyo) and the Miharu Kindergarten in Tokyo and Sapporo. The Ibi Kindergarten's Playworld project is called the "Hakken to Boken" project, which means "the discovery and the adventure." The Hakken to Boken project emphasizes art and imaginative play as its main activities. Ibi teachers selected these two activities because they argue that art and imaginative play provide children with the opportunity to explore both the real and imagined worlds. Ibi teachers also believe art and imaginative play through exploratory experiences are essential as a means of facilitating child development. The Playworld teachers at Ibi also argue that the active commitment on the part of the teacher is tantamount to children's social, emotional, and intellectual development when they engage in Hakken to Boken. In order for this to occur, teachers, like their young students, are encouraged to participate in both the imagined and real worlds in which children are experiencing art and play simultaneously.

The second Playworld project in Japan is the "Kodomo project," located in an after-school program in a Kindergarten that is connected to the Department of Education in the College of Arts at Rikkyo University and Playshop in the Miharu Kindergarten in Sapporo. The administrators and practitioners of the Kodomo project develop afterschool preschool programs around a play curriculum that challenges a common belief of educational policymakers who construe play as a hindrance to early formal education learning despite data that provide evidence indicating that the opposite is the case (Baumer, Ferholt & Lecusay, 2005; Ferholt, Nilsson & Lecusay, 2019; LCHC, 2020).

In addition to two Playworld Kindergartens in Japan, Playworlds have been forming in Finland since 2010. The origins of the Finnish Playworlds are based on the work of the play theorist Pentti Hakkarainen, particularly his theory of narrative learning (see Hakkarainen, 2004, 2008), as well as Lindqvist's (1995) original model of the Playworld, and that of Cole and his fifth dimension model (Cole, 1996). Playworlds in Finland were run by teachers and pre-service teachers whose primary function was to lead in the creation, design, and performance of the Playworlds. Finnish Playworlds are broader in scope than in other countries in that they include a larger age range of students, typically from four to eight years. As the LCHC (2020) has indicated, Playworlds in Finland are implemented in the pre-service education curriculum for future teachers. In the United States, the

LCHC at the University of California, San Diego is the principal organization that engages in Playworld projects. Like those in Finland, Playworld projects in the United States were inspired by the work of Pentti Hakkarainen of Finland and Gunilla Lindqvist of Sweden. Playworld research is also a growing field in Australia (Fleer 2019), China (Fleer, Li & Yan, 2018), Italy (Talamo, Pozzi & Mellini, 2010), Japan (Marjanovic-Shane et al. 2011), Lithuania (Hakkarainen, Bredikyte, Jakkula & Munter, 2013), Serbia (Marjanovic-Shane et al. 2011), Sweden (Nilsson, Ferholt & Lecusay, 2017), and the United States (Ferholt & Lecusay 2010).

I bring up Playworlds in this chapter devoted to play and STEAM learning because the implementation of Playworlds in constructive play environments related to STEAM subjects has been receiving more attention in recent years, particularly emanating from schools and child study centers in Australia. One of the key researchers on the subject of Playworlds and STEAM is Marilyn Fleer, Professor and Foundation Chair in Early Childhood Education and Development at Monash University in Melbourne. Fleer brought Playworlds to another level by including STEAM, in addition to the more common fiction and literary themes. In examining Playworlds and STEAM, Fleer (2020a, 2020b) investigated ways in which teachers can design motivating environments for children to participate in engineering thinking. Fleer conducted a 12-month study, which examined how teachers and young children learned about engineering principles collectively. In conducting her study, she performed digital video observations of the daily interactions of two teachers and 13 children between two early childhood classrooms when engineering periods occurred. The children who participated in the research ranged in age from four to six years. The results of her investigation, unlike previous research that focused on engineering affordances during free play, identify novel play pedagogies that support personally meaningful engineering learning of preschool children. According to Fleer, "The new practices, named as an *Engineering PlayWorld*, build imaginary situations, where children in teams act 'as if' they are engineers, meeting engineering problems and generating engineering solutions" (Fleer, 2020a, p. 1). The idea of children "acting 'as if' they are engineers" is a powerful outcome in that Playworlds can potentially bring all STEAM areas into the child's sphere of influence.

Bringing STEAM related concepts and activities to children as young as infants and toddlers has only recently been brought to attention. Research in infant cognition supports the notion that this age group can and do learn ideas in STEAM. In fact, a number of cognitive psychologists found evidence that demonstrates the existence of mathematical knowledge as early as the hours shortly after birth. One of the initial studies in this area was undertaken by Rochel Gelman and Charles Gallistel (1986), who found that relatively young infants—between five and eight months—were able to differentiate between slides projected on a screen showing two objects versus those showing three.

Karen Wynn (1992) studied the extent to which infants can comprehend number in terms of the placement and removal of objects. Her initial findings suggest that infants as young as only a few hours can differentiate between "one" and "more than one," and by four or five months can add and subtract using small numbers.

In addition to emergent mathematical thinking, another branch of cognitive development concerning infants and toddlers involves physical reasoning. One major question in this area has to do with the manner in which infants and young children predict and determine the outcomes of various physical events. Renee Baillargeon's (2002) research investigates various points during development when infants show signs of predicting outcomes of physical events. For example, through the method of inspection time, also referred to as preferential looking, it is posited that young infants spend a longer period of time engaged looking at a picture showing an object in mid-air and off a table than when looking at a picture showing the same object positioned on a table (the idea is that an object in mid-air will fall to the ground).

Grounding their work in the evidence of the existence of infant STEM related cognition found by Baillargeon, Gelman, Gallistel, and Wynn, Fleer, Fragkiadaki and Rai (2020) posit that engagement in STEM can begin during infancy. They reviewed the research literature on play and STEM in order to garner evidence to support the contention that STEM thinking begins during infancy and continues through the early childhood years. Despite the relative lack of research that exists in the area of STEM development during infancy and toddlerhood, Fleer et al. embrace the implementation of *Scientific Playworlds* (Fleer, 2019) as a means of introducing emergent STEM concepts to infants and toddlers through literary examples. In this situation, the teacher or parents facilitate the Playworld while both the children and adults act out and actively engage in emergent STEM activities. One particular example Fleer and colleagues use refers to the STEM concepts inherent in the story "Possum in the House" written by Kiersten Jensen and illustrated by Tony Oliver (1989)—specifically external biological characteristics, heredity, basic biological needs (such as sleep and nutrition), environment, and the concept of sound.

In equating the characteristics of children's cognitive skills through play with the work of eminent scientists (a comparison that my colleagues and I as well as others have supported with evidence for many years; see Bergen, 2009; Farenga & Ness, 2007; Farenga, Joyce & Ness, 2001a, 2001b, 2002; Farenga, Ness & Flynn, 2007; Ness, 2004; Ness & Diercks, 2005; Ness & Farenga, 2007; Ness et al., 2017), Fleer (2019) conducted case study research with three preschool teachers and 26 children to determine how imaginative play encourages scientific learning and how teachers support children's engagement in scientific play. During these case studies, Fleer concluded that while preschool teachers are adept in play pedagogy, transforming imaginary conditions to scientific narratives required additional pedagogical strategies. As Fleer indicates,

> the pedagogical principles of using a cultural device that mirrors the science experiences, creating imaginary scientific situations, collectively building

scientific problem situations, and imagining the relations between observable contexts and non-observable concepts, changed everyday practices into a scientific narrative and engagement.

(2019, p. 1257)

To this end, Fleer employs Scientific Playworlds as a pedagogical device that can be used to address the cultural underpinnings of scientific phenomena when combined with free play.

Conclusion

Previous research suggests that young children are occupied in play that emphasizes process-oriented skills when they have the opportunity to conceive, plan, and construct structures with blocks or other individual or attachable parts (Brophy & Evangelou, 2007). A consideration of the toys children use is necessary when examining the relationship between play and the development of STEAM thinking. Evidence suggests that the affordance that a particular toy or constructive play material offers contributes to the child's social and cognitive development (Ness & Farenga, 2016). Moreover, play objects can serve as the link between the act of play and the workaday life of both adults and children (Bradley, 2015; Zinguer, 2015). Constructive play materials can be divided into at least four categories based on their physical properties. Continuous play materials, the first category, are uncountable objects (e.g., paint, clay, and sand), and may contribute to perceptual knowledge such as right-left orientation and drawing. Countable play objects, the second category, are those such as blocks, bricks, planks, puzzles, and dominoes; objects that may contribute to memory development, verbal and perceptual knowledge, and quantitative skill. Microsymbolic toys, the third category, consist of dolls, miniature trucks and cars, small buildings, and minifigures. Macrosymbolic toys, the fourth category, include both manufactured and child-made play equipment and props for dramatic play (such as dresses, hats, shoes, costumes, and toy houses). Microsymbolic and macrosymbolic toys are said to influence memory, quantitative skills, and perceptual performance (Wolfgang & Stakenas, 1985). Play materials, then, are intrinsically valuable when considering play as an endeavor in the development of structure.

Through the use of ethnographic methods, the development of an analytical and systematic categorization of play objects used during constructive play can be helpful to the researcher or layperson who attempts to examine play within the context of STEAM. Although the terms "blocks" and "block play," which signify the tool and the task, respectively, are typically used in common parlance, their frequent use in constructive play discourse can be problematic due to lack of clarity and cultural specificity. Therefore, the term visuospatial constructive play objects (VCPOs) is used to refer to blocks (for example, standard wood blocks, plastic blocks, and foam blocks), bricks (plastic snap pieces such as LEGO and

MegaBloks), planks (1×3×15 cm wooden rectangular cuboids) as well as a host of other manufactured and natural objects used for constructive play (Ness & Farenga, 2016). Since constructive play can be differentiated from other types of play in that it considers the use of smaller objects as a means for constructing larger and often more elaborate structures, VCPOs are defined as those materials used during synthesis of structures that are either imagined or construed as a model of something in the everyday world. VCPOs can be tied or snapped together or touch each other and remain positioned by the force of gravity.

In the next chapter, we consider different categories of VCPOs—blocks, planks, bricks, and metal-based construction sets—as a way to better understand their strengths and weaknesses. Doing so will help the parent, researcher, and practitioner recognize and appreciate the materials that are most valuable in supporting children's cognitive development in STEAM.

References

Baillargeon, R. (2002). The acquisition of physical knowledge in infancy: A summary in eight lessons. In U. Goswami (Ed.), *Blackwell handbook of childhood cognitive development* (pp. 46–83). Oxford: Blackwell.

Baumer, S., Ferholt, B., & Lecusay, R. (2005). Promoting narrative competence through adult–child joint pretense: Lessons from the Scandinavian educational practice of Playworld. *Cognitive Development*, 20(4), 576–590.

Bergen, D. (2009). Play as the learning medium for future scientists, mathematicians, and engineers. *American Journal of Play*, 1(4), 413–428.

Boaler, J. (2016). *Mathematical mindsets: Unleashing students' potential through creative math, inspiring messages and innovative teaching.* San Francisco, CA: Jossey-Bass.

Bodrova, E., & Leong, D. J. (2015). Vygotskian and post-Vygotskian views on children's play. *American Journal of Play*, 7(3), 371–388.

Bradley, R. H. (2015). Children's housing and physical environments. In M. H. Bornstein & T. Leventhal (Eds.), *Handbook of child psychology and developmental science* (pp. 455–492). Hoboken, NJ: Wiley.

Brophy, S., & Evangelou, D. (2007). Precursors to engineering thinking (PET) project: Intentional Designs with Experimental Artifacts (IDEA). Paper presented at the American Society for Engineering Education Annual Conference and Exposition. American Society for Engineering Education, Honolulu.

Bruner, J. S., Jolly, A., & Sylva, K. (Eds.). (1976). *Play: Its role in development and evolution.* New York: Basic Books.

Bühler, K. (1927). *Die Krise der Psychologie.* Jena, Germany: G. Fischer.

Cole, M. (1996). From Moscow to the Fifth Dimension: An exploration in romantic science. In M. Cole & J. Wertsch (Eds.), *Contemporary implications of Vygotsky and Luria* (pp. 1–38). Worcester, MA: Clark University Press.

Courtney, R. (1989). *Play, drama, and thought: The intellectual background to dramatic education.* Toronto: Simon & Pierre.

Crystal, D. (2010). *The Cambridge encyclopedia of language.* New York: Cambridge University Press.

Deligiorgi, K. (2011). The proper *telos* of life: Schiller, Kant, and having autonomy as an end. *Inquiry*, 54(5), 494–511. doi:10.1080/0020174X.2011.608881.

Dweck, C. (2008). *Mindsets and math/science achievement*. New York: Carnegie Corporation of New York, Institute for Advanced Study, Commission on Mathematics and Science Education.
Eberle, S. G. (2014). The elements of play: Toward a philosophy and a definition of play. *American Journal of Play*, 6(2), 214–233.
Elkonin, D. B. (2005). The psychology of play. *Journal of Russian and East European Psychology*, 43(1), 11–21. doi:10.1080/10610405.2005.11059245.
Farenga, S. J., Joyce, B. A., & Ness, D. (2001a). Bridging the knowledge gap. *Science Scope*, 25(1): 10–14.
Farenga, S. J., Joyce, B. A., & Ness, D. (2001b). Mapping our environment: Where do we go next? *Science Scope*, 24(5): 48–51.
Farenga, S. J., Joyce, B. A., & Ness, D. (2002). Reaching the zone of optimal learning: The alignment of curriculum, instruction, and assessment. In R. Bybee (Ed.), *Learning science and the science of learning* (pp. 51–62). Washington, DC: National Science Teachers Association.
Farenga, S. J., & Ness, D. (2007). It's all in the pattern: Recognizing symmetry in architecture. *Science Scope*, 30(8), 70–73.
Farenga, S. J., Ness, D., & Flynn, G. V. (2007). Strategies for learning and metacognition: Identifying and remembering big ideas. *Science Scope*, 31(2), 82–88.
Ferholt, B. (2007). *Gunilla Lindqvist's theory of play and contemporary play theory*. Retrieved from: http://lchc.ucsd.edu/Projects/PAPER1%20copy-1.pdf.
Ferholt, B., & Lecusay, R. (2010). Adult and child development in the zone of proximal development: Socratic dialogue in a Playworld. *Mind, Culture and Activity*, 17(1), 59–83. doi:10.1080/10749030903342246.
Ferholt, B., Nilsson, M., & Lecusay, R. (2019). Preschool teachers being people alongside young children: The development of adults' relational competences in Playworlds. In S. Alcock and N. Stobbs (Eds.), *Rethinking play as pedagogy* (pp. 17–32). New York: Routledge.
Fleer, M. (2019). Scientific Playworlds: A model of teaching science in play-based settings. *Research in Science Education*, 49(5), 1257–1278.
Fleer, M. (2020a). Engineering PlayWorld—a model of practice to support children to collectively design, imagine and think using engineering concepts. *Research in Science Education*, 1–16. Retrieved from: https://doi.org/10.1007/s11165-020-09970-6.
Fleer, M. (2020b). Studying the relations between motives and motivation: How young children develop a motive orientation for collective engineering play. *Learning, Culture, and Social Interaction*, 24, [100355]. Retrieved from: https://doi.org/10.1016/j.lcsi.2019.100355.
Fleer, M., Fragkiadaki, G., & Rai, P. (2020): STEM begins in infancy: Conceptual PlayWorlds to support new practices for professionals and families. *International Journal of Birth and Parent Education*, 7(4), 27–31.
Fleer, M., Li, L., & Yan, Z. (2018). Problematising pedagogical imports and creating new conditions for children's development: A case from China. In M. Fleer, F. G. Rey, & P. P. E. Jones (Eds.), *Cultural-historical and critical psychology: Common ground, divergences and future pathways*. Dordrecht, Netherlands: Springer.
Forman, G. (1998) Constructive play. In D. Fromberg & D. Bergen (Eds.), *Play from birth to twelve and beyond: Contexts, perspectives, and meaning* (pp. 392–400). New York: Garland.
Gaskins, S., & Göncü, A. (1992). Cultural variation in play: A challenge to Piaget and Vygotsky. *The Quarterly Newsletter of the Laboratory of Comparative Human Cognition*, 14(2), 31–35.

Gaskins, S., Haight, W., & Lancy, D. F. (2007). The cultural construction of play. In A. Göncü & S. Gaskins (Eds.), *Play and development: Evolutionary, sociocultural, and functional perspectives* (pp. 179–202). Mahwah, NJ: Lawrence Erlbaum Associates.

Gelman, R., & Gallistel, C. R. (1986). *The child's understanding of number*. Cambridge, MA: Harvard University Press.

Gordon, G. (2008). What is play? In search of a universal definition. *Play and Culture Studies*, 8, 1–21.

Gould, S. J. (1996). *Full house*. New York: Harmony Books.

Groos, K. (1898). *The play of animals* (E. L. Baldwin, Trans.). New York: Appleton.

Groos, K. (1901). *The play of man* (E. L. Baldwin, Trans.). New York: Appleton.

Hakkarainen, P. (2004). *Narrative learning in the Kajaani Fifth Dimension*. Paper presented at the American Educational Research Association 2004 Annual Meeting, San Diego.

Hakkarainen, P. (2008). The challenges and possibilities of narrative learning approach in the Finnish early childhood education system. *International Journal of Educational Research*, 47(5), 292–300.

Hakkarainen, P., Bredikyte, M., Jakkula, K., & Munter, H. (2013). Adult play guidance and children's play development in a narrative play-world. *European Early Childhood Education Research Journal*, 21(2), 213–225.

Henricks, T. (2020). Play studies: A brief history. *American Journal of Play*, 12(2), 117–155.

Hirsh-Pasek, K., & Golinkoff, R. M. (2008). Why play = learning. In R. E. Tremblay, R. de V. Peters, & M. Boivin (Eds.), *Encyclopedia on early childhood development* (pp. 1–7). Montreal, QC, Canada: Centre of Excellence for Early Childhood Development.

Hughes, F. P. (2010). *Children, play, and development*. Thousand Oaks, CA: Sage.

Huta, V. (2013). Eudaimonia. In S. David, I. Boniwell, & A. C. Ayers (Eds.), *Oxford handbook of happiness* (pp. 201–213). Oxford, GB: Oxford University Press.

Jensen, K., & Oliver, T. (1989). *Possum in the house*. New York: Gareth Stevens Publishing.

Kricorian, K., Seu, M., Lopez, D., Ureta, E., & Equils, O. (2020). Factors influencing participation of underrepresented students in STEM fields: matched mentors and mindsets. *International Journal of STEM Education*, 7, 1–9.

Laboratory of Comparative Human Cognition (LCHC). (2020). *Playworlds: A recently emerging form of adult-child joint play*. Retrieved from: http://lchc.ucsd.edu/playworlds.

Lindqvist, G. (1995). *The aesthetics of play: A didactic study of play and culture in preschools*. Stockholm, Sweden: Gotab.

Marjanovic-Shane, A., Ferholt, B., Miyazaki, K., Nilsson, M., Rainio, A. P., Hakkarainen, P., Pesic, M., & Beljanski-Ristic, L. (2011). Playworlds—An art of development. In C. Lobman & B. E. O'Neill (Eds.), *Play and performance. Play and culture Studies* (pp. 3–32). Lanham, MD: University Press of America.

Mitchell, R. W. (2002). *Pretending and imagination in animals and children*. Cambridge: Cambridge University Press.

Ness, D. (2004). Mapping for Geographic Awareness. *Science Scope*, 28(3), 48–50.

Ness, D., & Diercks, M. (2005). Mapping your way to geographic awareness: Integrating cartography with literature, history, and science. *Science Scope*, 28(4), 59–63.

Ness, D., & Farenga, S. J. (2016). Blocks, bricks, & planks: Relationships between affordance and visuo-spatial constructive play objects. *American Journal of Play*, 8(2), 201–227.

Ness, D., & Farenga, S. J. (2007). *Knowledge under construction: The importance of play in developing children's spatial and geometric thinking*. Lanham, MD: Rowman & Littlefield Publishers.

Ness, D., Farenga, S. J., & Garofalo, S. G. (2017). *Spatial intelligence: Why it matters from birth through the lifespan*. New York: Routledge.

Nicolopoulou, A. (1993). Play, cognitive development, and the social world: Piaget, Vygotsky, and beyond. *Human Development*, 36(1), 1–23.

Nilsson, M., Ferholt, B., & Lecusay, R. (2017). The playing-exploring child: Reconceptualizing the relationship between play and learning in early childhood education. *Contemporary Issues in Early Childhood*, 1(15), 1–15. doi:10.1177/1463949117710800.

Piaget, J. (1951). *Play, dreams, and imitation in childhood* (C. Gattegno & F. M. Hodgson, Trans.). London: William Heinemann.

Prussin, L. (1995). *African nomadic architecture: Space, place, gender*. Washington, DC: Smithsonian Institution Press.

Roehr, S. (2003). Freedom and autonomy in Schiller. *Journal of the History of Ideas*, 64(1), 119–134.

Scarlett, W. G., Naudeau, S., Salonius-Pasternak, D., & Ponte, I. (2004). *Children's play*. Thousand Oaks, CA: Sage Publications.

Schiller, F. (1943 [1794]). *Schillers Werke, Nationalausgabe*, J. Petersen & H. Schneider (Eds.). Weimar: Hermann Böhlaus Nachfolger.

Smith, P. K. (2006). Evolutionary foundations and functions of play: An overview. In A. Göncü & S. Gaskins (Eds.), *Play and development: Evolutionary, sociocultural and functional perspectives* (pp. 21–49). Mahwah, NJ: Lawrence Erlbaum.

Sutton-Smith, B. (2009). *The ambiguity of play*. Cambridge, MA: Harvard University Press.

Sutton-Smith, B. (1966). Piaget on play: A critique. *Psychological Review*, 73, 104–110. doi:10.1037/h0022601.

Sutton-Smith, B. (1975). The useless made useful: Play as variability training. *The School Review*, 83(2), 197–214.

Talamo, A., Pozzi, S., & Mellini, B. (2010). Uniqueness of experience and virtual Playworlds: Playing is not just for fun. *Mind Culture and Activity*, 17(1): 23–41. doi:10.1080/10749030903342220.

Vygotsky, L. S. (1993 [1928]). The dynamics of child character. In R. W. Rieber & A. S. Carton (Eds.), *The collected works of L. S. Vygotsky: The fundamentals of defectology* (pp. 153–163). New York: Plenum.

Vygotsky, L. S. (1966 [1933]). Play and its role in the psychological development of the child. Lecture, Leningrad Pedagogical Institute. *Problems of Psychology*, 6, 62–76.

Ward, C. (1994). *Opportunities for childhoods in late twentieth-century Britain*. London: Falmer Press.

Weisberg, D. S., Zosh, J. M., Hirsh-Pasek, K., & Golinkoff, R. M. (2013). Talking it up: Play, language development, and the role of adult support. *American Journal of Play*, 6(1), 39–54.

Wolfgang, C. H., & Stakenas, R. G. (1985). An exploration of toy content of preschool children's home environments as a predictor of cognitive development. *Early Child Development and Care*, 19(4), 291–307.

Wynn, K. (1992). Addition and subtraction by human infants. *Nature*, 358, 749–750.

Zinguer, T. (2015). *Architecture in play: Intimations of modernism in architectural toys*. Charlottesville, VA: University of Virginia Press.

3
BLOCKS, BRICKS, AND PLANKS
Visuospatial Constructive Play Objects

In Chapter 1, we introduced the phrase "visuospatial constructive play objects" or VCPOs. My intention in this chapter's introduction is to expand on the meaning of VCPO so that readers will be comfortable encountering this term head on in this and later chapters. My colleague, Stephen Farenga and I coined the term because we found that there was no term (at least in the English language) that either defines or refers to all the small to mid-size parts or pieces that are used to design and construct larger structures when an individual is involved in constructive free play (Ness & Farenga, 2016). That is to say that block play can be differentiated from brick play and plank play as well as many other part types. Moreover, in our 2016 study, we wanted to determine whether parallels between block play and spatial cognition result from the type of object or play part that children or adolescents use when engaged in constructive free play.

In pursuing this goal, we developed an analytical framework of play objects used during constructive play, and established that the terms "blocks" (the term signifying the tool) and "block play" (the term signifying the task) are nonspecific and consequently, using these terms can become knotty when examining constructive play object types. These terms become more problematic when one attempts to study the extent to which children's constructive free play and their everyday, spontaneous concepts contribute to cognitive development (Casey, Andrews, Schindler, Kersh, Samper & Copley, 2008; Ness & Farenga, 2007, 2016) or spatial language development (Cohen & Emmons, 2017; Ferrara, Hirsh-Pasek, Newcombe, Golinkoff & Lam, 2011; Pruden & Levine, 2017). Therefore, rather than using the generic terms "blocks" or "bricks," we employed the term visuospatial constructive play objects (VCPOs; I would be delighted to learn of another term, other than an acronym, that someone might be interested in suggesting). VCPOs include blocks (for example, wood blocks, plastic blocks, and

DOI: 10.4324/9781003097815-4

foam blocks), bricks (such as LEGOs, MegaBloks, and the numerous other LEGO brick clones), and planks (1cm × 3cm × 15cm wooden rectangular cuboids), as well as other metal and plastic-produced pieces. As we indicated in our earlier work, VCPOs have the potential to offer cognitive researchers insight when they study the development of spatial thinking—in our present case, as it relates to STEAM. Constructive play, as we have considered in the previous chapter, differs from other play types because it requires the use of smaller, possibly more intricate parts that are assembled in such a manner whereby larger and conceivably more elaborate structures are constructed. Due to this unique feature of constructive free play, we further described VCPOs as materials that are either snapped together or remain erect due to gravity, and, when completed, represent the individual's imagination or construal of a structure based on everyday experiences.

Research on the affordance of play blocks, bricks, and planks, and VCPOs in general, as they relate to child development is sparse and research on their connections to STEAM concepts and architectural or mathematical thinking in particular is, to my knowledge, virtually non-existent. In terms of the former (which is the central focus of the next chapter), the relationship between VCPOs and their affordance from a developmental perspective can be traced back to studies on tool use among children and the animal kingdom (Köhler, 1921; Thurnwald, 1922; Vygotsky, 1928), particularly in connection with behaviors exhibited during play as discussed in the previous chapter. Moreover, this relationship has been highlighted in more recent studies that examine tool use from both a psychological and educational perspective on early childhood (Bjorklund & Gardiner, 2011; Pellegrini, 2009).

With this relatively brief introduction of VCPOs and the origin of this term, we will now dedicate the remainder of this chapter to discussing the many types of VCPOs that children play with, as well as those that stimulate cognitive development in STEAM subjects and those that may possibly limit creativity and development. The following sections are divided into four categories: blocks, planks, bricks (in addition to cloned and copyright-infringed brick companies), and metal constructive play toys. I then discuss the genderization of VCPOs and finally offer concluding remarks.

Blocks: STEAM Thinking through Block Play

Although there is virtually no research on the subject, the study of STEAM and the STEAM principles behind children's block constructions forms the overall thrust of this book. A number of reasons seem to account for the plethora of relationships between mathematics and natural sciences in preschool children's block constructions and the work of professional architects and engineers. To begin with, historical evidence corroborates these connections. For example, Balfanz (1999) discusses how Friedrich Wilhelm August Froebel's Gifts—both three- and two-dimensional materials that were designed and intended to promote young children's understanding of geometric concepts as well as those of tension and compression—influenced numerous individuals in different STEAM related fields. Froebel (1782–1852) was an eminent German philosopher and educator who is widely known as the inventor of Kindergarten. In addition to his numerous contributions to early childhood development and learning, Froebel, among others of his day, influenced the direction of education as both a professional and academic field in Europe and eventually in the United States and Canada. Froebel was the author of numerous publications. Perhaps the most noteworthy with regard to his educational mission is his work *On the Education of Man*, first published in 1826, in which he outlines and defines pedagogical principles (Froebel, 1887). In addition, educators, especially early childhood educators, are indebted to Froebel for his development and contribution of educational play materials for young children known as the Froebel Gifts. With a total of 20, these Gifts consisted of both two- and three-dimensional objects created specifically for the purpose of allowing the young child to explore and develop her mind through both mental and physical manipulation of objects. The main idea behind Froebel's Gifts was that each Gift was intended to follow a specific order in terms of development. The Gifts became more complex as children increased in age, and were made to help teachers identify children's perceptions and spatial ideas in a developmental manner. For our purposes, we will examine the first six.

The Gifts were created by Froebel to align with the different ages during early childhood from infancy to about five years of age. Gift 1 consisted of a single-colored small soft ball and a small ball of yarn—small enough to fit in the infant's hands. The purposes of Gift 1 were to engage the infant, develop the infant's gross motor skills and spatial thinking skills, as well as concepts of time, the contrast of colors, and the basic notion of gravity. Gift 2 was developed for children between one and two years, and consisted of a wooden sphere and cube. Referring to Gift 2 as "the child's delight," Froebel indicated that the very young child is presented with the sphere and cube and will undoubtedly notice that the sphere, when placed on an inclined plane, is active; it will produce sound as it moves. The sphere appears the same when the child moves in different directions while looking at it. Unlike the cube, which possesses flat surfaces, the sphere is curvilinear, and thus does not remain stationary when moved or placed on an inclined plane and possesses a different appearance when viewed from different directions. Gift 3, intended for children between two and three years, involved the cutting or division of the large cube into eight smaller cubes—small enough to fit into the child's hand. With Gift 3, the child takes apart the smaller cubes and reconstructs them, sometimes reconstructing the large cube from the small ones. This act of reconstruction forms the foundation of building structure—as we have maintained in Chapter 1 and through the rest of this book. Gift 4, also developed for children between two and three years, looks the same as the large cube, but in this case, the large cube is made of planks, which are twice as long as they are wide. This assembly offers the child greater construction possibilities and further development of structure. Gift 5, for children between the ages of three and four years, consists of several cubes that are divided into half and quarter pieces, thus providing the child with a fuller array of building possibilities. Gift 6, for children between the ages of four and five years, are more complex than the previous five Gifts in that they consist of cubes, planks, and triangular prisms for more advanced constructions.

In the architecture and engineering fields, as Brosterman (1997) indicates, Frank Lloyd Wright expressed his appreciation to Froebel and his ideas and techniques on numerous occasions. In one of his autobiographies, Wright recalled working with Froebel's Gifts to create geometric designs and models of buildings, which he further contended had a profound impact on his career (Lange, 2018). Wright was not the only architect who explicitly recognized Froebel's influence on later thinking. The Swiss architect Le Corbusier also acknowledged the importance of Froebelian Gifts as an important catalyst for his later endeavors in architecture. Le Corbusier, whose Kindergarten experience included a great deal of Froebelian influence, designed buildings that explicitly demonstrated Froebel's creative approach to the learning of geometry.

Widespread interest in research on pedagogical techniques of space and geometry did not occur until the 20th century; nevertheless, a number of prominent thinkers and educators of the late 18th and 19th centuries developed ways to foster children's thinking about the world through the use of specific objects. These objects were also essential in developing young children's ideas about mathematical concepts and scientific principles.

STEAM Thinking through Blocks in the Late 19th Century

Following Froebel, blocks became one of the most popular toys and play materials for children in both Europe and the United States (Provenzo & Brett, 1983; Hirsch, 1996). In the late 19th century, the Crandall family became one of the most successful manufacturers of children's blocks, and were credited with the creation and development of the interlocking block.

The Crandalls were by no means without competition, however. Friedrich Richter's Anker-Steinbaukasten, or anchor block (made of highly compressed sand), became quite popular in the United States in the late 19th century after its success in Germany and the rest of Europe. The importance of the Richter blocks, which were founded on the principles of Froebel's Gifts and Occupations, lay in their construction, which is designed to foster young children's intellectual development and flexibility in geometric thinking (Brosterman, 1997). Richter's stereometric manipulative (stereometry refers to the measurement of solid geometric figures) allowed children to not only explore with solid geometric blocks but extend the notion of shape identification to the actual measurement of solid bodies.

Montessori's Kindergarten

Maria Montessori, too, implemented blocks in her program as a means of developing geometric thinking and reasoning in the early years. Unlike earlier educators, Montessori, an Italian educator (trained as a physician), instilled an element of free choice in her method of facilitating young children's learning (Balfanz, 1999). Using her method, children developed ideas of various geometric shapes (circles, squares, triangles, ellipses, trapezoids, rhombuses, hexagons, and so forth) through exploratory activity. This is not to say, however, that her exercises and activities for children were deprived of structure; in fact, *The Montessori Method* (Montessori, 1964) contains nearly 400 pages of sequenced lessons that are to be balanced with the child's free choice activities. Montessori's method grew in popularity in Europe at the turn of the century, and, by 1912, had become a success in the United States.

By the end of the 1920s, Montessori's pedagogical methods had fallen into disrepute, particularly with the critiques of several educational psychologists of the time, William Kilpatrick and Edward L. Thorndike, both from Teachers College, Columbia University, in particular (Balfanz, 1999). While interest in educational theories in associationist psychology had waxed in popularity, the acceptance of the Montessori Method, despite its earlier success, had begun to wane. Kilpatrick wrote a scathing critique of Montessori's methods, describing them as insensitive to the social needs and development of the child. Moreover, he believed that her materials lacked a sense of differentiation and did not allow for creative expression on the part of the child. Thorndike, too, was a leading critic of the Montessori Method, and any other method or theoretical position emphasizing intellectual development at the expense of social development and personal hygiene in the early years. Nevertheless, despite overwhelming criticism, Montessori's method was not without merit in terms of the way her program and materials helped shape young children's spatial and geometric thinking and competencies.

Caroline Pratt and the Unit Block

Froebel was perhaps one of the first individuals to connect young children's cognitive skills with their use of tactile block materials—the Gifts or Occupations. After Froebel, the most noted individual to encourage the inclusion of blocks (particularly unit blocks) in the educational curriculum was Caroline Pratt. Unlike Montessori, whose emphasis seemed to be more on an educational theory in which the use of blocks played merely an incidental function, Pratt made unit blocks the paradigm of her educational curriculum and agenda. Much of Pratt's curriculum and educational ideology was based on intensive observation of children's cognitive behaviors during free play (see Provenzo & Brett, 1983). Her educational program, then, was founded on the notion that children's learning stems from spontaneous activity. Pratt's interest in children's spontaneous learning intensified after observing a Kindergarten class facilitated by Patty Smith Hill. Pratt was inspired by the children's use of floor blocks in Hill's classroom, and their ability to construct houses, buildings, cars, and wagons. Hill's maple floor blocks were manufactured in such a way as to represent real-life objects or phenomena. Some blocks were in the shape of circles (for the wheels of a car), while others were small 3" × 3" × 3" cubes and 36" × 3" × 3" rods. In her book, Pratt alludes to blocks being a central role in children's geometric thinking.

> Of all the materials which I had seen offered to children ... these blocks of Patty Hill's seems [sic] to me best suited for children's purposes. A simple geometric shape could become any number of things to a child. It could be a truck or a boat or the car of a train. He could build buildings with it from barns to skyscrapers. I could see children of my as yet unborn school constructing a complete community with blocks.
>
> *(Pratt, 1948, p. 28)*

Despite her penchant toward Hill's floor blocks, Pratt nevertheless strove to produce a type of block that did not necessarily resemble real-life models or phenomena. Instead, she searched for a block in which children were able to express their creativity—that is, children needed generic blocks, so that they had the opportunity to impose their own rules on constructing larger, life-like objects. Shortly before the founding of the City and Country School in Greenwich Village (New York City) in 1914, Pratt invented blocks based on a unit system with proportions of 1:2:4. Pratt's creation led to the prototypical block set that most American preschools have been using for the past several decades. The typical standard unit block that Pratt invented was in the dimensions of 14cm × 7cm × 3.5cm. Her primary motivation for founding the City and Country School was to identify what children tell us from their everyday goings on during free play time by intense observation. Pratt would then use the data she collected for the purpose of developing a curriculum that was child-centered (i.e., student-centered) rather than the typical grade school, which was based on a teacher-centered model that emphasized drill and practice with rote learning experiences. Pratt made the City and Country School into an observation and imagination laboratory in which teachers would gather information about children's invented strategies for the purpose of connecting their everyday play activities with blocks with concepts inherent in school subjects. Pratt was a steadfast advocate of the idea that play can inspire learning and that the school curriculum should be based on this premise. Pratt's general contribution to education was her intention, development, and subsequent publicizing and promotion of unit blocks in particular and, eventually, more common wood play blocks in general. Moreover, we are indebted to Pratt for the everyday use of wooden play blocks not only in schools but in homes as well.

Although Pratt had alluded to the power of blocks in building young children's cognitive skills and understanding of geometry, by the end of the 1920s, little if any research had been devoted to blocks and their possible connection with STEAM cognition. Despite the convincing arguments made by those who embraced and championed young children's use of blocks, as well as the Froebelian Gifts, evidence supporting types of play or activity engendering STEAM thinking through a cognitive or developmental perspective were lacking. It was not until the 1940s, with the work of Heinz Werner and Jean Piaget, that an understanding of the development of spatial and geometric concepts was developed.

Standard Wooden Play Blocks

Play blocks are often referred to as "wood blocks" or "standard unit blocks." They are extremely common in preschools and homes. Play blocks are constructed of numerous three-dimensional geometric figures. The most familiar of these figures are unit blocks, which are in the shape of a rectangular prism. Blocks that are double the size of unit blocks are called double unit blocks and those four times the length are called quadruple unit blocks. In addition to unit, double, and quadruple blocks, the standard block set usually consists of blocks in the form of arches, cylinders, and triangular prisms. Given their regularity in free play centers at the preschool or early elementary school grades, blocks are recognizable to most children from an ecological perspective because they have been touchstone materials in early childhood education settings for over a century (Lascarides & Hinitz, 2013).

History of Research on Block Play

Research regarding block play and its influence on social, emotional, and cognitive development is prevalent in the research literature. Blocks are the most examined of all the VCPOs. There has been more research literature on play blocks than on bricks and planks. Based on the work of Edward Thorndike and Raymond Cattell, early research on blocks tended to focus on stimulus-response conditions and the environmental influences of blocks on children. For example, Hulson and Reich (1931) studied children's play options during free play time, and Bailey (1933) examined the development of scales for determining children's motor manipulations and complexity of structure. A shift of research focus seems to have occurred in post-Second World War block studies with an increasing interest in gender and block play. A large number of these investigations have been based on Erikson's (1951) investigations, which essentially concluded there were differences in approach and intent between girls and boys when engaged in block play—namely, that girls generally construct open spaces and enclosures while boys build tower-like structures. While post-Erikson research has corroborated Erikson's findings (Schuster, 1973; Clance, 1975; Blackman, 1977; Wilcox, 1979), others have refuted his claims (Goodfader, 1982; Mayer, 1991). Other gender studies examined the amount of time boys and girls engaged in block activities (Beeson & Williams, 1979; Williams & Beeson, 1980; Kinsman & Berk, 1979) and the selection of block play with respect to other types of play (Massey, 1969; Rubin, 1977).

Provenzo and Brett (1983) and Hirsch (1996) have devoted entire volumes to the history, development, and use of blocks. Provenzo and Brett have provided a thorough treatment of the history of block building, theory and research, and the use of blocks in home and in the school environment. Hirsch's text is an edited volume that includes discussions on the functions of blocks within different subjects and across social domains. Brosterman's (1997) treatment of the history of Kindergarten parallels that of Provenzo and Brett in that it attempts to establish a historical underpinning of present-day blocks with that of the Gifts developed by Friedrich Froebel as well as connections between Froebelian Gifts and Frank Lloyd Wright's inspiration in architecture. Hewitt's (2001) history of blocks corroborates that of Brosterman in supporting the contention that block building builds mathematical knowledge.

The trade book market includes publications that advocate the importance of play in general and block play more specifically and its potential effects on intellectual development. In this regard, Pollman (2010) explained how blocks can serve as an important play type in the development of spatial abilities in mathematics, language, and science. While these publications serve a central purpose in emphasizing the seemingly intrinsic link between play and intellectual development as well as the need to implement blocks and bricks in the early childhood curriculum, they are lacking in terms of shedding light on how constructive play pieces promote spatial development from elementary school to middle-school and high-school grade levels in the areas of STEAM fields. Moreover, while block play does seem, at least intuitively, to be linked to the development of mathematical and scientific thinking, it is even more important to consider how certain types of block play can impede academic performance. We argue that the type of play object matters, and that certain themed play products can actually stifle cognitive growth, specifically in the area of creativity, and not necessarily enhance it (Farenga, Ness, Johnson & Johnson, 2011).

Another area in the research literature on block research concerns block construction stages. Guanella (1934) identified four stages—pre-organized, linear, bi-dimensional, and tri-dimensional—that are based entirely on childhood maturity. Forman's (1982) stages consider block activity from infancy and the grasping of a single block with both hands and ends with the building of symmetric constructions. Reifel (1984) presents a provocative framework for educational practitioners and researchers in understanding children's own ideas about spatial relationships. Basing his thesis on Piaget's theory of children's conception of space, Reifel organizes children's development of block constructions into several stages. Before discussing more advanced types of block constructions, Reifel treats particular spatial representations with blocks as discrete components within a so-called developmental progression.

Exploration in linking block play with psychological and educational research has been growing at a moderate pace since the 1990s, and much more so since 2015. I have reviewed many of these studies in other chapters of this book—particularly in Chapter 2 on our discussion of play and constructive activities and in Chapter 6, when I introduce our analysis of young children's VCPO play with an overview of research on emergent engineering and architectural thinking with blocks and bricks.

Anchor Stone Blocks

Anchor stone blocks are construction toys that are comparable to, but unlike, the standard wooden play blocks. These blocks have been produced in three colors: red brick, tan limestone, and blue slate. Due to their small size, they are not intended for very young children. Inspired by the Froebelian Gifts, anchor stone blocks were first created and designed by the brothers and aviation pioneers Otto and Gustav Lilienthal in the 1870s. Anchor stone blocks were made of a mixture of quartz sand, chalk, and linseed oil—materials that were smoother and more stable than Froebel's wooden Gifts. They were pressed in molds for easy use when constructing structures. The well-known toy manufacturer, Friedrich Adolf Richter, who started a toy factory in Rudolstadt, purchased the rights to the anchor stone blocks, also called Anker Steinbaukasten, in 1880 from the Lilienthal brothers who were struggling with debt. Richter popularized them throughout central and Eastern Europe and eventually the United States. Richter unveiled the first anchor stone block series with four different stone sets, and in 1887, he produced a Special Edition set that was a replica of the house in which Pope Leo XII was born. Richter was successful at marketing his products and commercialized the stone blocks through extensive advertising. As one of the pioneering toys that stimulated creativity, anchor stone blocks were praised by Thomas Edison as an ideal toy for modeling new projects. It has also been alleged that Albert Einstein, Max Born, J. Robert Oppenheimer, Ivan Sutherland, and Walter Gropius played with Anker stone blocks in their formative years and cited them as partly responsible for their inspiration in science, engineering, and architecture (Lepore, 2018).

Withstanding two world wars, the popularity of Anker stone blocks lasted for over 80 years, until, in 1963, the stone construction set fell out of favor. However, anchor stone blocks witnessed a rebirth in 1994, when Georg Plenge, a professor of acoustics at the Technical University in Berlin, brought them back to life and began the renaissance of anchor stone blocks, which were produced at the original factory in Rudolstadt, and are still being produced. Since their renaissance in 1994, anchor stone blocks have received several awards, which contributed to their renewed success. Anker has produced stone blocks with several different themes including the basic stone block set, the Brandenburg Gate set, numerous extension stone block sets, and mosaic puzzle block sets. Anker

Eurosource (2020) also offers various building plans that can be constructed from the extension stone block sets including, but not limited to, a small pyramid monument, an observation tower, an electricity generating station tower building, a memorial building grave chapel, speaker's platform building, a small city hall, a lighthouse tower, a school building, a river bridge, and a manor house.

Lincoln Logs

Invented by John Lloyd Wright, the second son of Frank Lloyd Wright, in 1916, Lincoln Logs consist of miniaturized logs with square notches that are used to construct both conventional buildings, like cabins and related houses, and military buildings, like forts and garrisons. It is not absolutely clear how Lincoln Logs got its name. The K'Nex Company claims that the toy was named after Abraham Lincoln, who, of course, was born in a log cabin, a fact which inspired the designer during World War I. Others claim that the designation comes from Frank Lloyd Wright's original middle name—Lincoln. The logs are of varying lengths but each one measures approximately two centimeters in diameter. Following the success of other VCPOs that will be discussed later in this chapter, namely, Meccano and Tinkertoys, Lincoln Logs evolved into a popular building constructive play toy and remains so to this very day. The uniqueness of Lincoln Logs lay in their construction, namely, logs that look like beams with notches. These notches are essential as they enable the logs to clamp together in 90-degree angles as a means of constructing rectangular buildings.

John Lloyd Wright got his inspiration to create Lincoln Logs from the time when he had accompanied his father to Japan in 1916 and 1917 for the purpose of designing the Imperial Hotel in Tokyo. More specifically, the younger Wright was fascinated by the way the Imperial Hotel was designed, that is, the interlocking beams that strengthened the structure and made it as earthquake-proof as possible (Wheeler, 2019). Upon their return to the United States, the younger Wright started the Red Square Toy Company in 1918 (which eventually was renamed John Lloyd Wright Manufacturing) after which he marketed Lincoln Logs. During the period between World War I and World War II, the patriotism in American society motivated interest in American history, particularly the military successes of Abraham Lincoln. John Lloyd Wright witnessed this and thus based his subsequent Lincoln Log models on the Uncle Tom's Cabin and Abraham Lincoln birthplace themes. As a result of the success of these themes, John Lloyd Wright and his team of manufacturers developed larger and more elaborate themes after World War II. Their current themes include more expansive subjects such as On the Trail, Sawmill Train Express, Fun on the Farm, Classic Meeting House, Classic Farm House, American Legends: Davy Crockett, Classic Lodge, and Classic Campfire Ranch. The Lincoln Logs construction set was one of the original inductees in the National Toy Hall of Fame in Rochester, New York in 1998–1999.

Montessori Blocks

Montessori Blocks are unique in that they are used solely in Montessori school environments for the purpose of developing children's sensory-motor skills and the five senses. Montessori Blocks have been useful play blocks that allow children in Montessori Schools to assess their own mistakes without the teacher having to assess them—a skill that promotes independence in approaches to problem solving. There are at least seven types of Montessori Blocks: cylinder blocks, pink towers, broad stairs, red rods, colored cylinders, binomial cubes, and trinomial cubes, as well as other geometric solids. These blocks are different from standard wooden play blocks because they are constructed in a way that allows the child to complete various sensory tasks (Lillard, 2008, 2013). Montessori designed sensorial exercises in order to account for every quality that the child can perceive through her five senses. Qualities that are perceived include size, shape, texture, volume in terms of sound, material composition, matching, weight, and temperature. In her book, *The Discovery of the Child*, Montessori (1948) categorized the sensorial exercises into eight different groups: visual (sight), haptic (touch), baric (differences in pressure and weight), thermic (differences in temperature), auditory (sound), olfactory (smell), gustatory (taste), and stereognostic (muscular movement).

The distinctiveness of all Montessori blocks is their individuality in structure for the purpose of focusing on a specific sensory-related activity. To begin, there is a fitted container block along with ten cylinder blocks each of differing sizes in terms of length and diameter. Each cylindrical block contains a knob that can be used by the child to remove the block from the larger fitted container block. Cylinder blocks were developed for young children to practice removal from and replacement in the same location on a fitted container block. When young children first engage in this task, they tend to be unable to replace a particular cylinder block in the same hole that can accommodate it on the large fitted container block. The general idea is that as the child develops, there is more likelihood that each cylinder block will be replaced in the same hole from which a particular cylinder block was removed.

The pink tower and broad stairs are similar in that their constructions were designed for the purpose of practicing the concept of "larger and smaller." The pink tower consists of pink cubes that vary in size in increments of 1cm. So the smallest cube is $1cm^2$, the second is $2cm^2$, and so on all the way to the largest cube which is $10cm^2$. The goal is for the child to identify the largest block and then put the second largest block on top of the largest block, the third largest on top of the second, and so forth. Any error that is produced, namely, placing a larger cube on top of a smaller one, is visual in nature. The child should identify this order of size both haptically and barically and be able to correct it. The brown broad stairs also consist of ten rectangular cuboids of different sizes. The purpose of the broad stairs is for the child to detect different thicknesses. The ten stairs are all 20cm long and vary in thickness from 1cm to 10cm. Like the pink tower, the broad stairs are placed one at a time on top of each other from the thickest to the thinnest. Again, the child uses haptic and baric perceptions when manipulating the broad stairs.

To familiarize the young child with the concept of "long and short," Montessori developed the red rod blocks. Again, there are ten rods in total and each rod has the same cross-sectional square-shaped dimension (2.5cm^2) but differing lengths. The shortest rod is 10cm and the lengths of each subsequent rod increases by 10cm (i.e., 10cm, 20cm, 30cm, etc.) so that the longest rod is 100cm, or 1m. The overarching purpose of red rod blocks is to have the child put the rods in the correct order from longest to shortest or vice versa. To do this, the child must make sure that one of the ends of each rod lines up with one of the ends of all the other rods so that the length can be determined. This action is similar to the seriation task of Piaget that determined, along with the many Piagetian conservation tasks, the stage in which the child belongs—more specifically, either the pre-operational stage or the concrete operational stage.

Unlike the cylinder blocks mentioned above, the colored cylinders do not have knobs. Rather, the colored cylinders have different attributes based on the color of the cylinders. Yellow cylinders vary in height and width in that the shortest cylinder is the thinnest and the tallest cylinder is the thickest. Red cylinders are all the same height but vary in terms of width. Blue cylinders are all the same width but vary in height. Lastly, like the red cylinders, green cylinders vary in height and width, but unlike their red counterparts, the shortest cylinder is the thickest and the longest one is the thinnest of the group. The colored cylinders help the young child in several ways, such as determining order of length, comparing them with the cylinder blocks, and constructing towers of the same or differing heights.

The monomial, binomial, and trinomial cubes are not necessarily used to teach young children mathematics; instead, they are mostly used to develop sensorimotor skills in this age group. Each binomial cube box contains one red cube, three black and red rectangular cuboids, three black and blue cuboids, and one blue cube. Together, the cubes and rectangular cuboids are representative of the following mathematical equation:

$$(a+b)^3 = a^3 + 3a^2b + 3ab^2 + b^3$$

The trinomial cube consists of one red cube and six black and red rectangular cuboids (differing in size), one blue cube and six black and blue rectangular cuboids (differing in size), one yellow cube and six black and yellow rectangular cuboids (differing in size), and six black rectangular cuboids (all the same size). Together, the cubes and rectangular cuboids of the trinomial cube represent the following mathematical equation:

$$(a+b+c)^3 = a^3 + 3a^2b + 3a^2c + b^3 + 3ab^2 + 3b^2c + c^3 + 3ac^2 + 3bc^2 + 6abc$$

Montessori sensorial block materials also include ten wooden, blue, geometric solids, which consist of a sphere, cone, ovoid, ellipsoid, triangle-based pyramid, square-based pyramid, cube, cylinder, rectangular prism, and triangular prism. These solids help children learn about three-dimensional figures. In the Montessori classroom, young children learn about geometric shapes by using the geometric cabinet, which contains various wooden shapes that are stored in drawers. Young children also have the opportunity to use constructive triangles, which allow them to create different quadrilaterals. To familiarize children with different shades of color, the Montessori sensorial materials include color tablets, which support visual acuity and the ability to discriminate between colors. Similar to the color tables are the baric tablets, which allow children to distinguish between varying tablet weights.

Tinkertoys

Observation and contemplation of children playing games with various objects is perhaps one of the best ways to invent or develop constructive play object toys. Such is the case with the Tinkertoy Construction Set, which was created by Charles Pajeau in 1914 after he observed children playing with sticks and empty thread spools. Pajeau, a stonemason from the Chicago area, started the Toy Tinker Company along with Robert Pettit and Gordon Tinker all of whom believed that the toy would have the potential to stimulate children's imaginations and creative abilities. Soon after their initial production, Tinkertoys were displayed at various exhibitions in the Chicago area. It was possible, then, to make an excellent model of the Ferris wheel with Tinkertoys, and, perhaps more importantly, since then, Tinkertoys have been used as models for numerous technological advances that took place at the Massachusetts Institute of Technology (MIT), Cornell University, and the Silicon Valley region. In 1975, during his time at MIT, Danny Hillis, along with his team of other students, created a computer made only from Tinkertoys that plays tic-tac-toe (Dewdney, 1989). The task emanated from a class project in which students were asked to construct a digital simulation from Tinkertoys. After examining the Tinkertoys, Hillis and his team realized that it was possible to create a logic device that converts the binary 1 signal to a 0 signal and vice versa. Hillis concluded that the Tinkertoy construction was computationally universal—which means that Tinkertoy parts can be organized in such a manner that a programmable computer can be assembled. These and related uses of Tinkertoys in technological research suggest that Tinkertoys can lead to increased creativity among children and adolescents.

The main part of the Tinkertoy Construction Set is the wooden spool, whose diameter is approximately 5cm. One hole is drilled all the way through the center of the spool and eight additional holes are drilled in 45-degree positions around the perimeter of the spool, but these holes are not drilled all the way through as they are used to hold sticks. The spools were so designed that they emulated the Pythagorean right triangle. In addition to the spool, the standard Tinkertoy set includes wheels, caps, couplings, pulleys, Part W, which is similar to the spool but differs in that it contains five holes on the circular surfaces and two grooves along the rim, short pointed sticks, and rods. Wheels are similar in shape to the spools, however wheels are thinner and larger in diameter than their spool counterparts. Originally made of wood, caps are now made of plastic. Caps are cylindrical pieces that hold closely-fitted rods. Couplings are also small cylindrical pieces that measure 5cm in length and over 1cm in diameter. These pieces have snug-fitting, blind-drilled holes in both ends, and a loose-fitting, through-drilled hole crosswise through the center of the piece. Pulleys are identical to spools with only one exception—they have loose-fitting center holes. Part W is roughly the same size as the spool, but, unlike the spool, Part W has perimeter holes that are in 90-degree positions. They also contain loose-fitting center holes and four tight-fitting, through-drilled holes that are parallel to the center hole, which allows for free-spinning parts and the creation of easily-moving gears.

Prior to 1992, Tinkertoy sticks had a diameter of approximately a 0.5cm. Originally made of wood, sticks produced after 1960 were colored, each stick color had a different length. The orange sticks are approximately 3cm long, the yellow stick is slightly over 5cm, the blue is slightly over 8cm, the red is about 13cm, the green is almost 19cm, and the purple is about 27.5cm. Spools are 3cm in diameter and the holes along the circumference of the spool are slightly under 1cm in depth. Larger Tinkertoy sets sometimes include an unfinished wooden rod without slotted ends having an intermediate length between green and purple in the form of a driveshaft. This driveshaft is generally turned with a small plastic crank. More recent Tinkertoy sets include battery-powered electric motors and at least one wooden double pulley, with a single snug-fitting, through-drilled center hole, and grooved circumferences at two diameters, allowing a variety of moving parts to operate at different speeds.

The Tinkertoy Construction Set was also one of the original inductees in the National Toy Hall of Fame in 1998–1999 (Strange, 1996; Strong National Museum of Play, 2020).

Brio

Brio is a toy company that bases most of its products on wood construction. The Brio company is perhaps most famous for its wooden train sets which include wooden tracks that fit together with puzzle tab and blank interlocking connectors at the ends of each piece of track. The Brio Company was founded in 1884 in the town of Boalt in Scania, the southernmost province of Sweden, by Ivar Bengtsson, a basket weaver by trade. In its first 20 years, the company specialized in different types of baskets. In 1902, Bengtsson and his family moved the company to a larger facility in the town of Osby, a profitable location given its close proximity to rail lines that linked many towns and cities in the region. In 1907, Bengtsson expanded the product line to include wooden toys. The first such toy was the Göinge Horse, which was a toy that young children were able to pull as they walked. This pulling toy became the starting point of Brio's wooden toy product line. Bengtsson turned his business over to his three young sons, who, in turn, changed the company name to Brio, which is an acronym that stands for Bröderna Ivarsson of Osby (Ivarsson Brothers of Osby). The company expanded exponentially in 1914 to the point that the company was able to sell toys, ceramics, glass, and porcelain merchandise.

It was not until 1958 that the Brio Company began to sell wooden train sets—the toy that the company is currently most famous for. As indicated above, the company produced wooden track pieces that were engineered with tab and blank interlocking connectors and side grooves that were gauged so that they can accommodate train cars. For the most part, Brio has produced non-motorized wooden train sets that children can assemble and play with by pulling the train cars that are connected by magnetic devices. Brio subsequently engineered wooden train toy products that are able to accommodate American wooden train brands, such as Whittle Shortline and Thomas and Friends Wooden Railway that are based on *Thomas the Tank Engine and Friends* characters.

Given the company's emphasis on wood products, Brio also has been producing wooden and, more recently, plastic construction sets. These sets include the Builder Construction Set, the Builder Activity Set, and the Builder Creative Set. Like the company's first toy, the Göinge Horse, Brio still manufactures wooden push and pull toys for older infants and toddlers.

Planks

Despite their general unfamiliarity, planks are excellent constructive play materials for several reasons. First, the very fact that all planks are the same shape and structure make them suitable for creativity in construction. In other words, children who regularly play with generic, no frills objects that are non-theme related may enhance self-regulatory behaviors during constructive play and may have a higher likelihood of engaging in creative tasks that involve synthesis and higher-order thinking skills (Amabile, Hennessey & Grossman, 1986; Amabile & Pillemer, 2012). Unlike blocks, which usually include at least eight different types, and bricks, which come in a cornucopia of themes with an even greater number of shapes and styles, planks are unique in that all planks look and feel the same; each one is in a ratio of 15:3:1 cm. They can be stacked, used as posts and lintels, or serve as foundations for larger structures. Second, planks are frequently used by professional architects as testing models prior to the development of blueprints. Further, Pottmann (2010) contends that planks serve as exemplary models of geodesic structures and other architectural constructions. Third, planks are not sold in themed packages. That is, aside from the typical description that is included in the plank box, one will not find elaborate instructions for constructing objects with planks. They do not come with a preconceived script; that is, superhero themes or intergalactic themes do not play any role in the manufacturing of planks.

Unlike blocks and bricks, planks are relatively new to the general public and the constructive play object market. They are seldom found in schools or in the home. At present, most children and adults may encounter planks in a small number of science museums and centers because some curators see planks as important tools for learning about concepts in the physical sciences. Given their consistent, uniform structure, planks are more amenable to proportion than are blocks and bricks. For example, a model representation of the Coliseum in Rome using planks will be more proportionate than that of blocks and bricks because planks present consistency in form and therefore do not come in multiple forms or shapes.

To my knowledge, there are only two plank companies in the world that actively manufacture and market planks for the school, museum, or home: the Kapla Company and the Keva Company. Invented in 1987 by Tom van der Bruggen from the Netherlands, Kapla is a portmanteau from the phrase *kabouter plankjes*, which is translated as "gnome planks." Bruggen was an art history student who had dreams of constructing his very own castle from a timeworn, abandoned barn in southern France along the Tarn River. Bruggen transformed the decrepit barn into his castle, which also featured a fountain, carriage entrance, and lateral towers. Bruggen made use of standard wooden play blocks to develop a blueprint for his refurbished castle. This is a fine example of a professional architect and future toy designer using VCPOs as a means of initially imagining his castle, and then identifying what he needed in order to construct it. The problem with standard wooden play blocks, however, was that they are unsuitable for developing architectural models that involve post-and-lintel construction, roofs, and floors. This dilemma inspired Bruggen to devise and eventually invent planks, a construction set that he intended to be used by people of all ages.

The Kapla plank set consists of identical, wooden planks—that is, same size, dimensions, and weight—measuring 11.7cm × 2.34cm × 0.78cm, essentially a length-width-thickness ratio of 15:3:1. This length-width-thickness ratio is different from that of the standard unit block, thus making the plank more useful in constructing model post-and-lintel structures along with roofs and floors. Like its Keva counterpart (to be discussed below), Kapla planks are positioned only by gravity when constructing models with them. In other words, they do not need any type of adhesive to remain standing—that is, no glue, nails, or screws; notwithstanding strong winds and other similar destructive forces of nature, Kapla planks remain stable without the use of affixers or fastening mechanisms.

Kapla planks can be placed or organized in three arrangements. The first way is flat, that is, with the length-by-width face down on the surface. The second way in which the Kapla plank can be arranged is on its side, which occurs when the length-by-thickness face is on the surface. And, lastly, it can be placed in an upright, vertical position with the width-by-thickness position on the surface. Kapla planks can be piled one on top of another or stacked as in a spiral. The Kapla Company manufactures planks out of pine wood. The majority of planks are wooden and not painted but some are painted in a variety of colors. They come in packages of a minimum of 40 pieces to at most 1,000 pieces. In an effort to promote STEAM through the use of Kapla planks, the Kapla Company produced four books that were written to support children's cognitive development through the use of planks. These Kapla books provide ways of connecting the use of Kapla planks with concepts in mathematics, physics, engineering, and technology, and, at the same time, expose children to art and architecture.

Like Kapla planks, Keva planks are wooden cuboids in roughly similar dimensions. Using US measurements, Keva planks are in the dimensions of 4.5in × 0.75in × 0.25in. KEVA planks are produced in Bridgewater, Virginia and owned by Mindware. Also like Kapla planks, Keva planks require no adhesives or fasteners; they remain erect after construction solely by gravity. Moreover, like Kapla planks, no instructions are needed to build with Keva planks. Unlike Kapla planks, which are made of pine wood, Keva planks are made of the less expensive maple. The first time I was introduced to planks was in 2011, in Balboa Park, San Diego, California, when I entered a huge room at the Reuben Hollis Fleet Science Center with my son. Museums can serve as ideal venues for engaging children in engineering and architectural talking and tinkering (Pagano, Haden, & Uttal, 2020; Tôugu, Marcus, Haden, & Uttal, 2017). This spacious room was filled with Keva planks and people of all ages, young children to older adults, were engaged in various types of plank constructions. We had an amazing experience constructing our own structures and observing those of other science center visitors. It was at that point that I realized that planks can have a strong influence on cognitive development and creativity—stronger than that of standard wooden play blocks, and much stronger than that of bricks (which will be discussed below and in Chapter 3). The rationale behind this realization is that both Keva and Kapla planks are all identical in size and weight and come without the instructions and themes that brick companies provide.

Keva planks are used in schools, libraries, makerspaces, and exhibits in numerous museums throughout the United States and parts of Canada. In addition to the Fleet Science Museum in San Diego, Keva planks can be found in the Da Vinci Science Center (Allentown, Pennsylvania), the Exploration Place of the Sedgwick County Science and Discovery Center (Wichita, Kansas), Science World (Vancouver, British Columbia), Turtle Bay Exploration Park (Redding, California), The Discovery—Terry Lee Wells Nevada Discovery Museum (Reno, Nevada), Lincoln Children's Museum (Lincoln, Nebraska), Museum of Life +

Science (Durham, North Carolina), the Lawrence Hall of Science (Berkeley, California), Mid-America Science Museum (Hot Springs National Park, Arkansas), Long Island Children's Museum (Garden City, New York), Peoria Play House Children's Museum (Peoria, Illinois), Rochester Museum and Science Center (Rochester, New York), Science Spectrum Science and Technology Museum (Lubbock, Texas), Markham Museum (Markham, Ontario), Echo Lake Aquarium and Science Center (Burlington, Vermont), Exploration Place (Wichita, Kansas), and the Children's Museum of Virginia (Portsmouth, Virginia). Keva planks are also an educational implement that can be used as a manipulative to teach not only STEAM subjects, but also geography, history, and the humanities.

Keva planks were highlighted as a highly recommended VCPO at Destination Imagination Global Finals that took place in Knoxville, Tennessee in 2011. *STEMosphere*, a student run science publication that hosts science blogs and podcasts, featured Keva planks at many of its annual events throughout the United States. World of Learning, a popular science blogpost, ranked Keva planks the "Number 1 tool for makerspaces."

Play Bricks

The term "brick" is the generic name for plastic pieces, usually in the shape of rectangular solids, which snap together. Other generic terms for "brick" are snap cubes and snap pieces. The public does not often hear the terms "brick" and "snap piece" because popular company trademarks—such as LEGOs, MegaBloks, KRE-O, or Cobi—are used much more frequently, thereby eclipsing the use of generic terms. While the term "brick" implies a rectangular solid or box shape, bricks come in a plethora of sizes and styles. In fact, they can appear in the form of flat or curved puzzle-like pieces.

LEGOs

The most popular brick is the LEGO brand. LEGOs come in numerous cuboidal shapes and thicknesses and can be found as generic pieces or as pieces for themed toys with instructions for assembly. The first LEGOs, established in 1930s by the Danish carpenter and joiner, Ole Kirk Kristiansen, were nothing like the generic plastic snap pieces; in fact, the first LEGO toy was a wooden duck on wheels known as Kirk's Sandgame. LEGOs, which, in Danish, is derived from the term "leg godt," or "play well," developed into a constructive play toy in the form of plastic bricks during the late 1940s. In fact, LEGO was not the first producer of plastic bricks (Lauwaert, 2008, 2009). This title goes to Hilary Page, who, in 1937, used new injection molding technology to develop the first plastic bricks with studs. Lauwaert (2008) maintains that Page was dissatisfied with wooden play pieces and wanted his construction toys to have more of a grasp and stay connected together. Accordingly, he formed British Plastic Toys Ltd., or Bri-Plax, and designed the interlocking building cube, which he patented in 1940 and called Kiddicraft Self-Locking Building Bricks. Unlike the world of past and contemporary LEGOs, Page's interlocking building cubes were stackable only with the studs facing upwards. Eventually, he engineered side slits, which allowed the bricks to be connected from side to side. In 1981, LEGO bought and thus procured the rights to Kiddicraft.

Original LEGO bricks came in the form of four- to eight-stud pieces that could be affixed together with a larger brick. The so-called LEGO interlocking principle—that is, a method of snapping pieces together—was invented and patented in 1958, and by the 1960s, Kiddicraft had developed bricks of numerous lengths and thicknesses. The so-called minifigure was developed in 1978. While not as time-honored as blocks in the preschool and elementary school play area, bricks have been an essential constructive play object type in preschools and early childhood grades since the 1960s. In 2005, LEGO unveiled its largest set up to that time—the 5,195-piece Millennium Falcon, which has turned out to be one of the few collector's items sold by LEGO. In 2020, LEGO began selling the Roman Coliseum—the largest brick set available having 9,036 pieces (Taggart, 2020). Ecologically, it can even be argued that children's familiarity with them in the play center environment has surpassed that of blocks because they are not only a staple play object type in schools but also prevalent in homes throughout the world.

In a landmark case in 2018, LEGO sued a number of LEGO clone companies headquartered in China for infringement of multiple copyrights. Clone companies, such as Lepin, simply duplicated the LEGO brand bricks and distributed them with their own names. LEGO clone companies are discussed in detail below.

In contrast to the research literature on blocks and their influence on creativity and spatial development, that of bricks is far less examined. Further, discussion of bricks is often embedded within the larger context of block studies, and, as a result, the block or brick literature has not taken their distinctive qualities and characteristics into consideration. That said, specific themes having to do with cognitive development and spatial thinking are hazier when examining the somewhat smaller literature on brick play. Yet, the common thread among these studies has focused on a putative conception that LEGOs, like blocks, promote cognitive gains. In tapping young children's everyday mathematical activities, Ginsburg and his colleagues developed six categories that reflect broad areas of emergent mathematical constructs evident during free play (Ginsburg, Pappas & Seo, 2001). Children's active free play that occurs in LEGO or block environments seems to engender the manifestation of two of these categories—namely, "Pattern and Shape" and "Spatial Relations." Moreover, this surfacing expression of pattern, shape, and spatial constructs is evident cross-culturally with no significant differences in terms of gender or social class (Ginsburg, Lin, Ness & Seo, 2003).

In a longitudinal study to determine whether brick play in the preschool years is correlated with higher levels of mathematical ability in middle and high school, Wolfgang, Stannard, and Jones (2003) found no relationship between three- and four-year-old children's LEGO play and level of mathematical achievement based on the awarding of letter grades in the third-, fifth-, and seventh-grade levels. Similar to their study on children's block play, their results for children's LEGO play were significant in terms of increased standardized test scores during seventh grade. However, Ko (2010) has questioned Wolfgang et al.'s sample size as statistically insignificant. In a related study, Hussain, Lindh, and Shukur (2006) attempted to determine whether an entire year of regularized LEGO play influenced children's performance in mathematics in school. While preliminary findings showed improvement in mathematics in the fifth grade, overall results were inconclusive. Verdine et al. (2014) measured spatial performance of three-year-old children using MegaBloks to determine possible relationships between spatial constructions and early mathematical skills and language. MegaBloks were used for the easy manipulation of the three-year-old age group. However, the unique properties of MegaBlocks and the ways in which they might be used as an important variable in construction were not considered. It is important to note, however, that brick studies consider brick play for measuring cognitive performances without considering the role of affordance as a potentially major factor in cognitive development.

LaQ

Earlier in this chapter, we said that bricks can come in the form of flat or curved puzzle-like pieces. LaQ is one such type. Developed and produced in Japan, LaQ is a fascinating brick-style, constructive play toy that enables the constructions of various figures, even spherical structures. In fact, the "Q" in the title stands for "kyuu" (球), which, in Japanese, is equivalent to the meaning of the term "sphere." The capacity to make spherical structures is due to the physical characteristics of the LaQ pieces, which include five different joint types and two surface types. While the two surface types, a square and a triangle, are flat surface pieces, the five varied joint types allow a structure to contain curvature.

Plastic Toy Companies and LEGO Clones

LEGO clones are pervasive and an international phenomenon. For all intents and purposes, LEGO clones are plastic toy snap bricks that are, for the most part, compatible with the LEGO brand, but are produced by a non-LEGO manufacturer. While China is the largest market for LEGO clones, many clone companies can be found in Europe and South America countries. Most clones are compatible with LEGOs, not only because they look like them but also because they possess studs that allow them to be affixed with LEGOs and other LEGO clones. Clones became much more prevalent when the patents covering LEGO bricks expired in 1978 (Austen, 2005). That being the case, lawsuits in which LEGO® has been the plaintiff and clone companies have all been defendants have been filed ever since the LEGO brand came into existence. In general, LEGO clones have been on the market since the 1960s. Many of them shut down or were purchased by and merged with other toy companies. In the following section, I provide descriptions of more than 30 plastic toy companies that include both original toy companies and LEGO clone companies, most of which are still in existence.

Airfix

Airfix is an injection-molding company based in the UK. As the oldest manufacturer in the UK of scale plastic model kits, Airfix has produced plastic toy model kits for the mass market since 1952. Airfix manufactures an extensive range of kits that are targeted at most scale modelers. Airfix subjects include military aircraft, civil aircraft, ships, galleons, automobiles, space figures, dioramas, and military vehicles. Airfix is a very popular company in the UK, so much so that any plastic modeling kit is called Airfix even if the product is made by a different company.

Airfix was originally founded in 1939 by Nicholas Kove, an émigré from Hungary who originally manufactured inflatable rubber toys. After World War II, Kove began working with plastic as the key material for his new toys, and shortly thereafter became the founder of the first toy company to use injection molding in the UK. In late 1940s, Kove was introduced to Harry Ferguson, a tractor manufacturer, who was interested in working with Airfix to make toy models of his tractors as a sales technique. Given the expense of the completed models, Ferguson and Kove decided to sell the models unmade with instructions for assembly. This process was successful and intrigued James Russon, an F. W. Woolworth top executive, who, in turn, approached Airfix and suggested that the Airfix Company use polystyrene plastic, a less expensive and more stable material, along with polybags to be sold retail by the Woolworth Company. In 1952, Airfix introduced the model of the Golden Hind, a famous British galleon captained by Sir Francis Drake in the late 16th century. As the sales of the Golden Hind were successful, it was then followed by a number of other toy themes, such as the 1953 model of the Supermarine Spitfire, a British fighter aircraft that was used during World War II.

Airfix suffered financial losses in the 1980s, due in part to the declining birth rate, the rising price of plastic (as a result of the rise in oil prices), and the onset of computer technology entering homes and schools. However, the brand made a comeback in 2006 and was subsequently purchased by Hornby, a British model railway brand. Ever since that time, Airfix has re-established itself as a household term throughout the UK and abroad.

Ausini

Ausini, like Sluban, discussed below, is a toy brick company from Guangdong province in China that made its way into Western markets, and therefore, the Ausini brand is more well-known to consumers than other toy bricks. They are easily obtainable through a number of online stores. Reviewers have generally placed Ausini bricks high on the list in terms of quality and comparison and compatibility to LEGOs. The company's most popular series are its Gun Series collection as well as its elaborate Trains collection. Other themes produced by Ausini include Castle, Pirates, City, and Army collections.

BanBao

BanBao, also known as Guangdong Jumbo Grand Plastic Moulding Industrial Co., Ltd., is a producer of educational building block toys that are now sold in over 60 countries. The product meets all the quality requirements set for educational building block toys. BanBao produces toys that accommodate children of every age group in early childhood. Unlike most other clone bricks, the building bricks and blocks produced by BanBao allow the individual to make unique structures and not just structures that follow prescriptive themes. The cubes are different shapes and colors. All BanBao building blocks fit neatly on blocks and bricks of other well-known brands, thus making the possibilities of construction boundless. Moreover, the BanBao themes accommodate children's potential to explore the boundaries of their own creativity. BanBao produces both blocks and bricks. BanBao blocks are much larger in size than their brick counterparts and are suitable for younger children, mostly between the ages of three and five. BanBao bricks are smaller in size when compared to the blocks, and are suitable for children older than five years. As indicated above, BanBao bricks are compatible, and can be interchanged, with other major brands of plastic building bricks. The BanBao brick has the same width and length as other brands, and the BanBao ToBee figures—unique to BanBao—are also interchangeable with other interlocking brick brands. When interchanging BanBao bricks with those of other brands, there is a small height difference but this can be solved easily in that the height of two standard BanBao bricks is the same as the height of two brand bricks and one slim brick of the typical generic Lego brick set.

Cada Bricks

Cada Bricks is a brand of play bricks that is produced by the Double Eagle Industry China Ltd. Double Eagle is located in Shantou, a city in the province of Guangdong in China, and is an internationally recognized Chinese toy brand for its remote control toy cars and trucks. Established in 2016, the Cada product line became a well-recognized building brick toy brand in mainland China by 2020.

Currently, the Cada Bricks toy is also a popular LEGO alternative in Germany and Russia. Cada Bricks consist mostly of interlocking plastic bricks that are compatible with other internationally renowned brick brands. Cada has also worked diligently to create its own set of designs. The building bricks series include, but are not limited to, super-cars, military themes, robots, construction and architecture, and other STEM based educational sets.

Cobi

Founded in 1987, Cobi is a construction block toy manufacturer headquartered in Warsaw, Poland and has sales offices in the Czech Republic, Germany, the UK, Hungary, Slovakia, and the United States. Cobi is one of the largest producers of construction blocks in Central and Eastern Europe. Its primary production facility is located in Mielec, Poland. In addition to being a toy importer and distributor, Cobi brands itself as a toy company that uses local raw materials and meets the international standards for child safety. In its nascent period, Cobi specialized in puzzles and board games. Then, in 1992, Cobi began to establish a line in plastic construction blocks. While both Cobi and LEGO produce themed products, they differ in that there is no such thing as a generic Cobi brick; Cobi's bricks come in all different shapes and sizes to more accurately represent a model of an object (army vehicle, tank, ship, airplane, etc.), while LEGO bricks have standard thicknesses. Like most VCPO companies that offer themed bricks, Cobi comes with instructions for their entire line of bricks.

Cobi produces blocks available in numerous themes. Their historical collection includes Pirates, Romans and Barbarians, The Battle of Grunwald (in celebration of the battle's 600th anniversary in 2010), Knights of Europe, and the RMS Titanic (in remembrance of its 100th anniversary in 2012). Other Cobi themes include World War I, World War II, Cobi Action Town (a city and its services made of bricks), Cobi Smithsonian (a collection of famous historical vehicles, vessels, and aircraft), Cobi Creative Power (the only non-themed collection), Cobi Electronic (construction of remotely-controlled vehicles with bricks), Cobi Football, Young Timer Collection (vintage car collection), Cobi Maserati (sports car collection), Cobi Skoda (collection for automotive enthusiasts), Armed Forces (tanks, planes, helicopters, and other military vehicles), and Top Gun Maverick (a fighter plane collection based on the action drama film *Top Gun: Maverick*^{TM}).

COGO

COGO is a LEGO-clone produced in the Shantou prefecture of China. Originally established in 1993, the Shantou Cheng Lee Plastic Company specializes in the manufacture of toy building bricks, hobby toys, and other plastic construction toys, as well as the export of numerous other miscellaneous toys. In addition to the Enlighten and Kazi toy brick brands, the Shantou Cheng Lee

Plastic Company also produces COGO bricks. Most clone brick bloggers have criticized the COGO brand for having weak plastic brick pieces and sharp edges. The Shantou Cheng Lee Plastic Company's market is directed at the households, mostly in southern China, that cannot afford higher-quality products. The COGO themes include City, Trains, Castles, Pirates, Army, Girls, and Brixbolt, which has a robot theme.

GUDI

GUDI is another LEGO-like brick that is produced in China. The company is currently a leading competitor among China's building blocks brands. GUDI, however, differs from LEGO and other competing brands in that the plastic material is harder, GUDI bricks have more luster, and the bricks fit more tightly than other brands. Even more noteworthy is that GUDI has been unwavering in attempting to produce original bricks with a strong and unbreakable design. GUDI themes include, but are not limited to, Army, Earth Border (a futuristic military theme), Star Hegemony, and City. Another positive attribute of GUDI is the price, which, according to many clone brick reviewers, is much more reasonable than other brands.

Jie Star

Jie Star is a relatively obscure constructive play brick company based in China. "Jie" is a Chinese term that alludes to the aphorism of speed and high performance. The term "Star" suggests excellence and innovation. The company, Shan Tou Jie Xing Toys Industrial Co. Ltd. began in 1998 as a producer of bricks, blocks, and musical toys for infants and toddlers. As a LEGO clone, Jie Star uses higher-quality plastic for the bricks than do other Chinese toy brick companies. Their most popular themes include Anti-Terrorism and Military.

Kazi/GBL

While there are numerous Kazi set collections, there is relatively little information available about the Kazi/GBL Company and its history. What is known is that Kazi/GBL is a LEGO clone brick toy company in China, which produces bricks that are compatible with most LEGO clones. The quality of the bricks is not as good as those of other companies. The most popular Kazi themes include Military, Pirate, and Red Alert, and the most popular theme of the GBL branch is the Trains line.

Kre-O

Kre-O, which comes from the Latin, *creo*, which means, "I create," is a LEGO clone produced in South Korea, and, as indicated below, is produced by Oxford Bricks

78 Blocks, Bricks, and Planks

and marketed and sold by Hasbro. Kre-O bricks are compatible with LEGO and MegaBloks. Unlike the standard Oxford themes mentioned above, Kre-O specializes in minifigures. Their trademark minifigure is the Kreon, a robotic, military-themed humanoid. The first Kreons, introduced in 2011, were based on the media franchise, Reformers, which depicts battles of sentient, living beings, namely autonomous robots—the good Autobots and the evil Decepticons—that can transform into animals and non-living objects like vehicles. In the following year, the Kre-O Battleship, based on the movie of the same year, was introduced. Other Kre-O themes include G. I. Joe, Star Trek, Cityville Invasion, and Dungeons and Dragons.

Loz

LOZ is part of the German company Loz Group Company Ltd. Founded in 1998, LOZ toy bricks and puzzles have been developed by German designers for the purpose of cultivating children's cognitive skills. The LOZ Diamond Block is a VCPO whose engineers have followed a trend since the first decade of the 21st century (which began with Nanoblock^{TM}) with the manufacturing of micro-building blocks, also known as mini-building blocks. The smallest size of the LOZ building block is 4mm x 4mm x 5mm. LOZ manufactures small sized blocks and bricks because the company believes that small pieces lead to greater creativity in building structures by providing children with the use of fine motor skills and attention to detail. LOZ micro-building blocks come in a variety of colors and, for purposes of safety, they have adjusted corners and smooth surfaces. Each micro-building block affixes with a tubed structure that is somewhat comparable to the LEGO stud. With LOZ micro-blocks, children have the opportunity to build structures like buildings or towers, or larger roadside environments. LOZ themes include anime images, inspired by Japanese comic books, architecture diamond blocks, and BrickHeadz, which allow children to create their own characters, and cartoon figures from Disney films, Sesame Street, and Pokémon.

MegaBloks

MegaBloks are LEGO-like figures that are much larger than their LEGO counterparts. They were created by Victor and Rita Bertrand, two Canadian toy developers. With the intention of expanding internationally, Victor Bertrand planned to create jumbo-sized bricks for toddlers and children under five years. He believed that LEGO bricks were not designed to accommodate the constructive play needs of younger children. The Bertrands unveiled the MegaBlok brick in 1984, and shortly thereafter, the MegaBlok became a huge success. By 1985, MegaBloks were popular throughout the United States and Canada, and in 1989, MegaBloks became a well-liked toy for toddlers in more than 30 European countries. By 1991, the Mega brand produced MegaBloks Micro, which essentially became a clone of LEGO bricks.

For the purpose of examining the spatial thinking abilities of very young children and toddlers, a number of studies have implemented MegaBloks, rather than brick companies that manufacture smaller bricks, as a toy used to investigate very young children's cognitive abilities related to spatial reasoning skills. Verdine et al. (2014) examined three-year-olds' spatial assembly skills as they manipulate MegaBloks. They also wanted to know the extent to which high levels of spatial assembly through the use of MegaBloks were related to early mathematical skills as well as the relation between spatial assembly skills and socio-economic status, gender, and parent-reported spatial language. The implementation of MegaBloks turned out to be a more suitable tool than the standard LEGO brick for examining the spatial skills and mathematical thinking of three-year-old children.

MacDonald, Dickson, Martineau, and Ahearn (2015) implemented MegaBloks as a tool for children to create video models. MegaBloks were used to build structures that resembled monsters and dogs. The general intention of this study was to examine the relationship between tasks that require delayed imitation and delayed matching on acquisition of daily living skills to children with autism using visual modeling.

Mis Ladrillos

Produced in Argentina, Mis Ladrillos is a plastic VCPO construction set that is a LEGO clone. The construction method requires one to join blocks by applying pressure and locking them when inserting the studs into the internal surface of another block. Mis Ladrillos is unique in terms of its adaptability with other LEGO clones as well as electrically powered devices. When first produced in the 1960s, Mis Ladrillos sets were made of rubber material, but this was changed to an unyielding plastic material shortly thereafter. The Mis Ladrillos Company emphasizes the combination of bricks with electrically powered devices, thus making each finished product mobile. Themes include electrically motorized vehicles, robotic figures, and moveable bridges.

Oxford Bricks

Oxford Co., Ltd. is a toy company based in Busan, South Korea, that produces interlocking bricks. As a rival LEGO clone brand that has been in existence since 1961, it is one of the oldest of all the clone brands. The smaller Oxford bricks are compatible with LEGO bricks. Oxford also manufactures larger bricks for young children. Like Rasti bricks, Oxford produces some of the strongest bricks on the toy brick market. A number of themes are available that are based on popular culture, such as Disney, Hello Kitty, Robocar Poli (a South Korean children's television series), and Pororo the Little Penguin (a computer-animated television series in South Korea). In addition to these highly popular themes, Oxford also manufactures common themes that include military, transportation, town and city, fire department, police department, spies, Three Kingdoms (based on Korean history), and Gwanggaeto the Great (a Korean monarch from the 4th and 5th centuries). Oxford manufactures bricks for the Kre-O toy company.

Qman Enlighten Bricks: Formerly Enlighten Bricks

Qman Enlighten Bricks is a Chinese manufacturer that produces toy bricks that are compatible with original brick companies such as LEGO. The company's toy brick sets are generally considered to be of high-quality materials. Qman Enlighten Bricks are considered to be the most original toy brick type apart from the LEGO brand. Founded in 1994, the Qman Enlighten brand is considered by most toy brick reviewers to be the highest-quality Chinese clone brand, and is the oldest and possibly the most well known of all Chinese clone bricks. In the company's early years, Qman Enlighten bricks were very similar to LEGO sets. In fact, the company still has some imitative versions of Pirates ships in its 2016 catalogue. Fortunately, at present, Qman Enlighten Bricks focuses on original designs and has come up with some of the most superior sets ever in the history of Chinese clone brands. The company's quality has increased dramatically and now includes Enlighten branded studs on their bricks. Combat Zones, Legendary Pirates and Space Adventure, Police, and City stand out among their most common themes. The most noteworthy package of the Enlightenment Company is its repair service, which covers the price of missing toy brick parts. Unlike other toy brick manufacturers, Qman Enlighten Bricks currently produces its own sets and does not replicate other brick sets.

Rasti

Rasti is a German and subsequently Argentinian plastic VCPO LEGO clone that is produced by the Knittax Company. The word "rasti" comes from the German verb, *rasten*, which means "to secure," "to rest," or "lock firmly in place." The Rasti toy was popular in Europe and Argentina between the 1960s and the 1980s. The toy was discontinued in Germany and then in Argentina for approximately 20 years, but it was then was resurrected by the company in 2007. The unique feature of the Rasti brick is the strength of its material; the plastic used to produce the Rasti brick is stronger and more durable than that of other companies, including LEGO. The engineering of the Rasti brick is distinctive in that it possesses studs that have an extended ring and elastic clamps underneath the ring. When one Rasti brick is connected to another, the clamps click in place, thereby locking on to the stud rings. The strength and durability is, at once, the hallmark of the Rasti brick and its shortcoming. The interlocking of the clamps with the stud rings is so strong that if one wants to separate the bricks, a small crow-bar, supplied in the Rasti set, is needed.

Sluban

Sluban is a newer brand of building blocks and, like BanBao, the company's bricks are compatible with other well-known brick brands including LEGO. Sluban bricks tend to be less expensive than other building blocks. Sluban produces a variety of themes, such as Land Forces, Star Dreamworks, Army, Aviation, Bricks Base, Builder, Carclub, Fire, Foodcourt, Kiddy Bricks, Legend Warriors, Police, Racing Team, and Space—all of which can be used for play construction by people of any age. Sluban began production in 2004 and is now available internationally. One of the company's primary missions is to produce bricks with high safety standards for all users, especially young children. With headquarters in Nieuwerkerk Ijssel, the Netherlands, Sluban is also known for producing toy brick products that accommodate children and adults of different world regions.

Star Diamond

Star Diamond is another toy brick brand from China. The Star Diamond toy brick brand of domestic building blocks has a slightly higher quality, color, luster, and compatibility when compared to other toy bricks. Clone brick reviewers rank Star Diamond as being fairly similar to LEGO. Star Diamond is relatively more affordable than other brands, but has, since shortly after its inception, been in competition in countries of East Asia with the more famous LEGO brand. Star Diamond themes include anime sets such as Seer, Balala The Fairies, GG-Bond, Robo Saviors, Kung Fu Panda, and Dino Brick, which is inspired by the Jurassic Park subject.

Stickle Bricks

The VCPO Stickle Bricks were invented by the English engineer, Denys Fisher, in 1969. Stickle bricks are plastic shapes that are 3–9cm long, and contain brushes of small plastic bits on one or more surfaces. The plastic fingers are important in that the adjacent stickle bricks of one plastic shape can interlock with another, allowing the shapes to adjoin in different ways. Stickle Bricks come in triangular, square, circular, rectangular, and animal-shaped pieces. These constructive play toys are suitable for toddlers and preschool children.

Tente

No longer in production, Tente was a VCPO that began to be manufactured in 1972. Produced in Spain, the company that originally produced Tente bricks sold the VCPO to Educa Borras, which discontinued the brick in 2008. This VCPO, which can be purchased today in toy specialty shops or through auction websites, is discussed here because of its uniqueness and contrast to the LEGO Company. Like LEGO, Tente consisted of interlocking plastic bricks, wheels, and minifigures. But that is where the similarities end for the most part. Tente focused its attention on producing brick themes based on transporting vehicles and vessels. Amongst the company's most popular themes were the cargo ship and ocean liner construction sets. The company also specialized in producing bricks based on military themes, such as navy and space warships. The principal difference between Tente and LEGO is the gauge of the stud that connects one brick to another. The Tente stud has a larger diameter than its LEGO counterpart, thus making Tente incompatible with LEGOs and LEGO clones. Moreover, there is a small central hole in the Tente brick that allows alternative ways of connecting the Tente brick with another Tente attachment.

Wange

Wange is a Chinese toy building block brand manufactured by the Wange Industrial Co. The company also brands its blocks as Ligao. Wange is an alternative brick brand that offers mostly architectural set themes. The sets are large and although the bags that contain plastic pieces are not numbered, the end result is usually sturdy and durable. The quality of Wange has improved since it first appeared on the market in 1999; so have its designs, including its own trademarked minifigures. The Pirates, Building (massive Creator style buildings and monuments), and Power Machinery are perhaps their most popular themes. Wange is also known for its intriguing line of model-like aircraft themes.

Winner

Winner is one of the more recent LEGO clone companies to enter the market. Winner has produced a theme called Journey to the West, one of four of the greatest classical novels of Chinese literature, which is based on a 16th-century Chinese novel by the novelist and poet, Wu Cheng'en. The novel was translated into English by Arthur David Waley, an English sinologist, who popularized the novel in the West and entitled it, *Monkey*. The company also produces the Snow White series, as well as an amusement park theme called Modern Paradise. The Military themes that Winner produces allows users to construct models that are more life-like than those of LEGO and other LEGO clone brands.

Woma

Woma is another Chinese LEGO clone brand that has produced bricks that are based on the older South Korean Oxford brick sets. As a LEGO clone, Woma, which is a fairly unknown company, manufactures bricks, which are generally stronger than those of other brands. The company's main themes are Military and

Special Weapons and Tactics (SWAT) and Police series. Woma tends to be more expensive than other clones.

Xipoo

Xipoo is a toy brick brand produced by the Shantou Xipoo Cultural and Educational Technology Co. Ltd. Reviews have indicated that the bricks are of fairly high quality in that the plastic studs allow for a tighter grip between bricks. Xipoo, like Ausini, has been sold in Western markets, but is not as well-known as other LEGO clones. The company's most successful themes include Weihe Warrior, essentially a set of brick robot warriors, and Military. The cost of Xipoo bricks tend to be less expensive than other clone brands.

Zome

When I teach mathematics methods to my college students, I find it essential to present concepts in geometry and spatial thinking. To this end, after we discuss two-dimensional geometric concepts, I find the time to discuss three-dimensional concepts—namely conversations about and activities with various polyhedra. In doing so, I ask each student to make a model of a polyhedron of his or her choice. To prepare for this activity, I provide each student with a handout of basic polyhedra—cubes, tetrahedrons, octahedrons, dodecahedrons, and various prisms. I also provide students with long toothpicks (straws can also be used) and spice drops or gumdrops (clay will do as well). I then explain to the students that polyhedra are closed shapes made out of polygons. Students have to learn special terminology when working with polyhedra, namely, face or plane (surface), edge (line segment), and vertex (corner or point). Then students begin to discover that there are two categories of three-dimensional figures—prism and polyhedron.

Next, I introduce the five regular, or platonic, solids—polyhedra in which all the faces have equal areas—by demonstrating their three-dimensional appearance when compared to their two-dimensional model. For example, the two-dimensional model of the cube is a set of six connected squares in the shape of a cross. Leonhard Euler's formula for polyhedra is then introduced. This formula is simply that the number of vertices plus the number of faces minus the number of edges equals two: $V + F - E = 2$. Finally, my students engage in simple polyhedron modeling using gumdrops and long toothpicks. Doing so allows them to learn the number of toothpicks and gumdrops needed to make a cube, a triangular- and square-based pyramid, a tetrahedron, and possibly more complex polyhedra. Students begin to realize that the gumdrop serves as a model of a vertex and the long toothpick or straw serves as a model for the edge.

I mention my class lesson on three-dimensional figures because the models of polyhedra that students make are quite similar to the Zome construction toy that children and adults use to construct both basic and elaborate models of polyhedra.

Zometool Inc., the Colorado-based company that manufactures Zome toy construction products, trademarked the term, zome, which was originally coined in 1968 by Steve Durkee of the Lama Foundation, who combined the words "dome" and "zonohedron" (a type of convex polyhedron that possesses central symmetries). Zome was originally used in the architectural world to refer to a building with uncommon geometries rather than the typical house or building that is designed as a series of rectangular enclosures. Later, in 1969, Steve Baer founded Zomeworks, which, in its early days, produced playground climbers and Zometoy modeling sets. Baer was fascinated by the extensive possibilities of building inventive structures in the form of non-traditional polyhedra. Ten years later, two admirers of Baer's work, geometer Marc Pelletier and architect Paul Hildebrandt, collaborated and invented the unique connector ball, which was the sensation behind the Zometool system. Baer and, later, Pelletier and Hildebrandt inspired many people in various fields, such as art, sculpture, and furniture design, and other architects emulated Baer's work as can be seen in various structures in North America and Europe.

As stated above, Zometool Inc., in Longmont, Colorado, produces the plastic Zometool Construction Set. Zometool evolved out of Baer's original company, Zomeworks. Vaguely similar to Tinkertoy, Zometool is often thought of as the definitive form of the ball-and-stick construction toy. Also, like planks, Zometool is used as a toy by people of all ages and can be used in schools and educational centers like libraries and museums for the purpose of teaching and learning all STEAM subjects. In fact, the Zome system refers to an advanced form of mathematics that fits within the realm of graduate-level geometry and topology. Zometool is essentially a construction set that is used to teach all STEAM subjects through spatial cognition. The Zometool components simply consist of small connector nodes and rods that are available in a large array of colors. The overall shape of a connector node, however, is more complex: It is called a non-uniform small rhombicosidodecahedron—a polyhedron with 20 triangular faces, 30 square faces, 12 pentagonal faces, 60 vertices, and 120 edges—each face of which contains a small hole in which a rod can be fitted. Both ends of the rods are designed to fit in the holes of the connector nodes. This allows for the conception and formation of a diversity of structures. Since the connector node has triangles, squares, and pentagons as faces, Pelletier and Hildebrandt used shape coding as a means of further developing the rods. They used the technology of hydraulics to form a mold as a means of constructing the connector node, which first appeared in 1992. Zometool Inc. kept the connector node the same so as to make it compatible with all rods. However, the company modified the rods by identifying each rod's cross-sectional shape with a specific color. So, for example, blue rods have rectangular cross-sections, yellow rods have triangular cross-sections, red rods have pentagonal cross-sections, and green rods have rhombus cross-sections.

Upon its initial launch in 1992, it took a while for the general public to become acquainted with Zometool. However, it was widely seen by academicians and researchers as a highly valuable tool for their work. From a mathematical perspective, the Zome system can serve as a model-for most polyhedra and other three-dimensional figures in geometry and topology, as shown in the Zometool models used by mathematicians Roger Penrose and John Conway (Hart & Picciotto, 2001). The Zome system is also extremely useful in modeling figures in the other STEAM subjects. After its synthesis and development, researchers in the natural sciences immediately saw uses for Zome in their research. In medicine, NASA used Zometool as a model to study the AIDS virus in space. In the field of chemistry, Dan Shechtman, the winner of the 2011 Nobel Prize in Chemistry, used the Zometool in a debate to show whether quasicrystals were real. In physics, Chris Quigg, a physicist from the Theoretical Physics Department at the Fermi National Accelerator Laboratory in Batavia, Illinois, has been using Zometool as a way of modeling the so-called Standard Model of particle physics. The Zometool configuration is demonstrated as a pair of interpenetrating tetrahedrals (three-dimensional figures with four-triangular faced configurations) that Quigg coined the Double Simplex (named after the Double Helix, which was identified by Rosalind Franklin, James Watson, and Francis Crick). His tactile and visual representation demonstrates more of the underlying order and structure of the Standard Model. In his blog post, Quigg elaborates on the importance of using hands-on tools for demonstrating and representing complex physics-related phenomena. What is important here is his position that physicists indeed engage in play as they are working, in this case with Zometool, as a means of developing theoretical assertions. In using Zometool as a representation of the Double Simplex, Quigg states:

> I want to represent what we know is true, what we hope might be true, and what we don't know—in other terms, to show the connections that are firmly established, those we believe must be there, and the open issues. I want also to show the aspect of play, of successive approximations, that animates the way scientists work.
>
> *(Quigg, 2003)*

Copyright Infringed LEGO Clones

The following toy brick companies, all of which are LEGO clone companies, have also been shown to duplicate many or all of the brick and minifigure types that are copyrighted by LEGO. However, when compared with LEGO, since these companies are relatively small in size and serve a tiny fraction of the brick toy market, few, if any, legal challenges have been taken against them. Bela, for example, is a LEGO clone that copied a number of sets from the LEGO brand. The specific series that are known to be copies include Chima, Ninjago, Ninja Turtles, Star Wars, Scooby Doo, Supreme Heroes (super heroes), Romantic (Disney), My World (Minecraft), Let's Go (automobiles), Fairy (elves), Nexo Knight, and Urban (city sets).

Big Elephant, another imitation LEGO clone brand, has attempted originality in that the company custom designs their brick sets. The company's series include Heroes Assemble, Chima, Ninja, My World (Minecraft), Pokémon, Future Knights, Walking Dead, and Ironman. The quality of plastic that Big Elephant uses tends to be of higher quality than most of the imitation brands.

Decool is another imitation LEGO clone that produces bricks and minifigures. Decool's minifigures probably have a closer resemblance to LEGO minifigures than any other brand. Decool replica sets of LEGO include Super Heroes, Technic, and Hero Factory. The company, however, has produced some original bricks and minifigures in its Army and SWAT collections.

Duo Le Pin is a relatively new clone brand that specializes in minifigure series. In addition to cloning LEGO, the brand also cloned some of the original collections of other LEGO clone companies. They replicate themes including Super Heroes, Star Wars, Army, SWAT, Friends, Disney, and Dragon Ball Z—a Japanese animated television series.

Lele originally began to clone LEGO minifigures and then cloned Star Wars, Dinosaur World (Jurassic World), Ninja, Heroes Gathering (super heroes), My World and Worldcraft (Minecraft), Nexo Soldiers, Friends, and Creators themes.

Lepin is perhaps one of the most popular of the imitation LEGO clone companies on the market. When compared to other companies, Lepin produces a relatively strong plastic brick. Lepin produces many themes copied from LEGO. These series include Technics, Nexo Knights, Super Hero, Ninja, Lord of the Rings, Harry Potter, The Simpsons, Angry Birds, Minecraft, and Chima.

Unlike other clone LEGO brands, POGO released most of its new collections one at a time, most likely for marketing reasons. POGO relies mostly on the Super Heroes and Star Wars themes. But the company has also copied The Big Bang Theory characters, The Beatles, The Lord of the Rings, as well as LEGO's Creator modular series. POGO has also released its own custom-made minifigures based on Assassin's Creed and the Game of Thrones.

Sheng Yuan is known in the brick collectors market as an imitative LEGO clone brand that produces high-quality minifigures. Copied brick sets include Heroes Assemble, Friends, Nick Knights, Space Wars, Ninja, and My World (Minecraft). Sometimes, the Sheng Yuan bricks cling so tightly that it is difficult to pull them apart.

Xinh has been in existence since the 1990s, perhaps the longest of all the imitation LEGO brands. The Xinh Company has grown since it included minifigures in its collections. The company has produced cloned themes such as Hero Factory, Super Heroes, Star Wars, Harry Potter, The Big Bank Theory, Ghostbusters, Watchmen and Ninjago.

Metal-Based VCPOs and STEAM: Meccano and Erector

Designed and created in 1898 by Frank Hornby, an English inventor, businessman, and politician, Meccano is a model construction system that consists of both metal and plastic pieces—metal strips, plates, angular posts and lintels, wheels, axles, and gears—that are used to make a large array of mechanical devices. These metal and plastic pieces connect together through the use of nuts and bolts. Meccano is a constructive play object that was no doubt a consequence of the Industrial Revolution in England. Although Hornby, himself, was not trained as an engineer, he based early models of the Meccano system on mechanical engineering principles. In general, the Meccano set provided children with educational opportunities to learn about simple machines—levers, wheels and axles, pulleys, inclined plans, wedges, and screws—and expand on them to construct more elaborate designs. The metal strips, plates, and girders are perforated so that pieces can be connected. A screwdriver, a spanner and a small wrench are the only tools needed to construct with Meccano sets (Marriott, 2012).

In the United States, slightly over a decade after Hornby began his work with Meccano, Alfred Carlton Gilbert first envisioned the idea of metal toy pieces representing railroads as he traveled from New Haven, Connecticut to New York City. Shortly thereafter, he invented the Erector Company in 1913. Motivated by the girders erected to support new electric railroad lines, Gilbert fashioned and produced building sets that provided children with everything they needed to construct their own miniature cities. Gilbert's first Erector set to be marketed and sold was the Erector Structural Steel and Electro-Mechanical Builder, which, by 1914, became one of the most popular constructive play toy sets in the United States. The A. C. Gilbert Company, which produced the Gilbert Erector, developed into a very successful company because Gilbert gradually added more construction parts and, therefore, more diversity in the Erector set. Gilbert's company became less profitable after his death in 1961 and fell into decline shortly thereafter. In attempting to compete with rival toy companies, the A. C. Gilbert Company began to produce less expensive Erector sets out of plastic. But this plan failed to materialize into a successful venture. The Erector name was purchased by different companies during the 1970s and 1980s but none of the companies were able to make it profitable.

Ever since Hornby's founding of Meccano and Gilbert's founding of Erector, some of the world's most influential inventors, scientists, engineers, and innovators, as indicated earlier, have used Erector and Meccano sets to bring to life their first creations as well as those they produced when they eventually became STEAM professionals. Some of the earliest connections between Meccano and STEAM included the use of Meccano as a model of the differential analyzer in the 1930s, a type of mechanical analogue computer that allowed the rather expedient solving of differential equations—a mathematical topic that is essential in most types of engineering (Robinson, 2005). In the late 1940s, William Sewell and William Glenn, both from the Yale School of Medicine, used Meccano to invent the first successful precursor to the artificial heart. Meccano and Erector have also been used as models in numerous inventions that support arts and entertainment, such as theme park rides and Ferris wheel models. These sets have also been used on a massive scale to create life-sized models of bridge structures.

In 2000, Meccano purchased Erector and now the merchandise is sold under the name Erector by Meccano, which comes under the umbrella of the Spin Master Ltd. family company. Erector by Meccano is now designing STEAM construction sets that respond to 21st-century themes in STEAM for a new generation of inventors, curious about science, technology, engineering, architecture, arts, and mathematics (McCullouch, 2019).

As discussed in the next chapter, because of the company's strong connection with the construction of objects from non-themed metallic, perforated pieces that are connected with screws, Meccano and Erector sets have inspired numerous renowned STEAM personalities and professionals, many of whom are Nobel prize-winning recipients. Probably because of its questionable nature with regard to safety and the well-being of young children, metal-based VCPOs have not been as popular a constructive play toy as have blocks, bricks, and planks. Yet, some of our most celebrated STEAM experts, such as Othmar Ammann, the Swiss-American civil engineer and designer of the George Washington Bridge, Verrazano-Narrows Bridge, Bayonne Bridge, and the Lincoln Tunnel, as well as Nobel Prize winners such as physicists Martin Perl, William Phillips, and Steven Chu (Sullivan, 2014), and chemist Harold Kroto (St. Fleur, 2016), used the Meccano model construction system as well as Erector sets in their childhood and early adult years to model their innovative ideas.

VCPOs and Genderization

Reference to Ammann, Chu, Kroto, Perl, Phillips, and other STEAM giants mentioned in previous chapters and sections above is essential to convey the point that promoting and fostering STEAM learning starts with constructive free play experiences during early childhood. But while it is important for teachers, educational and psychological researchers, and parents to recognize and appreciate how certain VCPOs have the potential to provide rich experiences for children and adults pursuing STEAM fields, it is perhaps more important to consider the unfortunate fact that inequality in the designing, manufacturing, and marketing of constructive free play VCPOs has persisted for decades—particularly from the standpoint of gender and socio-economic class. To be clear, constructive toy manufacturers have always aimed their marketing at boys. On the whole, these companies have masculinized VCPOs to the point that when girls become teenagers, they are already of the mindset that science, mathematics, and engineering are "male professions." Eschner (2017) captures the essence of this mindset in the opening line of her article: "Picture it: Christmas morning, 1922. Jimmy unwraps an Erector Set. Jane gets a Little Laundress ...."

As indicated above, much is known about Gilbert's accomplishment with the design and patent of the Erector Set and its successful marketing strategies and sales. But less is known about another toy sold by LaVelle, a spin-off sister company of the A. C. Gilbert Company that was established in the 1920s and tailored to girls. The name of the toy, the Little Laundress, was produced shortly after the Erector Set was established as an "alternative" for girls so that the company could market a toy to families with daughters (Pursell, 2018). The Little Laundress set consisted of small toy irons, a toy pre-electric washboard, a miniature wash pail, a small laundry bag, and a toy hang-dryer. It is possible that the Little Laundress toy "designed" for girls was inspired by a print from 1896 by the same title. Created by the well-known French painter, Pierre Bonnard, the Little Laundress portrayed a young female laundry worker carrying a large basket of washing along an abandoned alleyway in Paris. In addition to its representation of the feminization of laundry work, this print reflects the stark realities of child labor that existed in fin de siècle France, and certainly during the late 19th and early 20th centuries in the United States. During this period, approximately one-fifth to one-third of the Parisian population, mostly women and girls, were involved in the laundry industry (Lipton, 1980). It is no wonder, then, given the zeitgeist, that LaVelle would produce a toy tailored to girls that embodied an occupation intended to represent girls' work. Rebecca Onion (2016) pointed out that even in the early 20th century, young children were thought of as miniature scientists who engaged in curiosity and emergent experimentation. But in reality, this adult perception was assigned almost exclusively to boys. The technology historian Carroll Pursell (2018) clearly demonstrates gender disparity with regard to toy marketing in his history of toy production:

> Then as now, toys directed at boys were more numerous, more active, and more complex than those for girls. Boys were urged to investigate, experiment, and innovate—activities designed to develop each boy up to his highest capacity. Girls were not so encouraged, and were given dolls, small household tools, and appliances that prepared them not for success in the modern world of scientific and technological change but rather the more static domestic occupations of their mothers. No better example could be found than the offerings of the LaVelle Toy Company.
>
> *(p. 21)*

The Gilbert Company, which, as we discussed earlier, faded in the late 20th century and whose famed Erector set was purchased by Meccano, should not, I think, take sole responsibility for the genderization of toys; clearly, this has always been an endemic problem that has run rampant in virtually all toy retail companies. However, there are many blogs where people post contributions that place no blame whatsoever on toy companies. Unfortunately, a number of these individuals uphold chauvinistic bootstrap theory positions in claiming that all persons, female or male, are responsible for their own actions when it comes to entering certain professions such as those in STEAM. In paraphrasing their beliefs, they argue "If a parent provides STEM toys for girls, all the better; if not, so be it." Some STEM-oriented female blog contributors who espouse the bootstrap position have stated that they prospered in STEM related endeavors because it was their own decision and "not because they played or did not play with" constructive toys when they were young. But that's not the point: What is the point—and a fact—is that there is an overwhelming shortage of women in the STEAM professions (Ertl, Luttenberger & Paechter, 2017), and lack of cognitive experiences with VCPOs, particularly low-affordance VCPOs, in the early years contribute to this shortage. Making these toys available to both girls and boys should take place early in a child's life. Mazdeh (2011) has shown that early childhood experiences with the concepts and principles of engineering makes possible the development of technological literacy in women, and thus positively contributes to their pursuit and success in the engineering profession. Moreover, putting an end to all gender stereotypes is something relatively easy for parents to do; it starts during infancy and requires parents to expose their children to all types of play so that no one gender is stuck with any one stereotypical role in society.

Conclusions

In this chapter, we were introduced and exposed to numerous types of VCPOs that have been or are on the world toy market. We noticed that while wooden play block sets are perhaps the most widespread type of play block in preschools and homes, other forms of block types either have also been or still are manufactured and sold to a wide range of toy consumers. But perhaps most evident is the fact that brick toys have dominated the toy market ever since the onset of the toy brick in the 1930s and 1940s.

It is also important to note that much of the existing literature on toys—and in our case, VCPOs—has to do with the ways in which toys have inundated homes and preschools to the point that they undermine the meaning and magnitude of childcare, parental and custodial love of the child, and child development in general. For better or worse, toys have become one of the foremost influences on child cognition and acculturation for more than a century (Sutton-Smith, 1986). In fact, the Toy Industry Association (TIA) report produced by the U.S. Department of Commerce (2012) projected that the worldwide retail sales of toys was computed to be more than $80.280 billion in 2009. The ten most competitive markets in toy retail sales in 2021 were (in alphabetical order): Canada, China, France, Germany, India, Japan, South Korea, Spain, the UK, and the United States.

In his chapter on environment and parenting, Bradley (2002) discusses the toy culture in terms of its focus on consumerism and its potentially deleterious effects on children's cognitive, social, and emotional development. He argues that the material objects available in the home for recreation and learning affects what happens in the family environment. Bradley (2002) also acknowledges that while it is apparent how much parents are spending on toys and related learning materials for children, it should not be assumed that children have access to these materials. Moreover, because they have a strong influence on parental purchasing decisions, children have become adept consumers of toys (Calvert, 2008; Gunter & Furnham, 1998). Sutton-Smith (1986) proposes that parents and caregivers have been exploited by material markets—particularly toy markets—which do so in order to satisfy young children's hedonistic tendencies toward want and desire when it comes to their satisfaction and fulfillment. He states that these markets prey on the fears of parents who are busy or absent from home a good deal of the time that they are not engaging with their children sufficiently and who believe that they are not doing enough to help their children's cognitive, social, and emotional development. What these markets do is tap into parental fears by advertising all their toys and related play materials as "educational" or "child friendly."

To this end, as I will discuss in the next chapter, the popularity of a VCPO, or, for that matter, putative notions of a VCPO's influence on academic ability—in our case, STEAM subjects—does not automatically equate to its apparent role in supporting cognitive development. In fact, I will argue that most plastic snap brick toys, with the possible exception of generic LEGO and a very small number of LEGO themes, can potentially be more of a limitation than a benefit when it comes to facilitating intellectual development in children's emergent conceptions in STEAM. It should be noted, then, that LEGO clones, which are almost always themed and require step-by-step instructions for assembly, may conceivably undermine the intellectual welfare of the child.

References

Amabile, T. M., & Pillemer, J. (2012). Perspectives on the social psychology of creativity. *The Journal of Creative Behavior*, 46(1), 3–15.

Amabile, T. M., Hennessey, B. A., & Grossman, B. S. (1986). Social influences on creativity: The effects of contracted-for reward. *Journal of Personality and Social Psychology*, 50 (1), 14.

Anker Eurosource (2020). *Classic Anchor Blocks*. Rudolstadt, Germany: Anker Eurosource. Retrieved from: https://anchor-stone.eurosourcellc.com.

Austen, I. (2005, February 3). Lego plays hardball with right to bricks. *International Herald Tribune*, p. 11.

Bailey, M. (1933). A scale of block constructions for young children. *Child Development*, 4 (2), 121–139.

Balfanz, R. (1999). Why do we teach young children so little mathematics?: Some historical considerations. In J. V. Copley (Ed.), *Mathematics in the early years* (pp. 3–10). Reston, VA: National Council of Teachers of Mathematics.

Beeson, B., & Williams, A. (1979). *A study of sex stereotyping in child-selected play activities of preschool children*. Muncie, IN: Ball State University.

Bjorklund, D. F., & Gardiner, A. (2011). Object play and tool use: Developmental and evolutionary perspectives. In A. D. Pellegrini (Ed.), *Oxford handbook of the development of play* (pp. 153–171). New York: Oxford University Press.

Blackman, N. (1977). An investigation of the relation of historical change to the sexual identification of pre-adolescent as seen in dramatic block play. Unpublished doctoral dissertation, University of Maryland, College Park, Maryland.

Bradley, R. (2002). Environment and parenting. In M. Bornstein (Ed.), *Handbook of parenting* (2nd ed.). Hillsdale, NJ: Lawrence Erlbaum.

Brosterman, N. (1997). *Inventing Kindergarten*. New York: Harry N. Abrams, Inc., Publishers.

Calvert, S. (2008). Children as consumers: Advertising and marketing. *The Future of Children: Children and Electronic Media*, 18, 205–234.

Casey, B. M., Andrews, N., Schindler, H., Kersh, J. E., Samper, A., & Copley, J. (2008). The development of spatial skills through interventions involving block building activities. *Cognition and Instruction*, 26(3), 269–309.

Clance, P. (1975). Sex differences in play behavior of three age groups. Unpublished.

Cohen, L. E., & Emmons, J. (2017). Block play: Spatial language with preschool and school-aged children. *Early Child Development and Care*, 187(5–6), 967–977.

Dewdney, A. (1989). A Tinkertoy computer that plays tic-tac-toe. *Scientific American*, 261(4), 120–123.

Erikson, E. H. (1951) Sex differences in the play configurations of preadolescents. *The American Journal of Orthopsychiatry*, 21, 667–692.

Ertl, B., Luttenberger, S., & Paechter, M. (2017). The impact of gender stereotypes on the self-concept of female students in stem subjects with an under-representation of females. *Frontiers in Psychology*, 8(703). doi:10.3389/fpsyg.2017.00703.

Eschner, K. (2017, February 15). This sexist 1920s toy is part of the reason for the women in STEM gap: Boys got Erector sets—girls got this stellar consolation prize. *Smithsonian Magazine*. Retrieved from: https://www.smithsonianmag.com/smart-news/sexist-1920s-toy-part-reason-women-stem-gap-180962094.

Farenga, S., Ness, D., Johnson, D. D., & Johnson, B. (2010). *The importance of average: Playing the game of school to increase success and achievement*. Lanham, MD: Rowman & Littlefield Publishers.

Ferrara, K., Hirsh-Pasek, K., Newcombe, N. S., Golinkoff, R. M., & Lam, W. S. (2011). Block talk: Spatial language during block play. *Mind, Brain, and Education*, 5(3), 143–151.

Forman, G. E. (1982). A search for the origins of equivalence concepts through a microanalysis of block play. In G. E. Forman (Ed.), *Action and thought: From sensorimotor schemes to symbolic operations* (pp. 97–135). New York: Academic Press.

Froebel, F. W. (1887). *On the education of man*. New York: Appleton.

Ginsburg, H. P., Pappas, S., & Seo, K. H. (2001). Everyday mathematical knowledge: Asking young children what is developmentally appropriate. In S. L. Golbeck (Ed.), *Psychological perspectives on early childhood education: Reframing dilemmas in research and practice* (pp. 181–219). Mahwah, NJ: Lawrence Erlbaum Associates.

Ginsburg, H. P., Lin, C. L., Ness, D., & Seo, K. H. (2003). Young American and Chinese children's everyday mathematical activity. *Mathematical Thinking and Learning*, 5(4), 235–258.

Goodfader, R. A. (1982). Sex differences in the play constructions of pre-school children. *Smith College Studies in Social Work*, 52(2), 129–144.

Guanella, F. M. (1934). Block building activities of young children. Doctoral dissertation, Columbia University, New York.

Gunter, B., & Furnham, A. (1998). *Children as consumers: A psychological analysis of the young people's market*. New York: Psychology Press.

Hart, G. W., & Picciotto, H. (2001). *Zome geometry: Hands-on learning with Zome models*. Berkeley, CA: Key Curriculum Press.

Hewitt, K. (2001). Blocks as a tool for learning: Historical contemporary perspectives. *Young Children*, 56(1), 6–14.

Hirsch, E. S. (1996). *The block book*. Washington, DC: National Association for the Education of Young Children.

Hulson, E. L., & Reich, H. L. (1931). Blocks and the four-year-old. *Childhood Education*, 8(2), 66–68.

Hussain, S., Lindh, J., & Shukur, G. (2006). The effect of LEGO training on pupils' school performance in mathematics, problem-solving ability and attitude: Swedish data. *Journal of Educational Technology and Society*, 9, 182–194.

Kinsman, C., & Berk, L. (1979). Joining the block and housekeeping areas. *Young Children*, 35, 66–75.

Ko, P. (2010). The effect of a middle school robotics class on standardized math test scores. Doctoral dissertation, Texas State University–San Marcos.

Köhler, W. (1921). *Intelligenzprüfungen an Menschenaffen* [Measuring the intelligence of apes]. Berlin: Julius Springer.

Lange, A. (2018). *The design of childhood: How the material world shapes independent kids*. New York: Bloomsbury Publishing.

Lascarides, V. C., & Hinitz, B. F. (2013). *History of early childhood education*. New York: Routledge.

Lauwaert, M. (2008). Playing outside the box—on LEGO toys and the changing world of construction play. *History and Technology*, 24(3), 221–237.

Lauwaert, M. (2009). *The place of play: Toys and digital cultures*. Amsterdam, The Netherlands: Amsterdam University Press.

Lepore, F. E. (2018). *Finding Einstein's brain*. New Brunswick, NJ: Rutgers University Press.

Lillard, A. S. (2008). How important are the Montessori materials? *Montessori Life*, 20(4), 20–25.

Lillard, A. S. (2013). Playful learning and Montessori education. *American Journal of Play*, 5(2), 157–186.

Lipton, E. (1980). The laundress in late-nineteenth-century French culture: Imagery, ideology and Edgar Degas. *Art History*, 3(3), 295–313.

MacDonald, R. P., Dickson, C. A., Martineau, M., & Ahearn, W. H. (2015). Prerequisite skills that support learning through video modeling. *Education and Treatment of Children*, 38(1), 33–47.

Marriott, R. (2012). *Meccano*. London: Bloomsbury Publishing.

Massey, M. K. (1969). Kindergarten children's behavior in block building situations. Doctoral dissertation, Florida State University, Tallahassee, Florida.

Mayer, E. L. (1991). Towers and enclosed spaces: A preliminary report on gender differences in children's reactions to block structures. *Psychoanalytic Inquiry*, 11(4), 480–510.

Mazdeh, S. (2011). Women engineers and the influence of childhood technologic environment. Doctoral dissertation, Drexel University, Philadelphia, Pennsylvania.

McCullouch, J. (2019). Sketch: Maths, Meccano® and motivation. In A. James & C. Nerantzi (Eds.), *The power of play in higher education* (pp. 167–169). New York: Palgrave Macmillan.

Montessori, M. (1948). *The discovery of the child*. Madras: Kalakshet.

Montessori, M. (1964). *The Montessori method*. New York: Schocken Books.

Ness, D., & Farenga, S. J. (2007). *Knowledge under construction: The importance of play in developing children's spatial and geometric thinking*. Lanham, MD: Rowman & Littlefield Publishers.

Ness, D., & Farenga, S. J. (2016). Blocks, bricks, and planks: Relationships between affordance and visuo-spatial constructive play objects. *American Journal of Play*, 8(2), 201–227.

Onion, R. (2016). *Innocent experiments: Childhood and the culture of popular science in the United States*. Chapel Hill, NC: University of North Carolina Press.

Pagano, L. C., Haden, C. A., & Uttal, D. H. (2020). Museum program design supports parent–child engineering talk during tinkering and reminiscing. *Journal of Experimental Child Psychology*, 200. Retrieved from: https://doi.org/10.1016/j.jecp.2020.104944.

Pellegrini, A. D. (2009). *The role of play in human development*. New York, NY: Oxford University Press.

Pollman, M. J. (2010). *Blocks and beyond: Strengthening early math and science skills through spatial learning*. Baltimore: Brookes Publishing.

Pottmann, H. (2010). Architectural geometry as design knowledge. *Architectural Design*, 80, 72–77.

Pottmann, H., Asperl, A., Hofer, M., Kilian, A., & Bentley, D. (2007). *Architectural geometry* (Vol. 724). Exton, PA: Bentley Institute Press.

Pratt, C. (1948). *I learn from children: An adventure in progressive education*. New York: Simon & Schuster.

Provenzo, E. F., & Brett, A. (1983). *The complete block book*. Syracuse, NY: Syracuse University Press.

Pruden, S. M., & Levine, S. C. (2017). Parents' spatial language mediates a sex difference in preschoolers' spatial-language use. *Psychological Science*, 28(11), 1583–1596.

Pursell, C. (2018). A. C. Gilbert, toys, and the boy engineer. In C. Pursell (Ed.), *Technology in America: A history of individuals and ideas* (3rd ed.) (pp. 193–202). Cambridge, MA: MIT Press.

Quigg, C. (2003, May 30). Envisioning particles and interactions. Fermi National Accelerator Laboratory. Retrieved from: https://boudin.fnal.gov/~quigg/JGV/EnvPFintro.html.

Reifel, S. (1984). Block construction: Children's developmental landmarks in representation of space. *Young Children*, 40(1), 61–67.

Robinson, T. (2005). The Meccano set computers: A history of differential analyzers made from children's toys. *IEEE Control Systems Magazine*, 25(3), 74–83.

Rubin, K. (1977). The social and cognitive value of preschool toys and activities. *Canadian Journal of Behavioral Science*, 9, 382–385.

Schuster, J. (1973). Sex differences and within sex variations in children's block constructions. Doctoral dissertation, New York University.

St. Fleur, N. (2016, May 4). Harold Kroto, Nobel Prize-winning chemist, is dead at 76. *The New York Times*. Retrieved from: http://www.nytimes.com.

Strange, C. (1996). *Collector's guide to Tinker toys*. Paducah, KY: Collector Books.

Strong National Museum of Play (2020). *Tinkertoy*. Rochester, NY: Strong National Museum of Play. Retrieved from: https://www.toyhalloffame.org/toys/tinkertoy.

Sullivan, J. (2014, October 29). The five retro science kits that inspired a generation of tinkerers. *Discover Magazine*. Retrieved from: https://www.discovermagazine.com/technology/the-5-retro-science-kits-that-inspired-a-generation-of-tinkerers.

Sutton-Smith, B. (1986). *Toys as culture*. New York: Garland.

Taggart, E. (2020, November 17). LEGO unveils 9,036-piece Roman Colosseum—its largest set ever! *My Modern Met*. Retrieved from: https://mymodernmet.com/lego-colosseum.

Thurnwald, R. (1922). Psychologie des primitive Menschen [Psychology of primitive man]. In G. Kafka (Ed.), *Handbuch der vergleichenden Psychologie* (Vol. 1, pp. 147–320). Munich: Verlag von Ernst Reinhardt.

Tõugu, P., Marcus, M., Haden, C. A., & Uttal, D. H. (2017). Connecting play experiences and engineering learning in a children's museum. *Journal of Applied Developmental Psychology*, 53, 10–19.

U.S. Department of Commerce (2012). Dolls, toys, games, and children's vehicles NAICS Code 33993. Retrieved from: https://www.toyassociation.org/app_themes/tia/pdfs/facts/2012toyoutlook.pdf.

Verdine, B. N., Golinkoff, R. M., Hirsh-Pasek, K., Newcombe, N. S., Filipowicz, A. T., & Chang, A. (2014). Deconstructing building blocks: Preschoolers' spatial assembly performance relates to early mathematical skills. *Child Development*, 85(3), 1062–1076.

Vygotsky, L. (1928). Problema kul'turnogo razvitija rebenka [The problem of the cultural development of the child]. *Pedologija*, 1, 58–77.

Wheeler, M. (2019). Lincoln Logs creator: John Lloyd Wright. *Children's Book and Media Review*, 40(3), 58–90.

Wilcox, A. (1979). *Sex differences in the play configurations of pre-adolescents: A replication and revision.* Paper presented at the Annual Convention of the South Eastern Psychological Association, New Orleans, Louisiana, March 28–31, 1979.

Williams, A., & Beeson, B. (1980). *A follow-up study of sex stereotyping in child-selected play activities of preschool children.* Muncie, IN: Ball State University.

Wolfgang, C., Stannard, L., & Jones, I. (2003). Advanced constructional play with LEGOs among preschoolers as a predictor of later school achievement in mathematics. *Early Child Development and Care*, 173(5), 467–475.

4
SIMPLE VCPOS ARE BEST

In this chapter, our mission is twofold: We will first investigate how the various interpretations of affordance can be adopted for the purpose of categorizing VCPOs in terms of their effects on creativity, spatial development, and cognition in STEAM disciplines. We will then investigate whether certain VCPOs, namely, themed bricks, are helpful in the home or preschool in developing young children's knowledge in STEAM.

Reconsidering the Affordance of VCPOs

The psychological construct of affordance that was developed initially by James Gibson in the 1970s has shed a great deal of light on how we consider the ways in which objects or things in our environment interact with the everyday activities of the individual. Subsequent cognitive and social psychologists have followed in Gibson's path and have focused on the ways in which we as humans (and non-human organisms for that matter) deal with various things in our everyday environments (Greeno, 1994; Osiurak, Rossetti & Badets, 2017; Wagman, 2019).

When we consider affordance, one of the first things that comes to mind is what the onset of a particular object's features or characteristics offers the individual. We might think, in this case, that greater affordance of this feature is a good thing because it is seen to offer the individual greater benefit. Affordance can also be understood in terms of the individual, the environment, and the material objects within that environment, and how the individual uses specific objects in a collective manner as a means of building character and function. We can, thus, think of a large rock (or small boulder) as being something that is suitable for a small child to sit on or for an adult to use as a makeshift table (Krampen, 1989). In this example, affordance has to do with the ontological nature or disposition of

DOI: 10.4324/9781003097815-5

a given object that possesses some kind of function that can be exercised by an individual in a certain situation.

For James Gibson (1979), a pioneer in the psychological concept of affordance in the literature, affordances serve as the keystone attribute for any object or environment. Gibson treats affordances in such a way that links them with perception, a basic cognitive function. In doing so, Gibson shows that individuals have the ability to evaluate objects, environments, or events in terms of their affordances—in other words, what these objects or environments provide the individual for the purposes of mobility or intellectual development. Gibson's position has been embraced by contemporary cognitive and ecological psychologists, who have argued that the physiological underpinnings of perception failed to demonstrate the extent to which basic cognitive functions like perception, attention, and memory are based on mechanistic factors, and that an ecological approach was needed in order to gain a more robust understanding (Greeno, 1994; Reed, 1993; Withagen, de Poel, Araujo & Pepping, 2012).

The term "affordance" as defined by Gibson seems to have emanated from the work of Gestalt psychologists of the early 20th century. Gibson developed the concept of affordances from his earlier work with Laurence Crook (Gibson & Crook, 1938), which refers to the idea of valence. Gibson and Crook define positive or negative valences as "the meanings of objects by virtue of which we move toward some of them and away from others" (1938, pp. 454–455). For Gibson and Crook, positive valences are the meanings of objects we tend to move toward and, in contrast, negative valences are the meanings of objects we tend to move away from (Jones, 2003). Withagen et al. (2012) suggest that Gibson was influenced by the Gestaltist Kurt Koffka (1935) who proposed that properties of the environment that are action-relevant are instantly perceived by the observer. Gibson's notion of affordances has served as a way to explain how one can perceive the functions and properties of an object or objects instantaneously. Moreover, the notion of affordances demonstrates the inseparability of perception and action; we instantaneously perceive the operational properties of certain objects and how others might interact with them (such as a handle for holding a mug or a knob for turning to open a door), while the affordances of other objects might be more difficult to identify. For our purposes, affordance is critical in analyzing VCPOs because it allows the investigator to identify the individual's uses and intentions for use of the particular VCPO in question.

It is important to note that, with regard to spatial thinking and the use of VCPOs, the use of the term "affordance" in our context is only minimally associated with the Gibsonian view of the term. Gibson's definition of affordance brings to light the ways in which we refer to objects—VCPOs included—in our everyday lives. The general emphasis, then, is that the greater affordance an object possesses, the more it positively influences our way of life. Aside from this general Gibsonian view of affordance, my reason for using the affordance construct for the purpose of studying the development of VCPO use is to determine the extent to which affordances of VCPOs may influence the levels of complexity of spatial thinking and spatial sense—key cross-cutting concepts in STEAM disciplines. Affordance, then, has to do with the meaning of a VCPO in terms of what it gives the user in terms of maximizing potential in VCPO constructions that result in structural spatial behaviors. Someone who is interested in the affordance of VCPOs should ask what that specific VCPO offers the user. Does the VCPO provide the builder with a highly detailed set of instructions that make the construction process easier for the builder? Or, does the VCPO offer the builder little, if anything, in terms of affordance with regard to the detail and specificity of function? Moreover, how is a particular VCPO perceived by the builder or interpreter?

In order to understand affordance of VCPO use, examination of this study from a developmental standpoint is paramount—in particular, Piaget's notion of the interaction between empirical abstraction and reflective abstraction (Piaget, 1977). Piaget wanted to highlight the role of the object and that the development of mental constructions unfolds in large part through the individual's interactions with objects in the environment. Objects for our purposes are VCPOs. It should be clear that the different types of VCPOs possess a wealth of different characteristics that provide the child with ample experience to experiment with physical properties. Let's start with the idea of empirical abstractions and what it means with respect to the concept of the affordance of VCPOs.

Empirical abstractions are cognitive processes that are related to the properties of VCPOs. What are these properties? They may be in the shape of bricks (i.e., rectangular cuboids), wooden or synthetic as in the case of plastic, have mass, and be able to balance (or not). For example, VCPOs can be in the form of blocks, which have distinct colors and smooth surfaces to allow the sliding movement of one block over another. As another example, VCPOs can be in the form of bricks (i.e., LEGOs or MegaBloks) which contain studs for the purpose of affixing or snapping one brick to another. Thus, the properties of different VCPOs afford a variety of physical constraints that need to be grappled with in the initial stages of the construction process. Depending on the VCPO used at any given time, the smooth surfaces of wooden play blocks or the pip-laden surfaces of bricks present the individual with the awareness of the unique and seemingly innumerable possibilities of positioning and placement of individual pieces in the process of creating larger structures. Unlike bricks which cannot slide and must be affixed or interlocked in place, wood blocks and planks do not lock into place; rather, they remain in place based on how they are balanced due to their relative position to other blocks or planks. If a single block of a block structure is ever so subtly moved or slid, such movement can affect the stability of the entire structure in terms of its inertia and balance. Surely, we have seen occasions when someone removes a block from a block structure or a plank from a plank structure and the entire structure collapses. Due to the interlocking nature of pips, bricks, in contrast to blocks or planks, provide a totally different context that exhibits a different physical narrative with respect to inertia, balance, and mass. Accordingly, the child who encounters different VCPOs for the first time will have preconceived notions of how each VCPO type can be used.

Now that we have established that different VCPO types possess different forms, in part, resulting from their different surfaces, we can return to Piaget's notion of empirical and reflective abstractions. Again, empirical abstractions are cognitive processes that allow us as individuals to perceive (possibly initially) and eventually act on (i.e., use) a particular object based on its unique properties. So, when an empirical abstraction is realized, a reflective abstraction may follow. Reflective abstraction is a subsequent cognitive process (to empirical abstraction) that develops from the individual's contemplation of actions and the coordination of those actions, and forms the basis of the development of what Piaget calls logico-mathematical knowledge (Piaget, 1977).

Piaget distinguishes between different internal processes as a means of clarifying cognitive development. For instance, he differentiates between linguistic knowledge and logico-mathematical knowledge as two different internal cognitive processes. Logico-mathematical knowledge is comprised of the mental relationships that are formed from the individual's increased understanding of the properties of an object. When we think of a child building a structure, logico-mathematical knowledge is the result of the observable, behavioral processes that include, but are not limited to, classification, seriation, the concept of number, and spatial and temporal relationships. Each of these observable behavioral processes is affected by the level of affordance that is inherent in the properties of VCPOs. In recent studies, my colleagues and I use the placement of blocks for balance as an example of a child who reflects on balancing one block on another (Ness & Farenga, 2016; Ness, Farenga & Garofalo, 2017). The child, then, realizes that the block placed on top can only extend up to a certain point before it becomes unbalanced and subsequently falls (see Figure 4.1). In the figure, you can see that Block 1 (the movable block) and Block 2 (the stationary block) provide representative examples of empirical abstraction. However, reflective abstraction is the knowledge obtained from working with blocks and understanding the outcomes of acting upon the blocks. Pseudo-empirical abstraction refers to the transition between the empirical

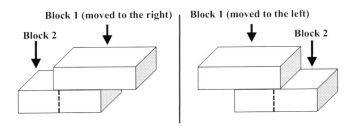

FIGURE 4.1 Representation of empirical, pseudo-empirical, and reflective abstractions

and reflective abstraction. The generalization that can be made from the pseudo-empirical abstraction is solely based on Isaac Newton's law of universal gravitation—that Block 1 will balance if it does not extend beyond Block 2, that is, beyond the halfway line (dotted line).

The interaction between empirical abstraction and reflective abstraction can be explained by pseudo-empirical abstraction, which, while transient, is based on the child's actions. With regard to children's VCPO play, pseudo-empirical abstraction, according to Piaget, is defined by the momentary contemplation of the properties and relations of VCPOs that result from the coordination of the child's actions. For example, a child discovers physical principles governing balance only after two or more blocks have actually been balanced. Piaget argued that reflective abstractions are extensions of pseudo-empirical abstractions because they are contemplations on the properties of objects that have been manipulated by the child. The child may then realize that the block on the top will balance, either midway to the left or midway to the right, and that the order of placing the block to the left or to the right will not change the result. Pseudo-empirical abstractions, then, are the contemplations that occur when a child is thinking about what is necessary to balance one block on another. More specifically, it is the knowledge that the child may have when realizing that the block will balance if it is placed midway or less on a same-size or larger block.

An important goal for us is to pay attention to how affordance levels of VCPOs affect the individual's concept formation as presented through empirical and reflective abstractions. Our understanding of the diversity of VCPOs, their levels of affordance, and their impact on the constructive play environment are crucial to one's understanding of Piagetian abstractions.

The importance of VCPO affordances is indirectly supported by Vygotsky (1966 [1933]), who maintained that things (in our case, VCPOs) themselves offer the child a variety of ways in which the child can construe what can be done in order for the thing in question to function effectively. Contemplating the mediation between action and play, Vygotsky elaborated on situational and environmental constraints and how children are bound to these constraints during play. In referring to Lewin's (1935) work on motivation and its effects on the environment and the child, Vygotsky argued that things, by their very nature, impose rules as to what the child must do to perform a particular task with these things. Just as a brush has to be manipulated by the painter for the purpose of releasing paint on canvas for painting a work of art, so, too, do VCPOs place demands on the user. To elaborate on Vygotsky's position, a LEGO minifigure possesses a clear-cut set of constraints in that it can only be used in a very limited number of occurrences and situations (e.g., on intergalactic missions, on horseback, or in the driver's seat of a truck). The LEGO minifigure, then, has a great deal of affordance because the user is generally clear about how it is to be used. In contrast, a unit block is simply a rectangular cuboid—the shape of a box. The same is true of a plank. The constraints of a unit block or a plank are somewhat ambiguous, thus exhibiting low levels of affordance and more possibilities and cognitive demands for the child.

In her groundbreaking study, McLoyd (1983) examined the effects of play objects in terms of their physical structure on pretend play of low-income children. Her results showed that high-structured objects, in contrast to low-structured objects, contributed to more non-interactive pretend play among three-and-a-half-year-old children, thus indicating that the more structured the object is, the less chance that children will continue to be engaged in pretend play.

My colleagues and I have suggested that the greater the affordance of a VCPO, the easier it is to use it in construction and, therefore, the more it impedes creativity, problem solving, spatial sense, and cognitive development overall (Ness et al., 2017). We argued that VCPOs with higher levels of affordance generally lead to more constraints on creative thinking. These constraints, which tend to place more restrictions on creativity, may lower the levels of interest and satisfaction and even motivation in completing a particular activity (Amabile, Hennessey & Grossman, 1986; Amabile & Pillemer, 2012; Deci & Ryan, 1980). One can also argue that the more intentionality in the manufacture and design of the material, the greater the affordance the object has and therefore the less potential for the individual's creative expression (Elkind, 2007; Hirsh-Pasek, Golinkoff, Berk & Singer, 2009).

We have also proposed the existence of an inverse relationship between the level of affordance of a particular VCPO and spatially-related cognitive skills, which can also contribute to the intrinsic motivation and creative fluency of the individual engaged in constructive free play (Ness et al., 2017; Ness & Farenga, 2016). This position can be summed up mathematically with the following inverse operation: $a = \frac{1}{X}$ where a refers to the affordance of an object and X (i.e., chi) is the acquisition of creativity and spatial thinking skills and their development. In other words, the affordance of a specific VCPO is inversely proportional to the acquisition of spatial skills as well as the development of creative processes. Greater affordance, then, brings about ease of use of the particular VCPO with which the child is playing. This ease of use leads the child to less interaction with materials, the limitations and disadvantages of problem-solving strategies required to complete a particular construction, and less overall time to complete a construction, and therefore, less time engaged in the constructive activity.

Scripted VCPOs, namely, the ones with specified narratives that are more often than not accompanied by detailed instructions for assembly, account for high levels of affordance, while non-scripted VCPOs tend to possess low levels of affordance. My colleagues and I contend that the more thematic, formulaic, or scripted the VCPO, the greater its level of affordance. From this standpoint, the child who uses highly thematic play objects will know what the end product might look like prior to the completion of the final structure. We can also say, then, that the grater the level of affordance, the less creativity and development of skills that emphasize spatial sense. For many of us, it may seem counterintuitive that certain VCPOs may have limitations on cognitive development. But this position is not necessarily an original one. Elias and Berk (2002) and Krafft and Berk (1998) suggest that over-structuring the child's environment may serve to limit creative and intellectual development and not necessarily enhance it.

Not only does the affordance level factor present itself as a central problem during the preschool and lower elementary grades; it is also problematic—perhaps to a greater extent—for students in the upper elementary grades and secondary grades. For the most part, activities and exercises are devised in ways that fail to take different points of view into account; the goal is to ensure predetermined results and not necessarily to make students think. Students' cognitive intrigue is often overlooked at the expense of accommodating a generally rigid curriculum. As defined in an earlier volume (Ness et al., 2017), cognitive intrigue is the curiosity that intrinsically motivates an individual to willingly engage and actively participate in an activity. The loss of cognitive intrigue may start by only using VCPOs or related play objects that have embedded within them predetermined conclusions, especially those that are reinforced by rote instruction in school. Examples of this reinforcement include toys, games, and lessons that serve only as ends in and of themselves and that require little, if any, cognitive intrigue of the individual. The following vignette from Farenga, Ness, Johnson and Johnson (2010) demonstrates this dilemma—namely, the use of themed VCPOs and the lack of development of cognitive intrigue of the child.

> The act of taking a tree branch and turning it into a magic wand may actually have more influence on promoting cognitive intrigue than a plastic, manufactured version of Darth Vader's light saber. At the time, my five-year-old son was invited to his friend's birthday party, where approximately 20 children played in the backyard, imagining that they were Star Wars characters. His friend having the birthday party is an avid fan of superheroes and Star Wars figures. So, Star Wars paraphernalia, mostly plastic multi-colored light sabers, were strewn through his parents' backyard. The "problem" was that although there were about 20 children, there were only 12 or 13 manufactured light sabers. What is a young child to do without a light saber—namely, one of the seven or eight who "weren't lucky enough" to get one? A couple of children among the seven or eight who didn't pick up light sabers picked up small hockey sticks and used these instead of the plastic light sabers. Others went with this idea and picked up generic objects that served as surrogates to the light sabers—such as a stick or a piece of wood—that they pretended were light sabers. The remaining two or three children were not interested at all in the surrogate objects and thus tried to negotiate with one of the children who had a plastic light saber. Over time, the children using the surrogate objects in lieu of the plastic sabers became more spirited, committed, and imaginative in their play than were the children

who had the manufactured plastic light sabers. This outcome was evidenced by a longer play period with fewer interruptions and a play activity that went beyond Darth Vader, Stormtroopers, and the magical wonder of the force. The novelty of the manufactured plastic light saber eventually wore off, but the use of the surrogate objects did not.

(p. 125)

This vignette makes clear that play involving the use of products manufactured with a specific theme may contribute to limitations of self-regulatory behaviors and even creative ideation. The form of play described above that engenders the use of manufactured systems has specified prescribed outcomes that are shown to be the case due to the user's need to follow specific instructions that must be followed to obtain a result based on the interests of the manufacturer and not those of the child. Moreover, these toy products often require repetitive actions with little to no latitude for the child's imaginative expression or variation of the activity. The position stressed here is supported by research suggesting that free play offers an opportunity to observe an intrinsically motivated action. This is extremely important because levels of intrinsically related activities are significantly correlated with creativity (Amabile et al., 1986; Amabile & Pillemer, 2012; Amabile & Pratt, 2016; Deci & Ryan, 1980).

The key point is that children's play using products manufactured with a specific design or function may limit or even stifle self-regulatory behaviors during both social and cognitive development. This form of play, which we refer to as high-stakes play, has a specifically defined outcome as prescribed by a set of instructions that must be followed in order to obtain a correct result. Central to this form of play are repetitive actions with no latitude for variation in the activity or freedom for the child's imaginative expression. High-stakes play is analogous to high-stakes test items designed to elicit specific responses from students. In other words, there is little creativity required of the student in designing her response. Many products come with a whole host of explicit and implicit scenarios for their use. Therefore, the development of scenarios required for play activities are no longer the child's responsibility, but that of the product's manufacturer (i.e., an adult). The creativity exhibited by the child to transform the tree branch into a magic wand, light saber, or conductor's baton is lost and what we see as the spark that ignites inquiry is ultimately extinguished. The ability to transform the stick into its new form parallels the important inquiry skills of devising a procedure to conduct an experiment. In each case, the participant is required to think ahead to continue the activity, which may have multiple possibilities depending on the variables encountered. It is a form of work, and each activity requires the participant to create a script which has the possibility of solving a problem. In some cases, the cognitive complexity involved in play related behaviors may exceed that in devising protocols for a science related investigation. Clearly, many human activities come complete with a variety of props. In fact, the creation of such materials is considered by many to be a unique human quality (Kinget, 1975). Our concern is that when the props come fully scripted, no room exists for seeing things any other way than for their original purpose.

LEGO and LEGO-Like Bricks Can Boost Cognitive Ability ... or Can They?

Thus far, we have discussed in great detail the affordances of VCPOs, a generally theoretical overview of how different VCPOs pose different types of challenges for the user or, in contrast, how they might make it easier for the child to use in the play environment. Many readers at this point might be wanting to ask the question of all questions: Are some constructive play objects better than others for stimulating children's thinking and cognitive development?

This question can also be asked another way: When comparing constructive play objects, do some VCPOs stifle or prevent cognitive growth? And if so, what are they? A follow-up question to this one is: Should our children still be playing with VCPOs that stifle cognitive growth if doing so is detrimental to their cognitive development?

Since the 1990s, numerous media outlets have emphasized the role that LEGO and LEGO-like bricks afford the child in terms of intellectual development. To a large extent, these sources are accurate in terms of how LEGO bricks and other related plastic snap pieces can aid in cognitive development, especially in STEAM related disciplines. For our purposes, an important goal is to pay attention to how the diversity of affordance levels of VCPOs affects conceptual knowledge as presented through empirical and reflective abstractions. Fundamental to understanding abstractions is our understanding of VCPOs, their levels of affordance, and their impact on the constructive play environment.

As I have mentioned in earlier chapters, research that examines the affordances of spatially related play objects—VCPOs—from a cognitive psychological perspective in terms of young children's cognitive growth and development is lacking. Most recently, Andrus, Bar-El, Msall, Uttal, and Worsley (2020) considered the extent to which Minecraft served as a supportive environment for studying spatial reasoning. They concluded that while Minecraft appears to be a spatially relevant platform for practicing spatial reasoning, the excitement combined with the gaudiness of this software may inhibit spatial skills.

In Chapter 1, we discussed how Wolfgang Ketterle, the Nobel Prize winner in Physics, alluded to the idea that themed play bricks do not capture the essence of creativity and ingenuity in STEAM. I would add, based on our examination of VCPO affordances above, that step-by-step instructions and guides do more harm than good when it comes to promoting and fostering creativity, spatial thinking, and cognitive development because the inclusion of instructions impedes critical and independent thinking skills and, perhaps most important, the player's imaginative ingenuities. In his article in the *BBC News Magazine* entitled "Has the imagination disappeared from LEGO?" Parkinson (2014) expounds on examples that support what we have discussed in terms of VCPO affordance in the present chapter. Parkinson comments that today LEGO produces approximately 3,000 different pieces for a plethora of themes such as Architecture, Batman™, Boost, BrickHeadz, City, Creator, DC Universe™, Disney™, Dots, Duplo®, Friends, Frozen 2, Harry Potter™, Hidden Side™, Ideas, Jurassic World™, LEGO® Art, LEGO® Brick Sketches™, LEGO® Education, LEGO® Originals, LEGO® Super Mario™, Marvel, Mindstorms®, Minecraft™, Minifigures, Minions, Monkie Kid, Ninjago®, Overwatch®, Powered UP, Serious Play®, Speed Champions, Spider-Man, Star Wars™, Stranger Things, Technic™, Trolls World Tour, Toy Story 4, Xtra, and numerous others. In other words, basic, standard 2" x 4" rectangular bricks, produced en masse, which we have indicated have lower levels of affordance than do themed bricks and thus show greater evidence of creativity, is no longer the norm. Sir Harry Kroto, the 1996 Nobel Prize winning chemist who we discussed in the previous chapter, went as far as to say that present-day LEGO and LEGO cloned toys, with their excess of themes and minifigures, are of little to no use in terms of their educational value, especially when it comes to STEAM subjects. Kroto argued that Meccano sets provide more value intellectually and educationally because they allow the player to simulate real-life scientific phenomena and engineering constructions.

Trawick-Smith and Savalli (2013) provide research to support the contention that themed toys, especially replica play toys, do more to inhibit young children's cognitive development than they do to promote it. Replica play toys is the term used to describe preschool toys that are manufactured as one piece. These toy types include miniature people, animals, vehicles, and the like. Trawick-Smith and Savalli indicate that replica play toys have not been considered in research that investigates their role in block building or children's intellectual development even though they have been recommended to preschools and Kindergartens for many years. They concluded that while replica play toys might be helpful in pretend play, they are distractions to children engaging in constructive play with blocks. Moreover, the levels of complexity of block structures and cooperative play with peers increased without the use of replica play toys. Parallel with replica play toys are themed brick minifigures. Trawick-Smith and Savalli's research, then, would support the conclusion that themed brick sets do more to discourage children from building more creative, complex structures than they do to encourage them.

It is also possible that the lack of interest on the part of toy companies in manufacturing generic bricks or blocks, which contributes to most of the present-day themed and purposeful VCPOs having starter instructions that inhibit creativity and cognitive development, might have to do with trends in constructive toy purchasing that tend to lean on the side of safety. While this factor might not be a factor that applies to all VCPOs, this problem is especially true of chemistry sets that allow children to engage in hands-on science exploration. As Sullivan

(2014) stated: "Most of today's successors [of science learning sets] manufacture safer—if perhaps less exciting—kits with booklets that discourage free-form experimentation while using nontoxic substances." The main point to be made here is not the lack of safety using toxic substances, but the need for manufacturers to include booklets and guides to experiment or to engage in creative STEAM activities.

The LEGO Company's practice of providing instructions and selling themed sets that have a specific purpose when constructed is not a new occurrence. In fact, LEGO has been selling themed kits that are accompanied by instruction booklets since 1964. In his technology blog, Swan (2014) indicates that accompanying instructions can have deleterious effects on players and constructors of LEGO sets that are manufactured to produce only one thing—such as a dragon or a construction that is licensed from a movie, like Star Wars or Harry Potter. But Swan offers a unique, novel conception of toy construction bricks, which has never previously been discussed or proposed at all in the research literature on play, spatial thinking, geometric thinking, architectural and engineering thinking, scientific and mathematical thinking, and STEAM thinking overall. And that conception of toy construction bricks has to do with the child's or player's action of taking apart brick models after they have been assembled—a cognitive, higher-order process that involves analytical processes. Swan further argues that themed brick sets that include instructions that have the player construct only one thing does not allow for disassembling. With themed sets, he argues, one cannot break them because doing so does not allow the player to rebuild the disassembled bricks into something else. He goes on to state that themed sets specifically manufactured to lead the player to produce single construction outcomes encourage preservation, which, in turn, make them less useful. In this regard, Swan, unlike the overwhelming majority of LEGO and LEGO clone players, favors destruction of brick constructions and refers to brick destruction as a positive thing. He calls the practice of brick disassembly creative destruction. Swan states:

> LEGO for me was always about creativity, remaking and improving on existing designs. Those things don't happen with sets that are designed to build a model of a single thing. But that's not the only problem—LEGO taught me the art of creative destruction—the need to break something in order to make something better. Single outcome sets encourage preservation rather than destruction, and sadly that makes them less useful, less educational (and in my opinion less fun). Good old generic LEGO (and the more sophisticated Technic sets), with endless possibilities on offer, haven't gone away, they've just been drowned in a sea of marketing for other brands.
>
> *(Swan, 2014)*

It is helpful to consider Swan's assertion that single outcome (i.e., themed) sets "encourage preservation," and not what he calls "creative destruction." In other words, builders of themed kits often seem to reach the prescriptive, step-by-step outcome for the sole purpose of the outcome—the final product in and of itself—and not for the enjoyment and satisfaction of constructing unique brick structures for the purpose of creativity and originality.

Notwithstanding the role of bricks in the analysis of VCPO affordance discussed above, I would go further than Swan to argue that the inclusion of instruction booklets, which offer not how something works but simply how to put something together, marked the decline of the toy brick industry in general. In addition to the points that Swan has articulated regarding the general rule of thumb of refraining from disassembly of themed brick sets, I contend that themed and instruction booklet laden brick sets impede progress—especially for young builders—in that they inhibit the child's imagination, which, therefore, fails to provide the necessary cognitive complexities that allow for further development in STEAM, social sciences, and language learning.

The problem of theming brick toys was further complicated and made worse when, in the early years of the first decade of the 21st century, LEGO distanced itself from its core audience of toy brick builders by appealing to children more interested in computer games and action figures than in construction and design. Accordingly, the company conceived of and subsequently planned themes based on its own characters, which included the action adventurer Jack Stone, introduced in 2001, and Galidor, which was based on a short-lived Canadian and American television series and showcased Nick Bluetooth, a teenager turned galactic warrior whose name was inspired by the 10th-century Danish king, Harald Gormsson. Galidor was released by LEGO in 2002. Neither Jack Stone nor Galidor involved much construction on the part of the child. The Super Glider in the Jack Stone series is constructed using only seven pieces. The Galidor TDN Module consists of merely nine parts. As a new line of sci-fi action figures, Galidor was the first LEGO toy that brought the company to a new toy category. This development made LEGO break from what it was always known for—the classical construction experience (Robertson, 2014). While Galidor was one of LEGO's most innovative themes, it failed to provide young children with the experiences that they so greatly need for expanding their imaginative powers and creativity.

Robertson (2014) maintained that the Jack Stone and Galidor series were introduced by LEGO as a result of research that appeared to suggest that most children do not like construction based activities. As a result, LEGO produced these brick construction sets that did not have any construction at all. This venture turned out to be a financial failure. LEGO staff eventually realized that parents whose children are averse to construction will not purchase LEGO or LEGO clone products. At the same time, those who do will be discontent with a toy brick manufacturer that produces themes that lack any sense of construction activity. Robertson further elaborated that LEGO discontinued Jack Stone and Galidor after only one year mainly because of its expense—injection molding and subsequent production costs for each new brick created was upward of $50,000.

Consequently, LEGO suffered large financial losses. And because these themes required more components than the typical LEGO brick and the few pieces that make up these figures were not compatible with other sets, the company concluded that the themes were too expensive to continue. Moreover, the Jack Stone and Galidor themes no longer appear as LEGO brick products. From this point onwards, LEGO continued to produce its usual themes, such as Star Wars, Harry Potter, and Marvel Comics, as a "happy medium." But its continuation of the company's many themes has not taken away from the fact that these themes have high affordance levels (as indicated earlier in this chapter), and therefore, fail to contribute to younger and older children's STEAM development.

Robertson (2014) goes further and states that LEGO will always provide instruction-laden booklets with their sets and will not be returning to the instruction-less times that existed prior to the 1960s. For children and players who wish to have some mode of preservation, some LEGO sets, such as LEGO Fusion, make it possible for builders to upload photographs of their completed set through a LEGO app. The implementation of this device allows children and other players to dismantle their finished products (even though most themed sets do not enable children to rebuild them in other ways than the intended theme). On this app, children can preserve their built products digitally, thus allowing the digital version of the brick figures to be combined with LEGO produced backgrounds so that builder's are able to make specific scenes that include their brick structures, such as resort towns, castles, and the like. This app, then, connects the child's constructive endeavors with the formation of online designs.

The idea that LEGO and LEGO clone companies will continue to produce sets that will always have instruction booklets demonstrates all the more clearly that themed brick sets have extremely high levels of affordance. In other words, as we have emphasized above, high affordance undermines the child's efforts to grow creatively and develop intellectually in STEAM related subjects in particular. Therefore, parents' and educational practitioner's ideal purchases of VCPOs for children are those that are uniform and come in generic pieces that do not have excesses of added features that enable affordance and thus detract from creativity and imagination.

In 2012, Norton, Mochon, and Ariely published an article entitled, "The IKEA effect: When labor leads to love" in the *Journal of Consumer Psychology*. In essence, the IKEA effect refers to "the increase in valuation of self-made products" (2012, p. 453). In coining the term "IKEA effect," they continue to

> suggest that labor alone can be sufficient to induce greater liking for the fruits of one's labor: even constructing a standardized bureau, an arduous, solitary task, can lead people to overvalue their (often poorly constructed) creations. We call this phenomenon the 'IKEA effect,' in honor of the Swedish manufacturer whose products typically arrive with some assembly required.
>
> *(Norton et al., 2012, p. 453)*

Their study stems from earlier research that suggests that the greater amount of time people put in to the effort of completing a project, the more they come to value that pursuit (Festinger, 1957). The IKEA effect occurs in other venues that require individuals to perform some duty or work in order to reap the benefits of outcomes. Examples include people who travel tens of hundreds of miles to pay a fee to go apple picking and find satisfaction in the work that it takes to pick the apples when they can easily get them at a local supermarket, or "Make-Your-Own ..." companies that require individuals to purchase the ingredients, equipment, or materials that are often more expensive than purchasing the actual merchandise retail. Furthermore, while the IKEA effect emphasizes the high level of satisfaction and valuation on the part of the assembler from putting pieces together, the end product is often shoddily constructed, and still considered of higher value by the assembler than if she were to buy the product as a single whole piece—according to the individual who followed directions for its assembly.

I bring up the IKEA effect because the problem with the overwhelming majority of do-it-yourself products is that the pieces come with assembly instructions, thus requiring little or no imagination or creativity on the part of the builder. In parallel with those who are influenced by the IKEA effect, I refer to individuals who purchase LEGO or LEGO cloned sets, all of which come with assembly instructions, as assemblers and not builders or constructors for the very reason that while finishing assembly of LEGO products increases one's valuation and sense of satisfaction when the brick theme is fully assembled, it does not account for what goes into the unique design of a finished product that was completed by someone using uniform bricks, blocks, or planks. Professional architects and engineers do not follow sets of instructions when they create blueprints of buildings, bridges, roads, tunnels, airports, towers, dams, and the like. So too should it be the case that parents consider providing their children with standard, uniform bricks, blocks, or planks that do not require the following of directions when engaged in constructive free play. The perennial problem with science and mathematics education is the ongoing fact that teachers either have to come close to teaching to the test in this test-heavy society or resort to giving their students worksheets that ask students to merely solve problems by following a specific procedure or algorithm or engaging in mind-numbing, rote skill and drill activities (Mayer, 2002). In the same manner, young children will benefit from being provided early on with basic VCPOs that allow for more creative outcomes and lead to higher levels of cognitive development.

The IKEA effect also raises the issue of levels of complexity of VCPO constructions. For example, professional furniture designers have their own unique engineering processes for making their products. These processes are not in the form of instructions but are based on STEAM related principles that undergird the successful production of a piece of furniture. So, the level of complexity in terms of the construction design of a product built by a furniture designer—and we can extend this to the unique work of other STEAM professionals—is much higher than that of a lay-person who is assembling a do-it-yourself furniture piece that requires instructions for completion.

Given the IKEA effect as it relates to complexity levels, research has shown that levels of complexity of young children's VCPO constructions and emergent mathematical skills, which are essential in one's success in STEAM professions, are related. Zhang, Chen, Yang, and Xu (2020) explored the cognitive underpinnings of young children's block-building ability and found that shape naming, shape recognition, and shape composition were determining factors contributing to higher levels of complexity in block structures. Similar to the results of Ginsburg and colleagues. (Ginsburg, Inoue & Seo, 1999; Ginsburg, Pappas & Seo, 2001; Ginsburg, Lin, Ness & Seo 2003), Trawick-Smith et al. (2017) examined preschool children's block play in naturalistic free play settings to determine the extent to which complexity of block structures is associated with mathematical cognition. They found that the level of social participation and the percentage of block structures built without replica play toys increased young children's levels of complexity during block play as well as their complexity in mathematical thinking. In studying developmental changes in spatial processing through block play, Ginsburg et al. (2003) corroborate Stiles and Stern's (2001) conclusion by finding correlation between age and the level of complexity of children's block constructions. Stiles and Stern also found that spatial strategy, a key skill in STEAM knowledge, changed with both the age and levels of complexity of children's constructions. Richardson, Hunt, and Richardson's (2014) work also substantiates Stiles and Stern by finding that controlling construction task complexity in order to examine relationships between children's block construction performance and their spatial-mathematical abilities demonstrated that greater complexity of block play resulted in higher levels of spatial and mathematical ability.

Conclusion

In this chapter, we have studied the roles of VCPOs by contemplating them in terms of their differences, and how these differences may affect levels of creativity, complexity, and cognitive ability connected with STEAM fields. And we did this by identifying the VCPO type and its position on the affordance continuum. It was concluded that VCPOs with the fewest theme-related pieces or intricate configurations of pieces tended to have lower levels of affordance, and, thus, a greater possibility of increasing STEAM cognition. Conversely, VCPOs with higher numbers of theme-related pieces, intricate configurations of pieces, or accompanying instruction or "how-to" booklets tended to produce higher levels of affordance, which may suggest deficits in STEAM knowledge and possibly more distractions in the construction process and lower, if any, evidence of creativity. We also questioned whether the LEGO bricks toy or its brick clone toy cousins are the right toys for children to play with in terms of fostering their cognitive development. Evidence was gathered in the first section of this chapter with support from current developmental, cognitive, and play research, which suggests that themed blocks or bricks with non-uniform pieces may fail to help children develop their recognition, understanding, and even appreciation of STEAM concepts, and that VCPOs with uniform pieces—that is, pieces that are all the same size, weight, and shape—may increase children's motivation and understanding in STEAM concepts.

In the next two chapters, we will delve into examples and stories that provide evidence of successful implementation of VCPOs for the purpose of increasing young children's exposure to STEAM. Chapter 5 focuses on mathematics, science, and technology, and Chapter 6 focuses on engineering and architecture.

References

Amabile, T. M., Hennessey, B. A., & Grossman, B. S. (1986). Social influences on creativity: The effects of contracted-for reward. *Journal of Personality and Social Psychology*, 50(1), 14.

Amabile, T. M., & Pillemer, J. (2012). Perspectives on the social psychology of creativity. *The Journal of Creative Behavior*, 46(1), 3–15.

Amabile, T. M., & Pratt, M. G. (2016). The dynamic componential model of creativity and innovation in organizations: Making progress, making meaning. *Research in Organizational Behavior*, 36, 157–183.

Andrus, B., Bar-El, D., Msall, C., Uttal, D., & Worsley, M. (2020, August). Minecraft as a generative platform for analyzing and practicing spatial reasoning. In J. Škilters, N. S. Newcombe, & D. Uttal (Eds.), *Spatial Cognition XII: German Conference on Spatial Cognition* (pp. 297–302). Berlin: Springer.

Deci, E. L., & Ryan, R. M. (1980). The empirical exploration of intrinsic motivational processes. In L. Berkowitz (Ed.), *Advances in experimental social psychology* (Vol. 13, pp. 39–80). New York: Academic Press.

Elias, C. L., & Berk, L. E. (2002). Self-regulation in young children: Is there a role for sociodramatic play? *Early Childhood Research Quarterly*, 17(2), 216–238.

Elkind, D. (2007). *The power of play: How spontaneous, imaginative activities lead to happier, healthier children.* Cambridge, MA: Da Capo Lifelong Books.

Farenga, S., Ness, D., Johnson, D. D., & Johnson, B. (2010). *The importance of average: Playing the game of school to increase success and achievement.* Lanham, MD: Rowman & Littlefield Publishers.

Festinger, L. (1957). *A theory of cognitive dissonance.* Stanford, CA: Stanford University Press.

Gibson, J. J. (1979). *The ecological approach to visual perception.* Boston: Houghton Mifflin.

Gibson, J. J., & Crook, L. E. (1938). A theoretical field-analysis of automobile-driving. *American Journal of Psychology*, 51, 453–471.

Ginsburg, H. P., Inoue, N., & Seo, K. H. (1999). Young children doing mathematics: Observations of everyday activities." In J. V. Copley (Ed.), *Mathematics in the early years* (pp. 88–99). Reston, VA: National Council of Teachers of Mathematics.

Ginsburg, H. P., Lin, C. L., Ness, D., & Seo, K. H. (2003). Young American and Chinese children's everyday mathematical activity. *Mathematical Thinking and Learning*, 5(4), 235–258.

Ginsburg, H. P., Pappas, S., & Seo, K. H. (2001). Everyday mathematical knowledge: Asking young children what is developmentally appropriate. In S. L. Golbeck (Ed.),

Psychological perspectives on early childhood education: Reframing dilemmas in research and practice (pp. 181–219). Mahwah, NJ: Lawrence Erlbaum Associates.

Greeno, J. M. (1994). Gibson's affordances. *Psychological Review*, 101(2), 336–342.

Hirsh-Pasek, K., Golinkoff, R. M., Berk, L. E., & Singer, D. (2009). *A mandate for playful learning in preschool: Presenting the evidence*. Oxford: Oxford University Press.

Jones, K. S. (2003). What is an affordance? *Ecological Psychology*, 15(2), 107–114.

Kinget, G. M. *On being human*. New York: Harcourt Brace Jovanovich, 1975.

Koffka, K. (1935). *Principles of Gestalt psychology*. London: Lund Humphries.

Krafft, K. C., & Berk, L. E. (1998). Private speech in two preschools: Significance of open-ended activities and make-believe play for verbal self-regulation. *Early Childhood Research Quarterly*, 13(4), 637–658.

Krampen, M. (1989). Semiotics in architecture and industrial/product design. *Design Issues*, 5(2), 124–140.

Lewin, K. (1935). *A dynamic theory of personality*. New York: McGraw-Hill.

Mayer, R. E. (2002). Rote versus meaningful learning. *Theory into Practice*, 41(4), 226–232.

McLoyd, V. (1983). The effects of the structure of play objects on the pretend play of low-income preschool children. *Child Development*, 54, 626–635. doi:10.2307/1130049.

Ness, D., & Farenga, S. J. (2016). Blocks, bricks, and planks: Relationships between affordance and visuo-spatial constructive play objects. *American Journal of Play*, 8(2), 201–227.

Ness, D., Farenga, S. J., & Garofalo, S. G. (2017). *Spatial intelligence: Why it matters from birth through the lifespan*. New York: Routledge.

Norton, M. I., Mochon, D., & Ariely, D. (2012). The IKEA effect: When labor leads to love. *Journal of Consumer Psychology*, 22(3), 453–460.

Osiurak, F., Rossetti, Y., & Badets, A. (2017). What is an affordance? 40 years later. *Neuroscience & Biobehavioral Reviews*, 77, 403–417.

Parkinson, J. (2014, November 26). Has the imagination disappeared from Lego? *BBC News Magazine*. Retrieved from: https://www.bbc.com/news/uk-politics-29992974.

Piaget, J. (1977). *Recherches sur l'abstraction réfléchissante. I. L'abstraction des relations logico-arithmétiques* [Research on the reflective abstraction 1: The abstraction of logical-mathematical relationships]. Paris: Presses Universitaires de France.

Reed, E. S. (1993). The intention to use a specific affordance: A conceptual framework for psychology. In R. H. Wozniak & K. W. Fischer (Eds.), *Development in context: Acting and thinking in specific environments* (pp. 45–76). Hillsdale, NJ: Lawrence Erlbaum Associates.

Richardson, M., Hunt, T. E., & Richardson, C. (2014). Children's construction task performance and spatial ability: Controlling task complexity and predicting mathematics performance. *Perceptual and Motor Skills*, 119(3), 741–757.

Robertson, D. (2014). *Brick by brick: How LEGO rewrote the rules of innovation and conquered the global toy industry*. New York: Crown Business.

Stiles, J., & Stern, C. (2001). Developmental change in spatial cognitive processing: Complexity effects and block construction performance in preschool children. *Journal of Cognition and Development*, 2(2), 157–187. doi:10.1207/S15327647JCD0202_3.

Sullivan, J. (2014, October 29). The five retro science kits that inspired a generation of tinkerers. *Discover Magazine*. Retrieved from: https://www.discovermagazine.com/technology/the-5-retro-science-kits-that-inspired-a-generation-of-tinkerers.

Swan, C. (2014, November 26). *The perils of modern Lego*. Chris Swan's Weblog. Retrieved from: https://blog.thestateofme.com/2013/01/01/the-perils-of-modern-lego.

Trawick-Smith, J., & Savalli, C. (2013). *A descriptive study of block play: Effects of replica play toys*. Paper presented at the Annual Play Research Roundtables of the Play Policy and Practice Interest Forum, National Association for the Education of Young Children, Washington, DC.

Trawick-Smith, J., Swaminathan, S., Baton, B., Danieluk, C., Marsh, S., & Szarwacki, M. (2017). Block play and mathematics learning in preschool: The effects of building complexity, peer and teacher interactions in the block area, and replica play materials. *Journal of Early Childhood Research*, 15(4), 433–448.

Vygotsky, L. (1966 [1933]). Play and its role in the psychological development of the child. Lecture, Leningrad Pedagogical Institute. *Problems of Psychology*, 6, 62–76.

Wagman, J. B. (2019). A guided tour of Gibson's theory of affordances. In J. B. Wagman & J. J. C. Blau (Eds.), *Perception as information detection: Reflections on Gibson's ecological approach to visual perception* (pp. 130–148). New York: Routledge.

Withagen, R., De Poel, H. J., Araújo, D., & Pepping, G. J. (2012). Affordances can invite behavior: Reconsidering the relationship between affordances and agency. *New Ideas in Psychology*, 30(2), 250–258.

Zhang, X., Chen, C., Yang, T., & Xu, X. (2020). Spatial skills associated with block building complexity in preschoolers. *Frontiers in Psychology*, 11, 2265. doi:10.3389/fpsyg.2020.563493.

5
YOUNG CHILDREN THINK LIKE SCIENTISTS AND MATHEMATICIANS

Science and mathematics education has been overwhelmed with reform movements and standards development over the last few decades in an attempt to increase science and mathematics literacy (NAS, 2019; NGSS, 2013; NRC, 1995). In 1989, the landmark report *Science for All Americans. Project 2061: Summary Statement*, tapped into the mood of policymakers, practitioners, and the general public regarding the condition of STEM education. As stated in the report, "A cascade of recent studies has made it abundantly clear that both by national standards and international norms, U.S. education is failing to adequately educate too many students—and hence failing the nation" (AAAS, 1989). Reports and commentaries of this kind are time-honored and persistently inundate the STEAM education community. Statements comparable to that of Project 2061 were made after the launching of Sputnik in 1957, the publishing of *A Nation at Risk* in 1983 (NCEE, 1983), after comparing test results from the Trends in International Mathematics and Science Study (TIMSS) and the Programme for International Student Assessment (PISA) study (Komatsu & Rappleye, 2021), and recently by the National Assessment of Educational Progress (Wilburn & Elias, 2020). Statements and reports making dire predictions about the state of American STEAM results on high-stakes tests will no doubt be a part of American STEAM education news for years to come. While there are perpetual obstacles that are thwarting the success of American students in STEAM, the bleak crises in educational outcomes have more to do with the lack of STEAM exposure to our youngest students that results in lower test scores later on and less to do with student STEAM test scores in upper elementary and secondary school (Johnson, Johnson, Ness & Farenga 2005; Johnson, Johnson, Farenga & Ness, 2008).

As a response to these national crises manufactured by cross-national comparisons, attempts have been made to reconstruct mathematics and science curricula,

DOI: 10.4324/9781003097815-6

retool teachers to update their current skills, increase graduation requirements, create new standards, and continue to test students, regardless of their socio-economic status (Johnson et al., 2005; Johnson et al., 2008). Past and present education reform movements whose mission it has been to increase mathematics and science achievement have aggravated, and not helped, the current state of STEAM knowledge in our schools. The widely held view among many educational administrators and policymakers that high achievement in science, mathematics, and technology translates to fact memorization and the successful performance of cookbook, "follow-the-directions" lab experiments is far removed from reality. Given that the problem of learning and teaching science and mathematics is qualitative (not quantitative), successful STEAM reasoning requires the individual to conduct inquiry-based activities and develop qualitatively grounded knowledge. Therefore, engaging in higher levels of scientific and mathematical inquiry involves the application of qualitatively related process skills, such as problem solving, problem posing, planning strategies, conducting investigations, and evaluating outcomes.

Past and current research in STEAM cognition suggests that scientists and mathematicians spend a vast amount of time solving problems using qualitative reasoning (Chi, Feltovich & Glaser, 1981; Chi & Glaser, 1981; Bransford, Brown & Cocking, 2000; Hattie & Donoghue, 2016). Observations of young children show parallels between the way they think and the thinking of STEAM experts and professionals (Forman, 2010; Ness & Farenga, 2007). An examination of what is essential in an expert's conceptual understanding toolkit and how they problem solve and problem pose is elaborated in Bransford, Brown, and Cocking's book *How People Learn* (2000), its newer edition How People Learn II (NAS, 2018), and demonstrated in a video documentary *Minds of Our Own* by the Annenberg Foundation (2008). These media show that experts place a great deal of emphasis on qualitative thinking skills to propose explanations and solve problems. The qualitative aspects in learning science and mathematics are what many early childhood researchers refer to when comparing the neo-Piagetian concept of the young child as scientist or mathematician and the Vygotskyan notion that the young child is an apprentice who uses language and cultural constructs to mediate cognitive development through adult-peer interactions (Driver, 1983; Ness & Farenga, 2007; Vygotsky, 1962). And yet, it is the qualitative element of teaching and learning science and mathematics that is often ignored during and after the early years and replaced by a greater emphasis on quantitative skills. The singular emphasis in too much science and mathematics learning in early childhood environments has swung from the qualitative nature of learning to the easier-to-assess rote, quantitative component of a subject. Furthermore, the quantitative focus is driven by high-stakes tests. Unfortunately, at present, young children in countless early childhood programs throughout the country are experiencing the one-time appealing qualitative elements of creativity and divergent thinking activities being devalued and replaced by the teaching of rote, mechanical algorithms, bereft of conceptual thinking and invented strategies, that search solely for singularly correct solutions (Johnson, Sevimli-Celik & Al-Mansour, 2013; Johnson et al., 2008). Therefore, it is imperative that early childhood schools and centers bring back curricula that promote qualitative thinking in STEAM. One element of this requires teachers to recognize, appreciate, and take anecdotal records of young children's propensities in scientific and mathematical thinking that is often embedded in fantasy that frequently occurs during free play.

Fantasy Leads to Young Children's Propensities in Science and Mathematics

As evidenced by Ginsburg and colleagues (Ginsburg, Inoue & Seo,1999; Ginsburg, Pappas & Seo, 2001; Ginsburg, Lin, Ness & Seo, 2003) and Rittle-Johnson, Zippert, and Boice (2019), young pre-school-aged children demonstrate an advanced proclivity in STEAM subjects that are far beyond their years: The young child who speaks as if she were a paleontologist providing a treatise on dinosaurs; the young child whose LEGO or block constructions cause professional architects and engineers to marvel; or the young child who displays a type of spatial ability to guide a school or family group through a zoological park like an orienteer. Each of these examples exhibits a child with intrinsic motivation and wonder.

VCPOs, mostly blocks and uniform LEGO pieces, have been successful tools in promoting motivation and wonder in children's science and math ideas. Ginsburg et al. (2003) noted that the constructive free play area, which contained blocks and bricks, allowed four- and five-year-old children to display evidence of knowledge in classification, enumeration, pattern and shape, and spatial relations—four out of six codes in a coding system designed to capture important features of emergent mathematical activity and its context. In addition, they found that this trait is evident across different cultures. Kamii, Miyakawa, and Kato (2004) discovered that a collection of spatial and mathematical thinking skills appear to develop concurrently during young children's active engagement in block play.

Young children problem solve and problem pose effortlessly. When given the opportunity, we can observe them playing with ordinary materials in creative and innovative ways. On many an occasion, adults demonstrate astonishment at the ephemeral interest a young child often shows when she receives what we think is a special birthday present. The present is often placed aside as the child becomes more engaged in the packaging in which the gift came. Without any special directions, many young children can take the discarded material and weave it into a medical bag to be a doctor, a garage for accommodating toys cars, or a doll's house for replicating daily household activities. As a result of sociodramatic and constructive play, the packaging material serves as the concrete prop that fosters the development of the abstract thinking that is sorely needed in our preschools. With its numerous roles, the packaging material provides the young child with a bridge between reality and fantasy allowing her to create and explore numerous STEAM concepts. Although perplexing to the adult, the child has a purpose and reason for her invented activity.

These observations support Piaget and Inhelder's (1956) contention that young children's development of STEAM thinking is qualitatively and quantitatively different from that of adults (see Carey, 1985). This is evidenced when we ask the child "Why did you make such a thing?" The child responds by giving the usual incredulous stare back, along with the common answer, "Why can't I do it?"

Thus far, educational administrators and policymakers have failed to revert back to the point in time when preschool and early elementary school children could engage in exploration, inquiry, and wonder. Instead, children today are inundated with tasks geared to high-stakes assessments through direct instruction (Bassok, Latham & Rorem, 2016; Zosh et al., 2017). Therefore, I propose that parents, caregivers, and early childhood and elementary practitioners reinvent their homes, preschool settings, and elementary school classrooms in order to foster the creative STEAM propensities of young children by simply recognizing and implementing fantasy. In sum, fantasy, as it contributes to creativity, is defined as the ability to take the lifeless and give it life, provide purpose for the purposeless, and provide opportunity where things seem unattainable. Fantasy affords the opportunity for the child to take on more responsibility for the activity and to move beyond her level of competence (Bodrova & Leong, 1996).

I am not suggesting that fantasy is a substitute for knowledge, rather, that active fantasy can enrich knowledge. As Egan (2012) puts it: "given the significance of fantasy in children's lives, we must develop educational theories and practices that not only encourage fantasy but are based directly on its principles and devoted to its exploration" (p. xi). Clearly, fantasy occurs in a social and cultural context that helps shape the development of cognitive skills (Berk & Winsler, 1995). Vygotsky (1962) proposed that children function at their highest intellectual level when engaged in sociodramatic and constructive free play. In doing so, he discussed the role of play in a child's development and the link between egocentric speech's emergence toward private speech and self-regulation. What adults may perceive to be so-called nonsense utterances by a child are, in fact, psychological mechanisms that the child uses to guide her behavior through fantasy (González Rey, 2016). Moreover, sociodramatic play serves as a context for developing self-regulation, which is considered a higher order executive function of metacognition, the concept of self-awareness of one's own thinking and actions (Elias & Berk, 2002; Krafft & Berk, 1998).

Self-Regulatory Behaviors, Creativity, and Play

Research suggests that the over-structuring of the child's environment may actually limit creativity and academic development (Rowe, 1973; Krafft & Berk, 1998; Elias & Berk, 2002). Over-structuring is a common problem with much science and mathematics learning. In this regard, exercises and activities are often planned to eliminate divergent options and instead to focus on directing children toward predetermined results. Also, these exercises require the child to yield answers that are structured to fit course assessments. Accordingly, the wonder of science is lost along with cognitive intrigue (Ness & Farenga, 2016), which is the wonder that stimulates and intrinsically motivates an individual to voluntarily engage in an activity. The loss of cognitive intrigue may also be instigated by the sole use of certain constructive play objects—exemplified by toys or games that are an end in and of themselves and require little of the individual other than to master the planned objective—with predetermined conclusions which are reinforced by rote learning. Therefore, the creativity that young children possess needs to be fostered throughout their development.

Conceptual Learning and Inquiry Related Skills: The Early Life of Richard Feynman

The process skills that allow young children to conduct inquiry—such as observing, questioning, manipulating materials, creating, and exploring—are the same skills required when they are puzzled and intrigued by scientific and mathematical ideas. The world of play and that of science and mathematics converge as young children begin to explore their surroundings. Research suggests a strong link between play and the development of emergent science and mathematics concepts (Ferrara, Hirsh-Pasek, Newcombe, Golinkoff & Lam, 2011; Ness & Farenga, 2007). Roeper argues that "through playful interaction children develop many concepts of science ..." (1988, p. 123). She makes this symbiotic relationship more explicit by positing that:

> Play and exploration remain the best learning tools for the young child. Children develop a sense of inner freedom and permission to reach out if they (and their goals and idiosyncratic ways of learning) are supported by the adults at the school. This security and freedom requires a flexible atmosphere with much opportunity for discovery, individualized and group learning, play, and stimulating enthusiastic adults who are learners themselves.
>
> *(1988, p. 133)*

The world of physical science is extremely important to young children in that it can provide a context for play, exploration, and wonder—activities that can be learned through child-initiated VCPO constructions (Ness & Farenga, 2007). Emergent science and mathematics concepts related to mass, matter, interaction of forces, symmetry, area, volume, and shape can be experienced through free play, which can, in turn, increase young children's experiences in pattern recognition. During the early childhood years, pattern recognition in the natural world can be thought of as an emergent behavior essential for the development of more complex process skills. In support, we consider the comments of the 1965 Nobel

Prize winner in physics, Richard P. Feynman, Professor of Physics at the California Institute of Technology (1950–1988), who reflected on his emergent science inquiries.

Feynman's moving article, "What is Science?" described how he was introduced to the field of science as a young boy by his father—a businessman (Feynman, 1969). He elaborated on how all of his early science related experiences were embedded in games and play. Through games, Feynman's father taught his son to search for patterns and relationships. He later realized and described his father's method as "insidious cleverness: first delight him in play and then slowly inject material of educational value!" (Feynman, 2000, p. 174). A second lesson from Feynman's recollection is his belief that knowing the name of an object is of little importance to the concept development and understanding of a phenomenon. Feynman recounts an occasion when a friend asked him to name a bird that could be seen in the distance. After responding that he did not know the name of the bird, his friend replied, "Your father doesn't teach you much about science" (Feynman, 2000, p. 177). Feynman's story continues with what can be argued to be one of the most critical lessons for learning science and mathematics. In explaining the essence of the bird—a brown-throated thrush, Feynman insists, "In German it's called a *halzenflugel,* and in Chinese they call it a *Zōng hóu é kǒuchuāng* (棕喉鵝口瘡) and even if you know all those names for it, you still know little about the bird" (2000, p. 177, emphasis added). In other words, the ability to name something tells us little, if anything at all, about the thing's or organism's essence.

Unfortunately, the name and definition recall of phenomena occupy a large part of the STEAM curriculum in early childhood and in later years. The memorizing of superficial information is what too many people still consider the overarching purpose of doing science and mathematics. What is more, many practitioners use high-stakes testing instruments, even at the preschool level, to measure this superficial kind of knowledge. Instead, the big ideas that are relevant to science and math and can lead to broad concept attainment are often ignored. Rather than learning the names of objects, children should observe "what goes on" (Feynman, 2000, p. 177) and develop an understanding through exploration.

Feynman's point about injecting play and exploration into learning is further elaborated by both Rowe (1973) and the National Aeronautic and Space Administration (NASA) (2008). Both Rowe and the authors from NASA use the study of kites to provide real-world experiences to demonstrate scientific and mathematical concepts. Through the activity of kite building, design, and testing, children have the opportunity to gain an understanding of concepts and process skills integrated with such STEAM subjects as physics, engineering, history, meteorology, mathematics, and the arts. The science and mathematics principles shown in Table 5.1 provide the opportunity for children, with peer and adult scaffolding, to develop conceptual understanding through application. Salomon and Perkins (1996) aptly describe the demonstration of the attainment of

TABLE 5.1 Concepts and process skills learned through kite building[1]

Science Fundamentals Three States of Matter Newton's Laws of Motion Newton's First Law Newton's Second Law – F=ma Newton's Third Law – Action & Reaction Torques (Moments) **Math Fundamentals** Functions Area Volume Scalars and Vectors Comparing Two Scalars – Ratio Comparing Two Vectors Vector Addition Vector Components Trigonometry Sine-Cosine-Tangent Ratios in Triangles Pythagorean Theorem **Kites** KiteModeler Interactive Simulator Kites Kite Construction Kite Geometry Control Line Bridle Point Geometry Kites – Newton's First Law Forces on a Kite Torques on a Kite Balance and Stability Launch and Flight Control Line Equations Determine Flight Altitude Altitude Equation Derivation Flight Altitude – Graphical Kite Safety	**The Atmosphere** Interactive Atmosphere Simulator Air Properties Definitions Air Pressure Air Temperature Air Density Earth Model – Imperial Units Earth Model – Metric Units Mars Model – Imperial Units Mars Model – Metric Units **Aerodynamics** Aerodynamics of Kites Dynamic Pressure Kite Center of Pressure Kite Torque Equation Kite Lift Equations Kite Drag Equations Inclination Effects Downwash Effects Density Effects Velocity Effects **Height** Determining Kite Weight Weight Equation Center of Gravity – cg Kite Center of Gravity **Aircraft Forces** Four Forces on an Airplane Wing Geometry Aerodynamic Forces Center of Pressure – cp Aerodynamic Center Lift Equation Lift Coefficient Drag Equation Drag Coefficient **Miscellaneous** Wright Brothers Aircraft Relative Velocity – Ground Reference Relative Velocity – Aircraft Reference Boundary Layer Bernoulli's Equation

knowledge as a performance of understanding. Upon further examination, we realize that kites are both toys and tools that allow the development of advanced concepts and process skills.

Free-play activities, particularly with low-affordance VCPOs, can provide children with the opportunity to experiment on the natural world and increase the locus of internal control (Rowe, 1973) and self-efficacy (Bandura, 1994). Further, close observation of children engaged in spontaneous science and math related activities provides support for the need to link the understanding of cause-and-effect relationships to one's internal locus of control, self-efficacy, and self-regulation. Children who play in an environment that encourages self-regulation will often take on challenges and spend more time engaged in attempting to search for answers. When observing young children, identify who can take an interest in a pile of unrelated materials and develop their own investigation. For example, what can be invented from a pile of interlocking triangle pieces or a pile of straws with some masking tape?

Language, STEAM, and Meaning

Observing and listening to children's discourse when engaged in STEAM play without intervention allows the practitioner, researcher, or parent to obtain an overall awareness of attitude, ability, and cognitive propensities. Language, in combination with the child's actions during an activity, can offer insight into what a child understands. The manner in which the child expresses similarities and differences in meaning of a term or phrase or action that allows inference of the child's intentions, may provide clues to the depth of that understanding. Because ideas or concepts only have meaning when they are placed in context with other ideas or concepts (Dou, Hazari, Dabney, Sonnert & Sadler, 2019; Lemke, 1990), the importance of listening to what the child says cannot be understated. In addition, the child may allude to emergent concepts without necessarily expressing them literally; so, evidence of the existence of these emergent concepts needs to be exposed and communicated. Through the question-and-answer technique known as "tacit dialoguing" (Ness & Farenga, 2007), children have the potential to uncover this evidence by explicitly stating what they think in their own words as they are engaging in the activity. Therefore, it is critical to have some form of verbal evidence when interpreting what the child says as this form of evidence can serve as a proxy for meaning.

The use of techniques, such as observation and tacit dialoguing, are formative processes that are used to gather verbal data that can help us infer children's intentions when encountering various materials during free play. The structure of the discourse is often quite orderly, as the children are manipulating materials or drawing graphic representations in order to create evidence of understanding.

In adult-structured group activities, some children jump straight into a scientific or mathematical investigation, almost as if they are pre-programmed, talking themselves through the activity while actively participating in it, while others contemplate the possibilities at hand, and have mini-discussions with themselves prior to active participation. But after a brief period, it is difficult to detect any difference between children who jump in and those who initially engage in reflection. Sometimes, the dialogue taking place is relevant solely to one of the children (e.g., thinking aloud), and at other times, it is relevant to the whole group. The group language related experience provides an opportunity for children to establish meaning through a product, which is the concrete expression that supplies meaning to the abstract idea by the use of words, diagrams, or pictures.

Feynman's childhood experience above also resonates with the importance of language in STEAM thinking as does the philosopher Ludwig Wittgenstein's famous "beetle-in-the-box" analogy. Wittgenstein's beetle-in-the-box analogy serves as the foundation for the problems associated with language and introspection. The analogy goes something like this: You are sent to a room with a lot of people. You may not even know anyone in the room. Everyone in this room is given a box, including you. The rule for opening the box and looking inside is simple—you may look at the contents of your box, but under no circumstances are you permitted to look at the contents of anyone else's box. It turns out that when you open your box, and you are asked what you see, you say: "Beetle!" It also turns out that when your neighbor opens her box, she says: "Beetle!" In fact, everyone in the room opens his or her box and says: "Beetle!" All the observer knows is that the word that is associated with opening the box and looking inside is "Beetle." In other words, the thing in your box might be a six-legged organism, walking from one corner of the box to another. The thing in your neighbor's box might be something that represents a ping-pong ball. The thing in a third person's box might be something representing a match stick. There might be nothing at all in a fourth person's box.

The connection between Wittgenstein's "beetle-in-the-box" thought experiment and the argument made here is this: Language use is culturally bound—it is not universal. When we use language in science or mathematics, we need to be circumspect when encountering language that muddies our ability to comprehend a concept. Unfortunately, in many preschools and elementary schools, young children learning science and mathematics spend a good deal of time learning abstract symbolism instead of the concepts themselves. This often results in the commonplace situation in which children may be able to identify a specific term for a concept without being able to explain the actual meaning of the concept. For example, many preschool and elementary school children are exposed in some way to specific terms related to the plant growth and rain formation processes associated with photosynthesis. By the time they reach the upper elementary-school, middle-school, high-school, and college level, students have difficulty explaining the role of carbon dioxide (CO_2) and its relationship to the mass of the tree. The producers of the Annenberg Project (2008) have shown that when college graduates were given a small tree log they were unable to correctly explain the one thing responsible for the log's composition. This outcome was extremely prevalent among college graduates even though photosynthesis is a universal concept in science that is introduced in some way in most levels of education. The producers of the Annenberg Project have stated that

> Just about everyone will agree that trees are made from sunlight, water, and soil the trees suck up from their roots. But the surprising truth is that trees are made from air! Trees are solar-powered machines that convert air into wood. Why is it that, despite the fact that photosynthesis is one of the most widely taught subjects in science, so few people really understand the central idea underlying this system?
>
> *(Annenberg Foundation, 2008)*

Bringing Play Back to School and STEAM

The Annenberg Project's presentation of the photosynthesis concept strongly suggests that the inquiry related behaviors developed during the exploration phase of an activity taking place during the early childhood years are especially important to the successful study of science in later years. Unfortunately, the problem with the lack of exploratory experiences is that preschools and elementary schools deemphasize the importance of play in developing conceptual knowledge. Hirsh-Pasek, Golinkoff, Berk, and Singer (2009) claim that the onset of No Child Left Behind (NCLB) was a big contributing factor to the marginalization or outright elimination of play time. In their own words: "Blocks were replaced with worksheets. Both free play and playful learning declined precipitously in U.S. preschools, where they were sidelined as an expendable diversion in favor of early preparation for school test-taking" (p. 9). As a result, preschool programs replaced playful learning with worksheets and skill and drill practice as "preparation" for STEAM subjects in elementary school. In fact, preschool and Kindergarten teachers expressed dismay when asked by school administrators to replace play blocks and other manipulatives with worksheets in order to follow the Common Core State Standards guidelines (Kinzer, Gerhardt & Coca, 2016). Research supported science and mathematics related behaviors and dispositions, which are essential for success in later school years, have been superseded by a strong focus on the learning of factual knowledge at the expense of more in-depth experience with analytical thinking. That is, the learning of concepts is sidelined as a result of an increasing lack of instructional time devoted to open-ended projects or playful learning in preschool and early elementary school. Conceptual knowledge does not come about from disconnected science or mathematics related tasks that overwhelmingly focus on labeling and recall, and that cover broader concepts superficially.

In support of playful learning (Hirsh-Pasek et al., 2009) for encouraging the development of conceptual understanding, Feynman's reminiscence above highlights two important arguments for conceptual development: 1) First, it requires consistency in so-called higher-order thinking skills over time; and 2) analytical thinking during STEAM learning must eclipse labeling and recall in that the former demonstrates a child's conceptual understanding, while the latter does not. As Feynman's example suggests, knowledge of the name of a bird tells one nothing about migration, flight, aerodynamics, reproduction, or any other concepts related to the bird. As emphasized by the National Research Council (NRC) (Bransford, Brown & Cocking, 2000), "Teachers must teach some subject matter in depth, providing many examples in which the same concept is at work and providing a firm foundation of factual knowledge" (p. 20).

In utilizing their prior knowledge, children, through playful learning, should be encouraged to create scientifically based explanations and be provided with the opportunity to explain their reasoning. These everyday child-developed explanations are what Vygotsky (1962) refers to as spontaneous concepts—concepts that deal with the child's conceptions, understandings, and explanations of the inner workings of the everyday world. These explanations may be incorrect, incomplete, partially correct, or correct in their structure. But the main point here is that these explanations are the formation of emergent theories that the young child acquires before formal science instruction. These emergent theories, based on the child's experiences, become her prior knowledge, which is a critical component that either fosters or hinders future learning. Even when confronted with contradictory evidence, children, like adults, are frequently reluctant to give up their prior beliefs. The extensive research carried out by the Annenberg Foundation (2008) on science and mathematics education has provided numerous examples to support the persistence of an individual's prior beliefs and how this either hinders or supports the acquisition of new information. In sum, both early childhood practitioners and parents need to engage in much more observation and less adult-directed activity in order to uncover what children know prior to formal instruction.

Many science and mathematics educators feel that children need to recognize the big ideas or the unifying concepts of science and mathematics in which to place their everyday experiences of the world (Fleer & Ridgway, 2007). According to the NRC (Bransford, Brown & Cocking 2000) and the National Academies of Sciences Engineering and Medicine (2018), the unifying concepts for the teaching of science and the mathematics that is connected to many scientific topics are: organization, cause-and-effect, systems, scales (relative and absolute), models, change, structure and function, variation, and diversity. Organization, a basic factor of science and mathematics content, calls for children to recognize the properties, characteristics, or attributes of things or organisms in their environment. In order to build organization skill, children should be exposed to descriptive features such as color, size, shape, texture, and odor. These attributes are encountered through children's interactions with objects in the everyday environment. Ness and Farenga (2007) suggest that these exploratory, attribute related interactions within the environment are the protobehaviors that

Thinking Like Scientists/Mathematicians 125

FIGURE 5.1 Proto-STEAM experience model
Source: Image used by permission of CERTA Research Corp.

contribute to basic and complex process skills (see Figure 5.1). As Figure 5.1 suggests, the learning of all types of knowledge emanates, for the most part, from free play. For this reason, play was placed at the center of the Proto-STEAM Experience Model. Protobehaviors, which are a result of play, are exploratory drives that cause the individual to come in contact with everyday phenomena through at least one of the five senses, which are then interpreted by neural networks. The mental representations or schemas that are formed from this event serve as patterns of understanding that the child will use to experience, analyze, and evaluate further encounters.

The following are some simple examples of encounters that young children experience every day. They take notice of the shapes of clouds in the sky, shadows at different times of the day, insects on plants, and the color of leaves on the trees. Couple these observations with additional observations, such as finding the conditions that are necessary to form long shadows, or determining when we see red, yellow, and orange leaves on trees. Next, record your observations to help you remember what you saw. Recording experiences is a simple activity that will enable children to remember and organize their observations. As another example, record the moon's phases on a calendar so children can check their predictions and make further predictions based on data that were collected. Many of the examples of common environmental observations help children recognize the big ideas in science and mathematics.

The scientific task of recording brings up another point in developing the young child's scientific and mathematical knowledge: the idea of predictable patterns, or cycles. The following are some of the many scientific cycle themes: day and night, moon phases, tides, seasons, animal migration, animal hibernations, water cycles, plant growth, metamorphosis (complete and incomplete), rocks, and weather. As children observe these cycles, they may notice that some changes occur more quickly than others. Children can compare the rate of change of a butterfly as it emerges from a chrysalis and compare that to the moon's phases from new moon to full moon. These science and mathematics experiences and recognition of patterns and relationships introduce the child to the concept of rate of change. The activities just mentioned will help children learn one of the most important constructs in doing science and mathematics: The scientific method. When children show evidence of recognizing patterns of change, they are then more successful in predicting outcomes, which, in turn, introduces the powerful idea of cause and effect. Children who begin to understand cause-and-effect relationships recognize that many things and organisms in the world behave in organized and predictable ways. At this point, children build control of the environment and acknowledge that outcomes are not possible without causes—one of the more powerful ideas behind all scientific thinking.

Scientific, Mathematical, and Technological Mindsets

It is essential for parents, caregivers, and practitioners to serve as guides in the child's quest in the development of scientific and mathematical thinking. But the problem is that many parents and teachers feel incapable of exposing children to scientific and mathematical topics. This is supported to a certain extent by research suggesting that early childhood and childhood practitioners possess a modest skill set for developing their students' formal science experiences (Garbett, 2003; Johnson, Johnson, Farenga & Ness, 2005; Nilsson & Elm, 2017). According to the NRC (2007), many childhood educators "have limited knowledge of science and limited opportunities to learn science" (p. 296). This statement parallels the present condition of engineering education among educators in general (Bers, 2008; Vincenti, 1990). Moreover, many of the states' teacher education curricula do not include the study of spatial and geometric thinking—an area that is critical for developing students' skill sets required in pre-engineering and engineering programs as well as other STEM related subjects. Therefore, an attempt to remedy the lack of inclusion of spatial thinking skill as a crosscutting concept is supported indirectly by the Next Generation Science Standards (NGSS) as an attempt to integrate disciplinary core ideas, science and engineering practices, and crosscutting concepts to the K-12 STEM curriculum (NNGSS Lead States, 2013).

One way to compensate for limited training is to develop a growth mindset about science and mathematics (Boaler, 2016) in early childhood and childhood professionals. In Chapter 2, we alluded to mindsets (Dweck, 2008) when we discussed the importance of making, recognizing, and fixing mistakes in STEAM and highlighted the fact that the act of making mistakes is part of play. Mindsets are brought up again here in that one's earlier experiences in STEAM related fields clearly have both positive and negative effects on later attitudes toward these subjects (Margot & Kettler, 2019; Nadelson et al., 2013). While perhaps not the case in other countries (Tao, 2019), early childhood practitioners in the United States, in particular, generally seem to show negative attitudes toward the exposure and orientation of science and mathematics and STEAM overall (Appleton, 2003; Jamil, Linder & Stegelin, 2018; McClure et al., 2017). The main cause of these negative attitudes is linked to their experiences in STEAM related areas at an earlier point in their lives. Many early childhood practitioners who have had these negative experiences during their early and formative years may develop negative ideas that congeal over time and eventually establish themselves as fixed mindsets. With respect to STEM subjects, people with fixed mindsets tend to believe that their ability to do science or mathematics is poor. They also seem to possess the "you either have [the skills in STEAM] or don't" mentality. People who have a fixed mindset place themselves in the category of "those who don't have what it takes to do well" in these subjects. They also believe that doing well in science and mathematics is an innate characteristic that successful STEAM students are born with. If infants, toddlers, and young children have any innate qualities at all, the one they do have is their inclination to explore, seek things out, and test and retest to see if their emergent theories can be supported by the evidence they come up with.

Now imagine what takes place when early childhood or elementary teachers and practitioners possess a fixed mindset in STEAM. In this unfortunate circumstance, teachers with negative attitudes about STEAM—and thus who possess a fixed mindset—who serve as role models for young children, can potentially influence their very young students to eventually stereotype who "is good" in science and mathematics and "who is not." This sequence of events has been a vicious circle for generations.

In order to avoid developing the no-win situation that follows from a fixed mindset, many early childhood and elementary educators need to develop what Dweck (2008) and Boaler (2016) refer to as the growth mindset. In stark contrast to the fixed mindset, those with the growth mindset believe that having high ability in STEAM subjects is the result of effort and hard work. These individuals believe that they could possibly succeed in STEAM if they put their mind and effort into these subjects. And even if they are laypersons in STEAM, people with a growth mindset find ways to think about STEAM in diverse, alternative ways. In other words, there is no such thing as "only one way" of solving a science or math problem. People with a growth mindset develop what 21st-century

STEAM educators refer to as problem-posing skills. Because of its increasing significance in the world of STEAM, problem posing is a process skill that was recently added to the NGSS standards. Earliest discussion in the research literature regarding problem posing in mathematics can be found in Silver (1994). Children who problem-pose create new problems or reformulate given ones (Tichá & Hošpesová, 2013) as a means of exploring a certain STEAM related situation. With a growth mindset, young children can be exposed to scientific or mathematical experiences needed in order to develop their own interpretations of real-life, everyday phenomena so that they can make something unclear in STEAM more meaningful and engaging (Stoyanova & Ellerton, 1996).

The importance of introducing problem posing at the early childhood level cannot be overstated. As we have learned in previous chapters, young children develop emergent scientific and mathematical ideas when they are engaged in play and are not restricted to formal or adult-imposed constraints. When young children participate in VCPO constructions, they begin to experience a number of scientific and mathematical phenomena, many of which will be discussed in the next chapter. For example, in Chapter 1, we examined Fernando's and Gabe's LEGO structures. In doing so, we learned that Fernando's structure remained standing while Gabe's did not. It turned out that Gabe placed several bricks that were jutting out so that the sides of his structure were uneven. In architectural and engineering terms, Gabe built cantilevers in his structure. That moment exemplifies an ideal situation for the adult caregiver to guide the child to investigate further the scientific concept of balance, which is also inherently connected to the Newton's law of universal gravitation. In this instance, the adult can use what we referred to above as the tacit dialoguing technique, which involves the parent or practitioner asking the child basic questions as to what specific characteristics of the structure keep making it fall. These types of questions provide engaging environments for the child to inquire about cause-and-effect relationships and to investigate ways that will prevent the structure from falling.

But this type of questioning cannot be productive for the young child if the adult either still possesses a fixed mindset about STEAM subjects or is unwilling to change to the much more powerful growth mindset. One way to start developing a growth mindset is to initially grapple with the understanding that maintaining a fixed mindset is unsustainable when facing challenges that require problem solving or problem posing, especially when it comes to the development of STEAM thinking. In response to this point, Maslyk (2016) argues that, in order for STEAM thinking and learning to thrive, it is up to practitioners, principals, and superintendents to provide conducive environments that promote and foster the growth mindset as a means of setting an example for our young children.

Mindset research has also been tangentially helpful in the area of self-efficacy, the ability of the individual to maintain a self-awareness of the extent to which one can be successful in a particular subject, profession, or academic domain.

Menon and Sadler (2016) conducted a mixed methods study that investigated variations in the science self-efficacy beliefs and science content knowledge of 18 pre-service teachers and how these two variables evolved over the semester in what was indicated to be a specialized science content course. Their results showed promising results—namely, statistically significant advances in pre-service teachers' science self-efficacy beliefs and conceptual knowledge in science content. They also found a positive relationship between advances in conceptual understanding in science and advances in science teaching self-efficacy. Menon and Sadler's qualitative analysis results showed positive changes in pre-service teachers' self-image in science. These teachers attributed their experiences in the science content course to the increased levels of confidence in engaging in science activities with future students.

In her work in Scientific Playworlds discussed in Chapter 2, Fleer (2019) alludes to the post-Piagetian notion of the young child as scientist when she states that "Eminent scientists, like Einstein, worked with theoretical contradiction, thought experiments, mental models, and visualisation—all characteristics of children's play" (p. 1257). In light of our earlier discussion on building self-efficacy and changing from a fixed to growth mindset, Fleer argues in support of an inextricable link between imagination in scientific thinking and the imagination that occurs during play. Moreover, Farenga and Joyce (1999) have argued that positive attitudes in science and mathematics can cultivate intrinsic motivation by tapping into young children's responsiveness in the exploration and interaction of their environments. Bringing up the work of Menon and Sadler (2016), Fleer (2019), and Farenga and Joyce (1999) allows us to recognize that acquiring self-efficacy or a growth mindset in science or mathematics is not really a difficult thing for practitioners and parents to do and that there is evidence to support this position.

Young children's science and mathematics related environments can be filled with numerous opportunities to learn. As early childhood specialists, we have the opportunity to either foster or change our dispositions toward STEAM so that our young students get the best out of it. We can start by introducing observation techniques—one of the most important process skills. From a phylogenetic standpoint, past civilizations took the act of observation to its zenith in that they could readily describe the motions of celestial bodies. Directionality, a fundamental component of spatial cognition, was intrinsically associated with acute observations and the concept of cardinal direction: east, west, north, and south. From an ontogenetic perspective, children should be encouraged to observe the world around them and identify patterns and relationships that support their understanding of the environment.

The following activity offers parents and early childhood practitioners an informal introduction to observational astronomy for young children. To begin with, children can be gradually introduced to the three most apparent celestial bodies—the sun, the moon, and stars. Each of these celestial bodies provides a variety of lessons that can be conducted over a set number of time intervals to help support conceptual understanding.

Activity: A simple activity that develops young children's observational skills is to watch the moon as it appears in the sky and record how changes happen over a period of time. In supporting children's recognition of patterns, it would be important to conduct the activity in the same location and at the same time for a period of at least three months. Children can draw the moon's shape and follow its transition from a full moon to a new moon and back to a full moon once again. The use of a calendar to record daily observations may make it easier to recognize patterns and relationships, which contribute to conceptual thinking. We concluded from Feynman's early experiences that labeling and recall alone are unhelpful in doing science and mathematics. However, when children recognize patterns, parents or practitioners may want to connect children's everyday terminology with new, conceptually systematic vocabulary that will help explain their discoveries. While making and recording their observations, children should always be encouraged to ask questions. The key point here is to nurture dialogue with children in order to foster questioning skills and motivation in STEAM. The following questions may help lay the foundation for conceptual knowledge: Describe the objects that you see when you look at the evening sky. Does the moon appear in the same location each night? If not, in which direction does the moon appear to be going? In which section of the sky does the moon appear? Is the moon only visible at night? Does the moon appear in the evening sky at the same time and location?

While these questions may seem simple to the reader, it is important to note that they represent similar questions to those posed to students majoring in earth science and physics. Because children's questions may arise, given that the answers to these questions are based entirely on observational data, practitioners and parents are always encouraged to consult internet resources, trade books, or to plan trips to a planetarium as a way to keep young children's wonder in STEAM subjects.

Note

1 This table is borrowed from the NASA Glenn Research Center website entitled *Kite Index*. (See NASA, 2008.)

References

American Association for the Advancement of Science (AAAS). (1989). *Science for All Americans. Project 2061: Summary statement.* Washington, DC: AAAS. Retrieved from: www.project2061.org/publications/articles/2061/sfaasum.htm.

Annenberg Foundation. (2008). *Minds of our own: Lessons from thin air.* Washington, DC: Annenberg Foundation. Retrieved from: www.learner.org/resources/series26.html#jump1.

Appleton, K. (2003). How do beginning primary school teachers cope with science? Toward an understanding of science teaching practice. *Journal for Research in Science Teaching*, 33, 1–25. Retrieved from: https://doi.org/10.1023/A:1023666618800.

Bandura, A. (1994). Self-efficacy. In V. S. Ramachaudran (Ed.), *Encyclopedia of human behavior*, Vol. 4 (pp. 71–81). New York: Academic Press.

Bassok, D., Latham, S., Rorem, A. (2016). Is Kindergarten the new first grade? *AERA Open*, 2(1). doi:10.1177/2332858415616358.

Berk L., & Winsler, A. (1995). *Scaffolding children's learning: Vygotsky and early childhood education*. Washington, DC: NAEYC.

Bers, M. U. (2008). *Blocks to robots: Learning with technology in the early childhood classroom*. New York: Teachers College Press.

Boaler, J. (2016). *Mathematical mindsets: Unleashing students' potential through creative math, inspiring messages and innovative teaching*. San Francisco, CA: Jossey-Bass.

Bodrova, E., & Leong, D. J. (1996). *Tools of the mind: The Vygotskian approach to early childhood education*. Englewood Cliffs, NJ: Merrill/Prentice Hall.

Bransford, J. D., Brown, A. L., & Cocking, R. R. (2000). *How people learn: Brain, mind, experience, and school*. Washington, DC: National Academy Press.

Carey, S. (1985). Are children fundamentally different kinds of thinkers and learners than adults? In S. Chipman, J. Segal, & R. Glaser (Eds.), *Thinking and learning skills*, Vol. 2. *Research and open questions* (pp. 485–517). Hillsdale, NJ: Lawrence Erlbaum Associates, Inc.

Chi, M. T., & Glaser, R. (1981). The measurement of expertise: Analysis of the development of knowledge and skills as a basis for assessing achievement. In E. L. Baker & Edys S.Quellmalz (Eds.), *Design, analysis, and policy in testing* (pp. 37–47). Thousand Oaks, CA: Sage Publications.

Chi, M. T., Feltovich, P. J., & Glaser, R. (1981). Categorization and representation of physics problems by experts and novices. *Cognitive Science*, 5, 121–152.

Common Core State Standards Initiative (2021). Preparing America's students for success. Retrieved from: www.corestandards.org.

Dou, R., Hazari, Z., Dabney, K., Sonnert, G., & Sadler, P. (2019). Early informal STEM experiences and STEM identity: The importance of talking science. *Science Education*, 103(3), 623–637.

Driver, R. 1983. *The pupil as scientist?*London: The Open University Press.

Dweck, C. (2008). *Mindsets and math/science achievement*. New York: Carnegie Corporation of New York, Institute for Advanced Study, Commission on Mathematics and Science Education.

Egan, K. (2012). *Primary understanding: Education in early childhood*. New York: Routledge.

Elias, C. L., & Berk, L. E. (2002). Self-regulation in young children: Is there a role for sociodramatic play? *Early Childhood Research Quarterly*, 17(2), 216–238.

Farenga, S. J., & Joyce, B. A. (1999). Science sensibility. *Science Scope*, 22(6), 6–9.

Ferrara, K., Hirsh-Pasek, K., Newcombe, N. S., Golinkoff, R. M., & Lam, W. S. (2011). Block talk: Spatial language during block play. *Mind, Brain, and Education*, 5(3), 143–151.

Feynman, R. P. (1969). What is science? *The Physics Teacher*, 7(6), 313–320.

Feynman, R. P. (2000). *The pleasure of finding things out*. New York: Basic Books.

Fleer, M. (2019). Scientific Playworlds: A model of teaching science in play-based settings. *Research in Science Education*, 49(5), 1257–1278.
Fleer, M., & Ridgway, A. (2007). Mapping the relations between everyday concepts and scientific concepts within playful learning environments. *Learning and Socio-cultural Theory: Exploring Modern Vygotskian Perspectives International Workshop 2007*, 1(1). Retrieved from: http://ro.uow.edu.au/llrg/vol1/iss1/2.
Forman, G. E. (2010). When 2-year-olds and 3-year-olds think like scientists. *Early Childhood Research and Practice*, 12(2). Retrieved from: http://ecrp.illinois.edu/v12n2/forman.html.
Garbett, D. (2003). Science education in early childhood teacher education: Putting forward a case to enhance student teachers' confidence and competence. *Research in Science Education*, 33(4), 467–481.
Ginsburg, H. P., Inoue, N., & Seo, K. H. (1999). Young children doing mathematics: Observations of everyday activities. In J. V. Copley (Ed.), *Mathematics in the early years* (pp. 88–99). Reston, VA: National Council of Teachers of Mathematics.
Ginsburg, H. P., Lin, C. L., Ness, D., & Seo, K. H. (2003). Young American and Chinese children's everyday mathematical activity. *Mathematical Thinking and Learning*, 5 (4), 235–258.
Ginsburg, H. P., Pappas, S., & Seo, K. H. (2001). Everyday mathematical knowledge: Asking young children what is developmentally appropriate. In S. L. Golbeck (Ed.), *Psychological perspectives on early childhood education: Reframing dilemmas in research and practice* (pp. 181–219). Mahwah, NJ: Lawrence Erlbaum Associates.
González Rey, F. (2016). Vygotsky's concept of "perezhivanie" in the psychology of art and at the final moment of his work: Advancing his legacy. *Mind, Culture, and Activity*, 23(4), 305–314.
Hattie, J. A. C., & Donoghue, G. M. (2016). Learning strategies: A synthesis and conceptual model. *Nature Partner Journals Science of Learning*, 1, 16013. doi:10.1038/npjscilearn.2016.13.
Hirsh-Pasek, K., Golinkoff, R. M., Berk, L. E., & Singer, D. (2009). *A mandate for playful learning in preschool: Presenting the evidence*. Oxford: Oxford University Press.
Jamil, F. M., Linder, S. M., & Stegelin, D. A. (2018). Early childhood teacher beliefs about STEAM education after a professional development conference. *Early Childhood Education Journal*, 46(4), 409–417.
Johnson, D. D., Johnson, B., Farenga, S. J., & Ness, D. (2008). *Stop high-stakes testing: An appeal to America's conscience*. Lanham, MD: Rowman & Littlefield.
Johnson, D. D., Johnson, B., Ness, D., & Farenga, S. J. (2005). *Trivializing teacher education: The accreditation squeeze*. Lanham, MD: Rowman & Littlefield.
Johnson, J. E., Sevimli-Celik, S. E., & Al-Mansour, M. O. (2013). Play in early childhood education. In O. N. Saracho & B. Spodek (Eds.), *Handbook of research on the education of young children* (pp. 265–274). New York: Routledge.
Kamii, C., Miyakawa, Y., & Kato, Y. (2004). The development of logico-mathematical knowledge in a block-building activity at ages 1–4. *Journal of Research in Childhood Education*, 19(1), 44–57.
Kinzer, C., Gerhardt, K., & Coca, N. (2016). Building a case for blocks as Kindergarten mathematics learning tools. *Early Childhood Education Journal*, 44(4), 389–402.
Komatsu, K., & Rappleye, J. (2021). Rearticulating PISA, globalisation, societies, and education. doi:10.1080/14767724.2021.1878014.

Krafft, K. C., & Berk, L. E. (1998). Private speech in two preschools: Significance of open-ended activities and make-believe play for verbal self-regulation. *Early Childhood Research Quarterly*, 13(4), 637–658.

Lemke, J. L. (1990). *Talking science: Language, learning, and values*. Norwood, NJ: Ablex Publishing.

Margot, K. C., & Kettler, T. (2019). Teachers' perception of STEM integration and education: A systematic literature review. *International Journal of STEM Education*, 6(1), 1–16.

Maslyk, J. (2016). *STEAM makers: Fostering creativity and innovation in the elementary classroom*. Thousand Oaks, CA: Corwin Press.

McClure, E. R., Guernsey, L., Clements, D. H., Bales, S. N., Nichols, J., Kendall-Taylor, N., & Levine, M. H. (2017). *STEM starts early: Grounding science, technology, engineering, and math education in early childhood*. New York, NY: The Joan Ganz Cooney Center at Sesame Workshop. Retrieved from: www.joanganzcooneycenter.org/publication/stem-starts-early.

Menon, D., & Sadler, T. D. (2016). Preservice elementary teachers' science self-efficacy beliefs and science content knowledge. *Journal of Science Teacher Education*, 27(6), 649–673.

Nadelson, L. S., Callahan, J., Pyke, P., Hay, A., Dance, M., & Pfiester, J. (2013). Teacher STEM perception and preparation: Inquiry-based STEM professional development for elementary teachers. *The Journal of Educational Research*, 106(2), 157–168.

National Academies of Sciences Engineering & Medicine (NAS) (2018). *How people learn II: Learners, contexts, and cultures*. Washington, DC: National Academies Press. Retrieved from: https://doi.org/10.17226/24783.

National Academies of Sciences Engineering & Medicine (NAS) (2019). *Achieving the promise of a diverse STEM workforce*. Washington, DC: National Academies Press. Retrieved from: https://www.nationalacademies.org/ocga/testimonies/116-session-1/mae-jemison/achieving-the-promise-of-a-diverse-stem-workforce.

National Aeronautic and Space Administration (NASA) Glenn Research Center (2008). *Kite index*. Cleveland, OH: NASA. Retrieved from: www.grc.nasa.gov/WWW/K-12/airplane/shortk.html.

National Commission of Excellence in Education (NCEE) (1983). *A nation at risk: The imperative for educational reform*. Washington, DC: United States Government Printing Office.

National Research Council (NRC) (1995). *National Science Education Standards (NSES)*. Retrieved from: www.nap.edu/html/nses.

National Research Council (NRC) (2007). *Taking science to school: Learning and teaching science in grades K-8*. Washington, DC: National Academies Press.

Ness, D., & Farenga, S. J. (2016). Blocks, bricks, and planks: Relationships between affordance and visuo-spatial constructive play objects. *American Journal of Play*, 8(2), 201–227.

Ness, D., & Farenga, S. J. (2007). *Knowledge under construction: The importance of play in developing children's spatial and geometric thinking*. Lanham, MD: Rowman & Littlefield Publishers.

Next Generation Science Standards (NGSS) Lead States (2013). *Next Generation Science Standards: For states, by states*. Washington, DC: The National Academies Press.

Nilsson, P., & Elm, A. (2017). Capturing and developing early childhood teachers' science pedagogical content knowledge through CoRes. *Journal of Science Teacher Education*, 28(5), 406–424.

Piaget, J., & Inhelder, B. (1956). *The child's conception of space* (F. J. Langdon & J. L. Lunzer, Trans.). London: Routledge and Kegan Paul.

Rittle-Johnson, B., Zippert, E. L., & Boice, K. L. (2019). The roles of patterning and spatial skills in early mathematics development. *Early Childhood Research Quarterly*, 46, 166–178.

Roeper, A. (1988). The early environment of the child: Experience in a continuing search for meaning. In P. F. Brandwein and A. H. Passow (Eds.), *Gifted young in science: Potential through performance* (pp. 121–139). Washington, DC: National Science Teachers Association.

Rowe, M. B. (1973). *Teaching science as continuous inquiry.* New York: McGraw-Hill.

Salomon, G., & Perkins, D. (1996). Learning in Wonderland: What do computers really offer education? In S. T. Kerr (Ed.), *Technology and the future of schooling: Ninety-fifth yearbook of the National Society for the Study of Education, Part 2* (pp. 111–130). Chicago, IL: University of Chicago Press.

Silver, E. A. (1994). On mathematical problem posing. *For the Learning of Mathematics*, 14(1), 19–28.

Stoyanova, E., & Ellerton, N. F. (1996). A framework for research into students' problem posing in school mathematics. In P. Clarkson (Ed.), *Technology in mathematics education* (pp. 518–525). Melbourne, Australia: Mathematics Education Research Group of Australasia.

Tao, Y. (2019). Kindergarten teachers' attitudes toward and confidence for integrated STEM education. *Journal for STEM Education Research*, 2(2), 154–171.

Tichá, M., & Hošpesová, A. (2013). Developing teachers' subject didactic competence through problem posing. *Educational Studies in Mathematics*, 83(1), 133–143.

Vincenti, W. (1990). *What engineers know and how they know it: Analytical studies from aeronautical history.* Baltimore, MD: The Johns Hopkins University Press.

Vygotsky, L. S. (1962). *Thinking and speech (Thought and language).* Cambridge, MA: MIT Press.

Wilburn, G., & Elias, J. (2020, October 28). *Grade 12 reading score declines, mathematics score unchanged on the nation's report card.* Washington, DC: National Assessment of Educational Progress (NAEP).

Zosh, J. M., Hopkins, E. J., Jensen, H., Liu, C., Neale, D., Hirsh-Pasek, K., Solis, S. L., & Whitebread, D. (2017). *Learning through play.* Billund, Denmark: LEGO Foundation.

6
YOUNG CHILDREN THINK LIKE ARCHITECTS AND ENGINEERS

Based on several years of studying children's cognitive propensities exhibited during free play, I have always argued that young children's constructive free play with VCPOs is analogous to the work of professional scientists, experts in technology, engineers, architects, and mathematicians (Ness, 2001; Ness & Farenga, 2007; Ness & Farenga, 2016; Ness, Farenga & Garofalo, 2017). As we have learned in the previous chapter, it is during their preschool years that young children have the potential, especially during free play, to be freer to think scientifically, mathematically, or architecturally in ways that don't stifle their creativity.

Parents and teachers all too often overlook the creativity in their children's or students' VCPO structures. Some adults, through no fault of their own, are simply unaware of or do not pay attention to children's structures. Other adults often pass children's structures off as "simply" trivial creations that are "not worthy" of further inspection. And once children enter school, their creative constructive work is often overlooked altogether. What is worse is that many preschools overlook the creativity of children because they are overwhelmed by school related factors such as preparing children for high-stakes testing that we mentioned in earlier chapters. The current testing craze—ever since the Bush Administration's No Child Left Behind Act—has placed such a heavy burden on children that it has contributed to children's intuition and creativity being almost completely ignored—two aspects of children's cognitive development that have been all but overlooked, even as early as the preschool level.

The objective of this chapter, then, is to convince the reader that children's work—and I am using work and play synonymously here—is completely analogous to that of the professional STEM expert. To do this, we will initially review the relatively recent literature on young children's free play and architectural and engineering principles. We will then reexamine some of the structures we saw in

Chapter 1, as well as other children's structures, and focus on precisely how each structure corresponds to specific concepts in architecture and engineering.

Research in Engineering Thinking

The study of engineering thinking during young children's engagement in free play is relatively novel in the research corpus of STEAM development. In fact, the majority of research in this area has been conducted since 2010. Evangelou's (2010) editorial discusses how STEM can be integrated into early childhood education in a contemporary and interdisciplinary context, and goes on to ponder whether such an integration is indeed practical and achievable. Mentioning the declining enrollments and waning enthusiasm for engineering studies, Evangelou suggests that researchers should examine how children think in terms of their emergent engineering knowledge—what she calls the field of developmental engineering. She argues that by doing so, we could draw from knowledge in different disciplines as a way to generate new knowledge and develop novel programs that demonstrate the need for more engineers in the world (see Adams et al., 2011).

Bairaktarova, Evangelou, Bagiati and Brophy (2011) examined the extent to which young children engage in activities that serve as antecedents to engineering thinking and actions. They sought to determine whether spontaneous, everyday free play and engagement with open, semi-structured, and structured play objects and play areas, including blocks, bricks, sandboxes, water tables, snap circuits, and puzzles, would uncover emergent cognition in engineering thinking. Bairaktarova and colleagues conducted naturalistic observation methodology of preschool children engaged in free play with the different play objects in different areas. Their work explains the various circumstances in which play with the above-mentioned objects facilitates young children's participation in engineering activities and development in engineering concepts. Their conclusions suggest that play environments can become conduits through which emergent engineering thinking can take place. They refer to these play environments as "engineering play."

Gold, Elicker, Choi, Anderson and Brophy (2015) observed 66 preschool children as they played with large, lightweight blocks as well as more traditional play materials, such as slides, ladders, swings, playhouses, sandboxes, action-figures and dolls, cooking and household toys, and writing and drawing materials, to understand their engineering play (Bairaktarova et al. 2011), a new paradigm that is based on emergent design and construction related concepts. Gold and colleagues examined engineering play and gender differences in the traditional playground, dramatic play area, and the block play area. They found no significant differences in terms of gender—both girls and boys engaged in emergent engineering behaviors fairly equally. However, they did find differences in the frequency of engineering play, and concluded that the large, lightweight blocks provided more engineering learning opportunities than did the traditional play materials. Moreover, their observations of preschoolers' social constructive play led to the identification of nine engineering play categories: communication of goals; design and construction; problem solving; creative/innovative ideas; solution testing/evaluating design; explanations of how things are built/work; following patterns and prototypes; logical mathematical thinking; and technical vocabulary.

Fleer (2020) focused most of her attention on the manner in which teachers engage their early childhood students in engineering practices. Using Hedegaard's (2008) educational experiment, which examines how school-based content knowledge in primary schools becomes personally meaningful to children, Fleer followed two teachers of two different classes for a one-year period. The objective was to observe these two teachers design environments that attempted to engage children's interest in engineering play through what she refers to as storying and imaginary PlayWorlds (Fleer, 2018), which are discussed in Chapter 2. Through the application of the cultural-historical concept of motives (Hedegaard, 2014), Fleer examined how four- and five-year-old children were predisposed to engineering practices and what she calls "a motive orientation to engineering." Her findings suggest that teachers introduce their students to emergent engineering concepts by creating environments that support motivation in this area. She further indicates that as children's tendencies toward engineering principles progress, imaginary storylines develop into engineering problems in which the children engage in problem solving. Fleer goes on to discuss the way in which children's free play becomes collaborative as their imaginary storylines merge into engineering play, which, in turn, supports conceptual learning in engineering.

In support of the notion that children's collaborative play is analogous to the collaborative manner in which professional engineers engage in their work, Gold and Elicker (2020) asked whether observing children's play from a social constructivist perspective in terms of engineering enables parents and teachers to foster and promote the children's STEM learning. They also investigated whether engineering play supports collaborative play in general. Gold and Elicker argue that engineering play is useful because, on the one hand, it enables the researcher to understand collaborative play as it relates to social constructive play, and on the other, it strengthens young children's interest and motivation in learning early STEM concepts.

Gold, Elicker, Kellerman, Christ, Mishra and Howe (2020) studied the connections between engineering play with wooden unit blocks and mathematics and spatial skills of children both with and without disabilities. They referred to their previous study (Gold et al., 2015) to classify the preschoolers' behaviors in terms of nine engineering play categories. Their participants included 110 preschool students in all, 48 of whom were female and 28 of whom were children with disabilities. The ages of the children ranged from 49 to 72 months. They found a significant correlation between engineering play and spatial horizontal rotation skills. Moreover, they found a positive correlation between engineering play and geometry for children with disabilities. Results also suggest that engineering play and mathematics and spatial development are interrelated. They further concluded that engineering play is an important educational endeavor in developing cognitive skills and school readiness for preschoolers in general.

Bodnar, Anastasio, Enszer and Burkey (2016) focused on a different level of education and examined the types of engineering curriculum that engage and motivate students at the undergraduate level. Accordingly, they studied existing research that concentrated on the use of educational games to teach undergraduate engineering students, and reviewed the principal features that include examples from a variety of engineering specializations. Bodnar and colleagues' review was conducted by completing a thorough search of the existing literature in a number of different science and engineering databases as well as the ERIC Education Research Abstract database using keywords that were germane to games in engineering education. They found 62 publications that were suitable for further examination. They concluded that research on the implementation of engineering-based games in the undergraduate engineering classroom support the successful inclusion of games as a means of teaching engineering concepts—in terms of both student learning and attitudes toward engineering learning. Like Bodnar and her colleagues, Kothmann (2019) focuses on engineering play for students of engineering. In agreement with Bodnar et al., he contends that play is an essential feature of any successful engineering program in that it provides a platform on which students can discover new ways of designing and planning constructions, devices, and mechanisms that advance society.

While the research literature on STEAM education, like those discussed above, has addressed the application of psychological learning theories for the development of STEM thinking (Schunn & Silk, 2011), theories that deal with the integration of engineering thinking and spatial cognition by combining the epistemological and ontological perspectives on advancing a STEM learning theory needs further investigation.

Research in Architectural Thinking

It is evident that architects possess a unique set of spatial skills that are essential for them to successfully design structures (Gerber et al., 2019). Although there has been an increase in research that has examined emergent engineering concepts recently, research on the development of architectural thinking from the standpoint of young children's free play environments is sparse. Most of the research on architecture and play, specifically when one uses the keywords "architecture," "play," and "children," has to do with the manner in which school buildings and playgrounds are designed and constructed.

To date, only two publications, to my knowledge, consider the role of architectural cognition from a developmental perspective. The first publication is a book entitled *The Design of Childhood: How the Material World Shapes Independent*

Kids by Alexandra Lange (2018). In this important book, Lange delineates the history of the "block" conception—from its origins as a learning tool described in John Locke's (1880 [1693]) account of a father who began to use lettered blocks to educate his children after he became dissatisfied with instruction through repetition and recitation, followed by Froebel's invention of the Gifts (wooden figures representing different configurations for young children to experience) and the rapidly growing use and dispersion of wooden play blocks in preschools and Kindergartens and eventually in homes, the creation and development of plastic bricks, and finally software that helps enhance spatial skills and 3-D printing. *The Design of Childhood* is devoted to the material world of children from an architect and design critic's perspective. In the first chapter, Lange points out that while play blocks seem so simple in appearance, they actually serve as a channel and springboard for scientific and architectural inquiry.

To take Lange's argument a step further, blocks can be seen analogically as cognitive metaphorical training wheels; scientists might use blocks or similar manipulatives as a way to characterize newly discovered physical phenomena, while architects might work with blocks or VCPOs to represent possible future structures. Blocks are dynamic for both children and professional scientists, mathematicians, architects, and engineers because they enable haptic and tactile sensorial interactions to help make cognitive schema more deliberate and intentional through the detection of recognizable patterns and relationships. There is a reciprocal relationship here as well—that is, our initial thoughts, conceptions, and non-written, informal hypotheses have the potential to be subsequently represented by the physical or virtual VCPO. I would even suggest a cyclic process in that hands-on materials can generate novel ideas, which then allow for reconfigurations of hands-on models that consequently lead to adjustments and modifications of our earlier mental notions.

This interconnection between senses parallels Vygotsky's (1986 [1934]) theoretical position regarding concept formation. Vygotsky distinguishes between two seemingly contrasting—but actually symbiotic—concepts: 1) spontaneous, or everyday, concepts; and 2) scientific, conceptually systematic concepts. Spontaneous concepts are those that individuals develop within the everyday context. These concepts are like little reflections, in that they concern the situational, practical, and empirical (what individuals are able to conclude based on what they see). Scientific concepts (also called conventionally systematic concepts) are those that refer to a hierarchical system of interrelated ideas. They are highly organized and systematic. Scientific concepts can be in the form of formal school instruction, which makes the student self-conscious of content. Through scientific concepts, then, systematization develops cognitive processes. Vygotsky maintained that instruction in scientific concepts, which involves systematization, is very helpful because it provides individuals with more extensive frameworks in which to place their everyday, spontaneous concepts. As an example, a young student might have developed the spontaneous concept of the relationship between tension and compression—a key concept in engineering and physics. But her concept is primarily based on an image of someone pulling on a rope during a tug-of-war and pushing down on a spring. If we ask her to define the relationship between tension and compression, she might reply, "It's when you stretch something and then push it back." Formal instruction—in which the teacher enables the student to learn that tension is the force exerted by an object being pulled upon from opposite ends, and that compression is the equal and opposite force exerted on an object that presses or pushes inward on it thus causing the object to compact—can give the student a broader framework in which to place her spontaneous concept and help her understand what the concept of tension and compression really is. Vygotsky, then, believed that spontaneous concepts moved in an upward manner while scientific concepts had a downward movement. In Vygotsky's own words:

> In working its slow way upward, an everyday concept clears a path for the scientific concept and its downward development. It creates a series of structures necessary for the evolution of a concept's more [nascent], elementary aspects, which give it body and vitality. Scientific concepts, in turn, supply structures for the upward development of the child's spontaneous concepts toward consciousness and deliberate use.
>
> *(1986, p. 194)*

In light of the intrinsic relationships among block and brick play, spatially related virtual games and software (such as Minecraft and computer-aided design), and the activities of architects and engineers, Lange (2018) introduces and elaborates on a play system called ZOOB (which stands for Zoology, Ontology, Ontogeny, and Botany) that was created and developed by the artist and inventor Michael Joaquin Grey. The ZOOB system consists of five parts, each of which is slightly less than 6.5cm in length and has a notch in the middle that allows pieces to connect. These pieces have ball- or horseshoe-shaped, socket-like ends (or one of each) for snapping into place and come in five different colors with each of the five types of pieces having a distinct color. Interestingly, ZOOB has allowed not only artists, but also scientists and engineers with different specializations to develop models of physical phenomena within their own domain. What makes the discussion about ZOOB important is that Lange demonstrates how a seemingly expensive stereolithographic process of making plastic pieces and parts in the 1990s led to the more innovative and relatively inexpensive techniques of 3-D printers. Through historical examples from the 17th century to the present, Lange points out how stereotomic developments—namely, the cutting of solids, mostly of wood and stone, and eventually plastic, to create various forms of blocks and bricks—led to increased interest in novel configurations of VCPOs that transformed the ways in which we play and use imagination and eventually put our embryonic, playful ideas into practical and actionable outcomes.

The second publication, also a book, is one by Ann Gadzikowski entitled *Young Architects at Play: STEM Activities for Young Children* (2021), which is an engaging volume that provides educational practitioners with the tools necessary to generate in children a fascination for architecture through thought-provoking projects and exploration. Earlier in Chapter 4, the reader may recall our examination of the affordance of different VCPO types. We concluded that due to their rather high affordance, bricks do not provide the same type of challenge and creative development that blocks and planks do. In corroboration with this finding, Gadzikowski is perhaps one of the first investigators of play materials who has discussed the limited possibilities that children may have in terms of challenge and originality when playing with LEGO bricks—particularly those that have popular themes. She has underscored "that due to this interlocking system, LEGO [bricks] can't provide the same level of challenge and creativity as wooden unit blocks" (Gadzikowski, 2021, p. 23). I couldn't agree with her more. In this regard, the theoretical position that connects VCPOs with affordance discussed earlier substantiates Gadzikowski's experiences with young children and their level of challenge with various constructive play materials. But based on the affordance model explained in Chapter 4, it can be taken a step further in that planks have demonstrated even less affordance than that of unit blocks, thus providing more intellectual possibilities with planks than with other VCPO types. Similar to Swan (2014), who, to my knowledge, was perhaps the first to elaborate on the equal importance of deconstruction (he calls it "creative destruction") and construction with play bricks, Gadzikowski also discusses the important role of deconstruction—which can be construed as both a philosophy and process similar to Piagetian constructivism but in reverse—as a means of cognitive development in STEM. She emphasizes the role of deconstructing from a social-emotional perspective. As an example, Gadzikowski describes the real-life ephemeral nature of children's constructions in that on almost all occasions, no adhesive is used to keep their constructions permanent. These constructions are often disassembled or razed deliberately. This intentionality of constructing and knocking down a block or brick structure, Gadzikowski argues, might be a sign of the child's sense of power—a feeling that provides her with total control over a situation.

While Gadzikowski (2021) has elaborated on the social and emotional role of deconstructing block structures, it is also important for practitioners to learn about the cognitive resources that can be potentially tapped during the process of deconstructing VCPO structures. Like the act of constructing, deconstructing, assuming it is not in the form of intentional destruction, is an example of higher-order thinking skills. In what has been commonly referred to as Bloom's *Taxonomy of Educational Objectives*, Bloom and Krathwohl (1956) elaborated on higher-order skills as those that exhibit the child's ability to analyze and synthesize phenomena. Unlike so-called lower thinking skills (i.e., labeling, explaining, and, to some extent, applying a particular concept or skill), when a young child is engaged in the building process of VCPO structures, she is in the act of creating, or synthesizing, something made of smaller parts. The same is true for deconstruction, which is the process of analyzing, and involves comparing, contrasting, discerning, and critiquing. Doing so contributes to the development of the brain's cerebellum and cerebral cortex from both ontogenetic and phylogenetic perspectives (Balsters, Whelan, Robertson, & Ramnani, 2013; Leiner, Leiner, & Dow, 1986; Vandervert, 2017). Play, then, greatly contributes to the development of higher-order thinking abilities that will better enable young children to succeed in future schooling and professional life.

One of a handful of studies on children's free play that tangentially relates to architectural thinking is that of Zinguer (2015), who has dug deeply into the world of architectural toys. Her work is more of a historical perspective on architectural toys used when children engage in play than one on architectural cognition and development. Her research is essentially an exposé of the development of architecturally related toys over the last two centuries—from the time of Froebel to the present. What is also valuable about her findings is that they focus on the changing attitudes with regard to architectural form, and perhaps more importantly, how these toys developed in terms of technological advances and how these advances linked in with architecture in the real world. Rather than including plastic toys, such as toy bricks, she focuses on toys that are made of wood, stone, metal, and paper. She begins with a discussion of Froebel's Gifts and their impact on the development of Kindergarten. The next major development, Zinguer suggests, was the creation of Anker Stone Blocks, which proved an essential constructive toy for the construction of fortresses, garrisons, castles, and churches. Her next focus was the impact that Meccano and Erector Sets had on the developing child, and how these toys helped to connect the young child's everyday constructive free play with the older child's or adolescent's cognitive development of architectural concepts that are fundamental to the work of professional architects. Zinguer then examines the role that architectural toys have played in more recent times—specifically, The Toy of 1950 and the House of Cards of 1952, which enabled the child to work with lightweight cardboard pieces that resemble the fundamental concepts and processes of prefabrication.

A second study that indirectly relates to the development of architectural thinking through play is the work of Ginoulhiac (2018). In his research on architectural toys, Ginoulhiac touches upon our discussion in Chapter 4—namely, the affordance of constructive play objects. He is the only researcher who could remotely be said to consider this area by investigating the extent to which various architecturally related toys assist children's play actions that somehow associate with the curriculum examined in professional schools of architecture. The architectural toys that Ginoulhiac suggests should be used are those that are not complicated in structure and possess little in the way of direct instruction. Another tangentially related study that examines the role of gesture and architectural thinking is that of Park, Brösamle, and Hölscher (2020). But these researchers are not investigating gesture from the perspective of young children's emergent architectural thinking.

My earlier inquiry is the only research, to my knowledge, that considers young children's architectural development as they engage in everyday activities during free play (Ness, 2001; Ness & Farenga 2007). Using naturalistic observation techniques (Ginsburg, Inoue & Seo, 1999; Ginsburg, Pappas & Seo, 2001; Ginsburg, Lin, Ness & Seo, 2003; Lincoln & Guba, 1985), Ness (2001) devoted more than 1,000 hours to the identification of specific spatial, mathematical, and architectural activities in which four- and five-year-old children were engaged. In total, 13 codes were identified. In the remainder of the chapter, I discuss how to code STEAM related behaviors in greater detail. In addition, after numerous adjustments and modifications to the original 13 codes, a further four codes were identified. These codes allowed for a more robust understanding of the total time in which young children were engaged in spatial and architecturally related behaviors from the standpoint of three areas of inquiry: gender, socio-economic status, and age. The results of the study revealed no significant differences in time spent on spatial and architecturally-related activity in terms of gender and socio-economic class, but there were significant differences between ages (Ness, 2001; Ness & Farenga, 2007).

In sum, there is clearly a research void in the area of children's architectural cognition and development, particularly in the realm of everyday activities during free play. I see this as an open opportunity for future research in spatial thinking and STEAM development, and more generally, in cognitive development.

The Development of VCPO (Block) Building

The role of VCPOs, blocks, or LEGO pieces, in particular, in early childhood education has become a central theme in developmental psychology and the early childhood education research literature over the last three decades. Two pioneering books in this area include the work of Provenzo and Brett (1983) and Hirsch (1996), both of which are discussed in more detail in Chapter 3. Brosterman (1997) is helpful in establishing the historical background regarding the connection between these two areas of inquiry.

Up to this point, we have discussed the research related to the ways in which VCPOs can serve as learning devices. However, few studies have examined how VCPOs may serve as a cognitive devise in enhancing young children's STEAM thinking. One of the few studies that seems to explore this area is Stuart Reifel's (1984) discussion of the development of block play. Reifel presents a provocative framework for educational practitioners and researchers in understanding children's own ideas about spatial relationships through block play. Basing his thesis on Piaget's theory of intellectual development as it relates to the child's concept of space (Piaget & Inhelder, 1963), Reifel organizes the child's development of block constructions into several stages. Before discussing more advanced types of block constructions, Reifel treats particular spatial representations with blocks as discrete components within a developmental progression.

Following Piaget's thesis that children acquire knowledge of proximity of objects before they develop an understanding of enclosure, Reifel argues that children's initial block constructions, mostly prior to four years, are a result of the process of either piling blocks on top of one another, thus creating vertical structures, or of placing individual blocks beside or next to other blocks in a horizontal manner. During and after their fourth year, children progress to another level in which defining characteristics of block construction includes the necessity for inner space—that is, enclosure. Constructions of this kind include various types of enclosed, or arch-like structures. Consequently, his framework involves four elemental block structure types: the row, in which individual blocks are placed beside one another in a horizontal fashion; the stack, in which individual blocks are placed on top of one another in a vertical fashion; the flat enclosure, in which blocks are placed beside one another in a way that produces inner space, that is, space surrounded by blocks touching one another; and arch-like enclosure, in which one or more blocks are suspended by at least two other blocks.

Despite Reifel's attempt to develop stages in the progression of spatial representations with blocks, he omits the child's development of order and continuity—two very important spatial relations in the child's understanding of space. Also, in Reifel's study, children were assigned adult-directed tasks (i.e., told what to do) of building with blocks and describing what the "outcome" is or "should be." It is possible that there were several outcomes in the course of construction. Studies that require adult-directed activities may be one reason why there seems to be a lack understanding in terms of the young child's unique, everyday, spontaneous ideas regarding representation of spatial structures.

It is a bit vague as to what Reifel means by having a "better spatial understanding." An adult who has a limited sense of direction does not necessarily have a better or worse spatial understanding than another individual. One aspect that can be considered as a follow-up to Reifel's thesis concerns the connection between block building and both formal and informal STEAM learning. Finally, the enclosed structure, which Reifel refers to as "arch[ed]," does not appear to be based on the same principles that architects or engineers—and preschool children in their everyday context—use for the building or construction of arches or vaulted buildings. Instead, Reifel's enclosures, which he refers to as "arches," are closer in resemblance to the trabeated system of building—that is, the use of posts and beams, or the appearance of a rectangular arrangement of objects or material, whose physical arrangement is based on both tension (beams) and compression (posts), as opposed to a circular or semi-circular one, whose physical constraints are those based on compression alone.

One of Reifel's (1981, 1984) and Reifel and Greenfield's (1982, 1983) major findings regarding the development of children's block play was that block complexity increases with age. We can extend this idea to state that VCPO complexity

Thinking Like Architects/Engineers 145

increases with age. As stated above, the young child begins by placing a VCPO *beside* or next to another VCPO. So, the earliest organization of the young child's VCPO construction is horizontal placement. In the next stage of VCPO development, the young child places a VCPO *on* or on top of another VCPO. This arrangement demonstrates an organization of VCPOs in vertical placement. In the third stage of VCPO development, the young child places a VCPO *in* other VCPOs or between two VCPOs. We can also conclude that in the second stage, the young child advances beyond the placement of a VCPO beside another VCPO with the placement of VCPOs in the form of *rows*. Likewise, we can conclude that in the third stage, the young child advances beyond the placement of a VCPO on or on top of another VCPO with the continual placement of VCPOs *on* top of one another in the form of *piles* or *towers*. The last stage in the initial phase of block building is the extension of placing VCPOs in rows, in towers, or within or between other VCPOs by the creation of elaborate enclosures—similar to the enclosure described below in the scenario with Alejandro and Karl. Thus, the entire progression of the young child's development of VCPO constructions can be summarized by the schematic in Figure 6.1.

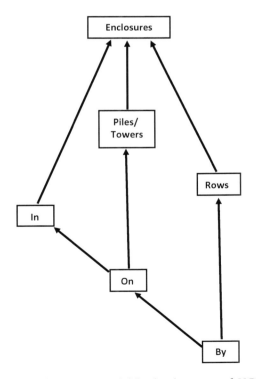

FIGURE 6.1 Progression of the young child's development of VCPO constructions schematic

An examination of the developmental progression of children's VCPO constructions after the initial four stages outlined by Reifel and presented as a schematic in Figure 6.1 needs to be based on levels of complexity of VCPO constructions. Tian, Luo, and Cheung (2020) reviewed the literature on developmental changes in block play as it relates to age with respect to increased levels of complexity. They also examined different scales that have been used to measure block construction complexity and subsequently proposed a conceptual model of the abilities associated with block construction. While some researchers, including Tian, Luo, and Cheung, have attempted to categorize the stages of block building development (Bailey, 1933; Gregory & Whiren, 2003; Stiles & Stern, 2001; Trawick-Smith et al., 2017), few, if any, have done so in naturalistic settings—those in which children have access to blocks, bricks, and other VCPOs without adult intervention or adult-directed activities. In the next chapter, I provide a bottom-up system of coding STEAM related behaviors in terms of spatial development using VCPOs for construction. It is a bottom-up, or inductive, approach in that the codes were identified based on the observations of young children made by the researcher, similar to the research of Ginsburg and his colleagues (Ginsburg et al., 1999, Ginsburg et al., 2001, Ginsburg et al., 2003, Ginsburg & Ertle, 2016), who identified the early mathematics codes evident in young children's free play activities.

Analysis of Children's VCPO Structures through the Lens of Professional Engineers and Architects

Now we consider specific examples of young children engaged in STEAM related constructive play activities and their specific connection to the ideas and work of professional architects and engineers. To do this, I took specific architectural features, such as foundations, posts, beams, beams that are cantilevered, and the scientific processes of tension and compression, and identified how they function in the young child's process of constructing and the finished structure. I then compared and contrasted each young child's structures with analyses of professional engineers and architects. In particular, I have mostly referred to the writing of Mario Salvadori, the internationally renowned structural engineer and professor of both civil engineering and architecture at Columbia University, who, in his prose, takes seemingly complex concepts in engineering and architecture and makes them clear and understandable for the early childhood practitioner, the parent, and even students of engineering or architecture see Salvadori, 1964, 1980, 1990).

Children's Foundations as Models of Real-Life Foundations

We begin with Kathryn's structure, namely, the foundation (see Figure 6.2). Her large, rather complex structure is clearly one in which the four-and-a-half year-

Thinking Like Architects/Engineers 147

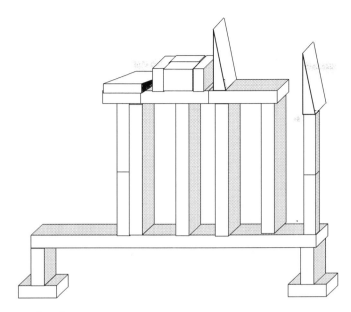

FIGURE 6.2 Kathryn's structure

old paid close attention to the foundation. Figure 6.3 focuses on Kathryn's attention to the foundation. In this figure, you will notice that she had placed unit blocks with their large faces face down. She then placed unit blocks vertically and on top of the faced down blocks. A quadruple block acting as a beam was then placed on top of the vertical unit blocks, thus producing the lower part of her rather intricate structure.

We see, then, that there are parallels between Kathryn's foundational base and that of a foundational base produced by a civil engineer. Figure 6.4 is an analogous raft foundation that would have been erected by a professional engineer as demonstrated by Salvadori (1964, p. 65). So, Kathryn's foundation in Figure 6.3 is similar to that of the engineer's raft foundation in Figure 6.4 depicted by Heller in Salvadori's text. This is because closer inspection of Kathryn's foundation

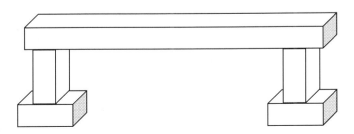

FIGURE 6.3 Kathryn's foundation

148 Thinking Like Architects/Engineers

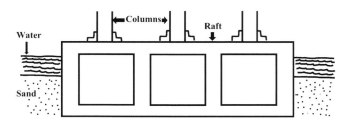

FIGURE 6.4 An engineer's raft foundation

construction reveals basic properties of balance that are essential in the professional engineer's blueprints and eventual construction. The steel girders serving as columns in the engineer's draft of the raft foundation are modeled by blocks when inspecting Kathryn's placement of the unit blocks in vertical fashion on top of horizontally placed unit blocks which serve as the base and also represent the raft in the engineer's drawing.

In this particular case, Salvadori discusses the issue of stability, and how "stability is concerned with the danger of unacceptable motions of the building as a whole" (1964, p. 62). Salvadori uses the example of a tall building that is adversely affected by hurricane wind. If the building is not properly rooted in the ground or balanced by its own weight, there is the possibility of it toppling over. The following is an example of a child's structure that risks toppling over due to heavier weight placed on top of it, thus making it unstable.

Figure 6.5 is an example of Gabe's structure discussed in Chapter 1. Gabe's structure is unstable for at least two reasons. First, and perhaps foremost, his base

FIGURE 6.5 Image of Gabe's structure

lacks any type of firm foundation to support the weight that is above it. Thus, the base, which lacks any firm foundation, creates instability and a greater risk that Gabe's structure will topple over. The second reason for the instability of Gabe's structure, and something we will discuss in greater detail later in this chapter, is that the weight of the upper part of the structure consists of cantilever construction. Now, cantilever construction in and of itself is not something that contributes to instability. But, if there is little to no support in the base of the structure, then a cantilevered structure has a greater possibility of toppling and thus has less resistance to outside forces. Salvadori uses the diagram shown in Figure 6.6 to illustrate the instability of a structure due to wind or some related external force.

Salvadori argues that the building is unstable in rotation. He states that this phenomenon is particularly true of tall and narrow buildings with poor foundations. Salvadori shows this by asking readers to blow on a slim cardboard box resting on a rough surface. As an everyday example, Salvadori mentions the foundational problem of the Leaning Tower of Pisa. The danger of rotational instability is evident, it is not well balanced, and it is supported on soil of uneven settlement. If the soil under a building settles unevenly, the possibility exists that the building will rotate—that is, eventually topple. The Leaning Tower of Pisa is a great example of a building in rotation.

Let us pause for a moment and think about all the events or situations that can lead to the toppling of a structure in the preschool block area. We will then compare these events or situations to what occurs in the everyday goings on in the world of professional architecture and civil engineering. We have already indicated some of the things that threaten the stability of a structure in the preschool. Reflecting on Gabe's structure, we noticed that the lack of a strong foundation can lead to instability. We also noticed that the building of cantilevered construction—especially with a weak base—can lead to a structure toppling over. Additional events that can lead to a preschool structure's instability include, but are not limited to, wind or a strong breeze created when a child runs by the structure, undo pressure exerted on a structure, such as a child pushing down strongly on a structure, or any external forces—that is, forces inside the preschool

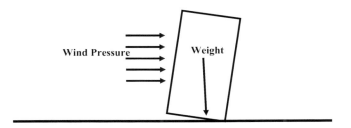

FIGURE 6.6 Instability of a structure due to wind

that may contribute to the structure toppling, such as an outside wind, or even an earthquake whose epicenter is in relatively close proximity to the preschool.

The Architect's and Civil Engineer's Foundations

Let us now consider what events or situations can adversely affect real-life structures designed by architects and built by civil engineers. Some of these things overlap with those that adversely affect structures built by preschoolers. Clearly, strong winds and earthquakes can adversely affect the stability of structures. Very strong winds are what led to the collapse of the Tacoma Narrows Bridge in 1940. Salvadori discusses wind disasters by using a scarf as an example. He states:

> If a scarf is held out of the window of a moving car, it oscillates rapidly up and down. The "flutter" produced by the constant rush of wind on the scarf is called an aerodynamic oscillation. The reader may produce such an oscillation by blowing against the edge of a thin piece of paper.
> *(1964, p. 34)*

He goes on to make the comparison with the Tacoma Narrows Bridge:

> Aerodynamic oscillations were produced by a wind of constant and fairly low velocity blowing for six consecutive hours against the suspension bridge at Tacoma, Washington; the oscillations increased steadily in magnitude, twisting and bending the bridge, until it collapsed.
> *(1964, p. 34)*

So, clearly, wind plays a major role as an event that can pose severe consequences to structures. Salvadori also discusses the devastating nature of earthquakes to structures. He claims:

> Most of the loads applied to architectural structures do not have impact characteristics, except those due to earthquakes. An earthquake is a jerky motion of the ground. This series of randomly variable jerks is transmitted to a building through its foundations, and produces much larger jerky motions of the higher building floors. Inasmuch as earthquakes are unpredictable, and their action on a building depends on the structural characteristics of the building itself, earthquake design is a complex chapter of structural theory. It is only in the last few years that enough information on earthquake motions and on dynamic building characteristics has been gathered to allow safe, simplified calculations based on "equivalent static loads." Tall buildings thus correctly designed have survived earthquakes that destroyed smaller, inadequate buildings.
> *(1964, p. 32)*

Salvadori's position and research regarding earthquakes and structures are clearly analogous to the way we would examine earthquakes, albeit rare, and the structures constructed by preschoolers. So, one way in which professional engineers have extended on young children's VCPO representations of structural foundations is by the process of "lifting" the actual building's foundation above the earth. In other words, engineers draw up plans in which the building is constructed on top of flexible pads that isolate the building's foundation from the ground. In the event of an earthquake, then, only the foundation moves while the building above the foundation remains stable and sound. For easy movement in the event of an earthquake, the flexible pads that isolate the building's foundation are made of steel, rubber, and lead. I mention the importance of steel here because some of the first tall buildings and skyscrapers of the late 19th and early 20th centuries, which were indeed actually smaller than today's skyscrapers, were planned using wrought iron (and not steel) as the material that made up the inner post-and-lintel frame system. Wrought iron is a construction material made by heating iron ore in a furnace and then beating it with a hammer or flattening it with heavy rollers to remove impurities and increase ductility. But because of its relative stiffness, a material's resistance to elastic deformation—that is, the ability to sway and not snap or buckle, wrought iron proved not to be the ideal framing for tall buildings. So steel, an alloy of iron and carbon as well as smaller amounts of manganese and chromium, turned out to be much more ductile than wrought iron, and therefore, more useful for taller structures.

Given the engineering feat of developing and inventing flexible pads that isolate the building's foundation from the actual building structure, one activity that would be useful for young children engaged in constructive free play would be to provide opportunities for them to think about how they would model the base of a building that has a moveable system so that it would allow the structure to remain standing on top of a table when someone shakes the table in a way that the jerky motions of an earthquake would shake the ground beneath us. While this is a very challenging task, it is one in which young children would have to think of alternative possibilities and different variables that might need to be added or taken away—such as substituting metal pieces for wood or plastic brick pieces. While it is most likely that their "movable foundations" will fail under conditions of shaking, it is important to engage children, as we have stated earlier, in activities that accommodate failure as a means of finding alternative possibilities and theories that may lead to solutions.

Beams in Children's VCPO Constructions

We will now examine beams in children's VCPO constructions. What is a beam? Beams are among the most frequently used structural elements. This is as true for the emergent architect and engineer preschooler as it is for the professional architect and engineer. Since the majority of loads are vertical and the majority of usable surfaces are horizontal, beams are used extensively to transfer vertical loads horizontally. What does this all mean? Simple! As people, we are vertical loads in the homes in which we live or the buildings in which we work. Cross beams are what hold the floors in these structures in place; without the crossbeams, we would not have floors on which to walk, sit, recline, or lie down.

In Kathryn's structure (Figure 6.2), the first beam that is situated on the two foundations is a quadruple unit block—the longest block in the typical preschool wood block set. This block serves Kathryn's structure as a simply supported beam. As indicated by Salvadori (1964), a beam is said to be simply supported when it is supported at both ends, so that the ends are free to rotate and the beam itself is free to expand or contract longitudinally. Figure 6.7 is an example of a simply supported beam with pressure being exerted upon it.

Salvadori continues by stating that a simply supported beam transfers a load applied at midspan, half to one support and half to the other. With load placed on it, the beam bends and deflects. The midspan section of the beam moved downward as a result of symmetry, but nevertheless remains horizontal.

Let us now analyze the beams that are located at the top of Kathryn's structure. These three horizontal structural elements are being supported and suspended by five columns. The two beams on the right are simply supported beams. But the one on the left is a cantilevered beam. It is called a cantilevered beam because a cantilever is any structural element that is held in place at one end, usually by a strong wall or column, while the other end hangs in midair without support. In Kathryn's structure, the cantilevered beam is held in place at one end by the top of two columns below the beam and a wedge-shaped block placed above it. The other end of the beam is not supported by anything, thus making it a cantilevered beam.

From a professional architect's and engineer's perspective, Salvadori (1964) uses the example of a thin, steel ruler clamped between a person's fingers at one end. He argues that the length (L) of the cantilever will determine the extent to which the ruler will deflect or bend (d). After applying pressure (p), the deflection of the loaded tip of the cantilevered ruler increases rapidly with the cantilevered length; doubling the length of the cantilevered ruler increases the deflection by a factor of eight, which is the cube of the length's ratio (see Figure 6.8).

It is important to note, however, that deflection rates change based on the type of material used. For example, steel is stronger than aluminum which deflects

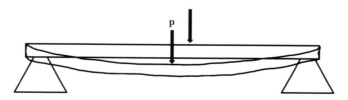

FIGURE 6.7 Simply supported beam with pressure being exerted downward

FIGURE 6.8 The deflection of the loaded tip of the cantilevered ruler

three times as much as steel. On a much smaller scale, Kathryn's cantilever constructions are quite short, and thus have little, if any, deflection, which means that her structure is stable for the most part. But Gabe's tall brick structure, which had several cantilevered bricks, repeatedly fell down because the deflection was greater due to the length of the cantilever on the structure furthest from the floor on which he was building his structure.

The most common example of cantilevered construction in the real world of architecture and engineering is the balcony or terrace that juts out of the building proper. A most exaggerated real-world representation of the cantilevered structure is the so-called Jenga Building, located at 56 Leonard Street in New York City. While it has numerous cantilevers, the Jenga Building remains erect because the building's cantilevers are balanced—that is, there are cantilevers on all four sides of the building—an architectural and engineering feat that allowed for a successful cantilevered structure.

Alejandro and Karl's Pavilion

We move now to Alejandro and Karl's structure—a large complex, and pavilion-like structure that is made up of hundreds of unit blocks, cylindrical blocks, and other wooden block types in the block center. Alejandro begins the structure by taking four cylindrical blocks and places them far enough from each other so that he can place quadruple blocks on them as lintels, thus creating a post-and-lintel structure. Figure 6.9 demonstrates what Alejandro created initially as a post-and-lintel structure.

He then continues to use quadruple blocks as slats, placed on the top and flush together, thus resembling a first level of a multilevel building (See Figure 6.10). Karl comes along and notices what Alejandro is building. Karl starts to build a very similar structure on the floor in very close proximity to Alejandro. Karl suggests to Alejandro that they could build the structure together. Alejandro agrees, and so he takes apart his structure and works together with Karl. They initially come up with the structure seen in Figure 6.10.

What Alejandro and Karl created is a structure that is extremely similar to that of a professional architect or civil engineer. Salvadori states that ever since the earliest time in human history, the problem of sheltering human beings from the weather and the outside elements in general has been solved by the building of an

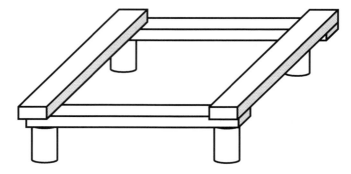

FIGURE 6.9 Alejandro's structural base

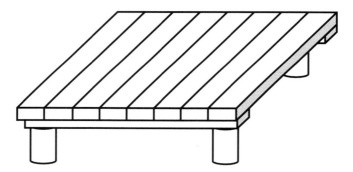

FIGURE 6.10 The second level to Alejandro's structure

enclosure of walls topped off by a roof. In prehistoric times, the walls and roof were made of stone without any distinction between the supporting structure and the protecting "skin." A separation of the supporting and protecting functions leads to the simplest "framed" system: the post-and-lintel or post-and-beam system (see Figure 6.11). Salvadori defined lintel and posts as follows:

> The lintel is a beam simply supported on the posts, and carrying the roof load. The posts are vertical struts compressed by the lintel. The posts must also resist some horizontal loads, such as wind pressure; this resistance comes from a bending capacity in the case of wooden or steel posts, from their own weight in stone or masonry piers. Some connection between post and lintel must also be provided, lest the wind blow the roof away.

As Salvadori points out, the foundations of the posts carry the roof and post loads to the ground by means of footings which spread the load and guarantee that soil deflections are limited. The posts and the foundations are essentially under compression, and this is typical of the post-and-lintel system.

Thinking Like Architects/Engineers 155

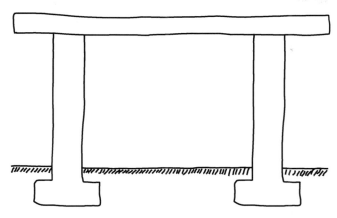

FIGURE 6.11 The post-and-lintel foundation system: the "simplest framed system"
Source: Salvadori, 1964, p. 168.

Returning to Alejandro and Karl's structure, it is important to note that the boys create a post-and-lintel system as a means of supporting more levels, and thus, more blocks. In the Space-Architecture Coding System (SPARC) coding system that will be introduced in the next chapter, I refer to post-and-lintel or post-and-beam systems as trabeated construction—which means structures that are constructed of horizontal beams instead of arches. A visiting professor of architecture was invited to view my video recordings of four- and five-year-old children during constructive free play and concluded, as I indicate in the next chapter, that the structural design of Alejandro and Karl's structure parallels that of the professional architect's blueprint for the framing systems of most buildings—again, more evidence that suggests the particularly similar relationship between the planning and constructions of STEAM professionals and young children's VCPO constructions.

We notice something very interesting in what happens next in Alejandro and Karl's structure: the boys initially notice that they can cover the sides of their structure, namely, the walls. They do this by taking 12 quadruple blocks and placing three on each side of the structure so that each wall is built. Prior to the process of walling their structure, a fascinating mathematical discussion took place. After Alejandro agreed to put walls on all four sides, he said, "Okay, we're gonna need 8 …" When I show my students this discussion, they are amazed at how spontaneously Alejandro did informal multiplication during block play. He intuitively knew that square or rectangular structures have four sides, and he thought that each side would need two quadruple blocks to cover it—even though the boys actually needed three for each side, or 12 quadruple blocks altogether.

In the previous chapter, we emphasized the importance of observing young children in their everyday environment during free play because we can learn so much in terms of what Vygotsky calls their everyday, spontaneous concepts. But we also stated that observing is not enough; we must also record our observations of what they are doing, and it is perhaps best to focus on one child at a time.

The moment when Alejandro said "We're gonna need 8 ..." is an ideal example that supports the importance of observing and recording observations for at least three reasons. First, it demonstrates evidence that young children do mathematical activities in their informal, everyday environments. This is important because even with all the research that now supports the finding that young children not only think mathematically but also invent their own strategies for solving mathematical and other STEAM related problems, there are still many preschool, elementary school, and secondary school practitioners who either don't know, or don't want to believe that mathematical thinking is part of the everyday life of the young child before the start of formal schooling and instruction. The goal of STEAM researchers, then, is to put STEAM research into practice by convincing preschool and elementary school teachers, administrators and parents of the importance of informal STEAM behaviors of young children.

Second, Alejandro's "We're gonna need 8 ..." example provides the opportunity for both teachers and parents to think about how young children process STEAM concepts. When I show this and other excerpts of children engaged in STEAM constructive play activities to my undergraduate and graduate students, I ask them to hypothesize in an introspective manner what the child was thinking based on the events and actions that occurred on the digital excerpt. In class, my students and I discuss the "We're gonna need 8 ..." example to see what led Alejandro to the point where he makes that utterance. As we engage in discussion, many ideas come up. My students come to the conclusion, for example, that early childhood experiences with constructive play objects and familiarity with the appearance of buildings—that they generally have four sides—led Alejandro to decide that four sides need to be covered. They also hypothesized that Alejandro was involved in informal measurement ideas—that one horizontal quadruple block would not be enough to cover each of the four sides of their structure. And that might be the reason why Alejandro did not say that they needed four quadruple blocks, that is, one for each side. Instead, his informal measurement ideas suggested to him that there needed to be two quadruple blocks for each side. My students' observations support research that shows the emergence of ideas of measurement very early in the child's life (Milburn, Lonigan, DeFlorio & Klein, 2019).

And third, while it is very important to recognize and appreciate young children's spontaneous STEAM ideas, it is simply not enough to recognize, observe, and record these traits. It is crucial to realizing the importance of everyday STEAM thinking that the teacher picks up on these spontaneous, informal ideas and relates them to the formal concepts that will be essential for further STEAM learning. Alejandro's "We're gonna need 8 ..." statement displays his informal, emergent knowledge of multiplication, which the teacher can then develop. While impressive for the observer and listener, Alejandro's statement is not unique in the sense that all children use invented, mostly verbal strategies to solve problems in their everyday world. This gives all the more reason for first-, second-, third-, and fourth-grade teachers to begin identifying and recognizing their students' informal and often out-of-school knowledge in which they often invent their own strategies and connect this knowledge to the structured, formal concepts that are essential for success in STEAM in the later grades. Vygotsky's theory of concept development supports the link between children's spontaneous concepts that they acquire outside school with what he calls scientific concepts, which are those concepts that are conventionally systematic in that they have been formalized for more advanced thinking in a particular academic domain (Hedegaard, 2007).

Also of note is the extent to which the blocks above, on higher levels, are causing stress, due to their weight, on the base—which we mentioned above was constructed of four cylindrical blocks (as corners of a square) and quadruple unit blocks in the form of crossbeams. Engineers and physical scientists refer to a base like the one constructed by Alejandro and Karl as being in a state of compression, which, as we learned in Chapter 1, is an internal force that causes a structural element—the four cylindrical blocks supporting Alejandro and Karl's structure—to shorten. While the quadruple unit blocks acting like crossbeams are holding a good deal of downward force from the heavy blocks above, they are actually in a state of tension as the downward force is causing the quadruple block to stretch ever so slightly. Salvadori sums up tension and compression succinctly, and does so in a manner that will help early childhood practitioners and parents explain the concepts formally to young students. He writes:

> We cannot always put our arm where the structure is and "feel" [the] forces [of tension and compression], but it is still quite easy to recognize them. Take a thin rubber band and pull it with your hands. You are putting the rubber band in tension and the band becomes longer ... You now know that whenever a part of a structure becomes longer it is in tension. Take a rubber sponge and push on it: the sponge becomes shorter in the direction in which you push. Whenever a part of a structure becomes shorter, it is in compression ...
>
> *(1990, p. 13)*

Going back to Alejandro and Karl's structure, now that the structure contains four walls, the boys go on to do something equally fascinating: they build a second floor to their original structure. Their method of building a second floor is, again, an analogue to what the professional architect or engineer would do: they take an additional four cylindrical blocks and place them directly above the locations of the original four cylindrical blocks. Figure 6.12 shows Alejandro and Karl's structure up to this point. A new pair of horizontal lintels are placed on top of the two pairs of cylindrical blocks as shown in Figure 6.12.

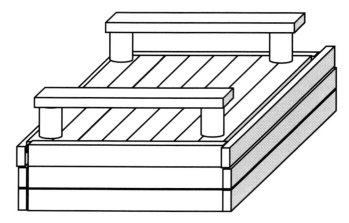

FIGURE 6.12 Alejandro and Karl's structure with a second floor construction

From the perspective of the professional architect and civil engineer, post-and-lintel, or trabeated, systems may be built one on top of another to frame multistory buildings. In this case, the lintels are supported by vertical columns, or walls of stone or masonry as high as the entire building as seen in Figure 6.13. In terms of the post-and-lintel support, the parallel activity that took place in Alejandro and Karl's construction was the use of the quadruple blocks to serve as walls of the structure. In terms of the construction of actual buildings, construction of this kind, while capable of carrying vertical loads, is not well suited to resist horizontal loads, and is easily damaged by hurricane winds and earthquakes because masonry or stone elements have little bending resistance, and therefore a strong connection between the horizontal and the vertical structural elements is not easily developed.

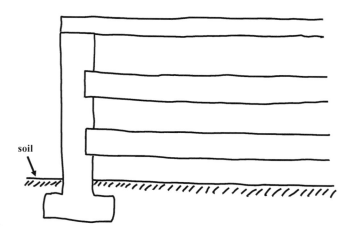

FIGURE 6.13 Lintels are supported by vertical columns

Salvadori discusses the development of floor systems. He states that the framed structure that encloses the inner space defined by the post-and-lintel frame will need to be covered by a "skin," which he defines as walls and ceilings. Salvadori asserts:

> The columns and beams of a framed structure are its resisting "skeleton." In order to enclose the space defined by the skeleton and to make it usable, the exterior of the building is covered with a "skin" and the floor areas are spanned by horizontal floor systems. The skin of modern buildings is often made of metal or concrete or glass, and called a curtain wall. The floor structure consists of long-span beams connecting the main frames, of secondary beams or joists spanning the distance between the main beams, and of slabs of concrete or steel decks, spanning the distance between the secondary beams ...
>
> *(1964, p. 185)*

This description of floor systems of the professional architect or engineer is consistent with the unfolding of Alejandro and Karl's structure and how they developed additional floors from quadruple unit blocks, similar to manner in which wooden floors in homes and buildings are laid on the floor skeleton.

The structure that Alejandro and Karl built collaboratively turned out to be a huge accomplishment that entailed the use of many emergent and informal STEAM concepts. Toward the end, Alejandro and Karl stated that they needed to construct a garage for cars. The structure had three levels and all of the sides were covered with blocks that acted as the walls of the building. The activity required the use of almost all of the preschool's wooden play blocks, so other children were obliged to join in with Alejandro and Karl's construction activity if they wished to continue to participate in a construction activity.

In this excerpt we witnessed evidence that young children's block structures are, by their very nature, conceptual representations of real-life constructions that are planned and developed by professional architects and engineers. They can be seen as blueprints of the architect's blueprints because they are founded on the very same principles that are followed by STEAM professionals.

Anna's Plank Structure

We now examine one of the most detailed and precise of structures—and that is Anna's plank structure. There are two reasons why Anna's structure is so detailed: Anna's age—she is nine years older than the preschoolers whose structures we examined in the previous pages (and chapters)—and the fact that she is using Kapla planks as a form of constructive play material (i.e., VCPO). Anna is 13 years' old—quite a bit older than the preschoolers we studied earlier. But that fact gives us all the more reason to study children's VCPO activities at all age levels.

Studying pre-adolescent and adolescent children's VCPO constructions is instructive for several reasons. First, it gives us a sense of what they can construct—given that they are almost entirely alienated from VCPOs after their childhood years as a result of following rigid curriculum frameworks that teachers of all grade levels are often obligated to follow. Teachers are often expected to adhere to rigid guidelines that prevent older children and pre-adolescents from demonstrating their creativity and precocity when it comes to constructing and synthesizing new structures.

Second, more often than not, older children and adolescents possess a certain level of precision that might not be found among younger children. They often pay closer attention to a structure's foundation, ensuring that the structure doesn't collapse. Their greater attention to detail, given the correlation between physiological changes and differences in motor development, allows older children and pre-adolescents to focus more attention on the finer elements related to various architectural and engineering topics that we have discussed thus far in this book. For example, while young children possess an intuitive knowledge of balance and gravity, older children will often plan ahead when they are thinking of including a cantilever in their structure. That is, they might not be as haphazard as many younger children in their placement of specific VCPO pieces when engaged in the construction of cantilevers. Or they might plan a larger foundation to support the upper parts of the structure.

Moreover, older and pre-adolescent children can use VCPOs as a way to model something they are doing in school that is related to STEAM. As we have seen in Chapter 3, older students and adults might use Tinkertoys, generic bricks, or Meccano sets to develop models of real-life scientific and other STEAM related phenomena. For example, generic bricks, if manipulated in an organized manner, can be useful in representing chemical compounds. This can be done particularly well by identifying each element in the compound with a particular color or a particular size. We have also seen older children participate in VCPO activities that enable the individual to create structures that can be used to model technological devices, and, in some cases, deliver results when input is given to them—as we mentioned with Danny Hillis's creation of such a device using Tinkertoys.

There is some research that examines adolescents' involvement in block play. Casey, Pezaris, and Bassi (2012) examined the role of block play in terms of gender, and found that girls construct with blocks in a different manner from boys—a similar outcome to Erikson's (1951, 1963) classic studies of gender and block play. Casey et al. (2012) found that boys performed better than girls in block building skills and structural balance and learned that structural balance is a key element that not only differentiates girls from boys, but also may serve as a contributing factor for predicting mathematics achievement. Kato and Morita (2009) found similar results among adolescent girls and boys in Japan.

As I mentioned above, Anna uses Kapla planks for her construction. She starts off by taking two planks and placing them adjacent to one another so that they are touching along the long side. She does this until she has taken four pairs of planks and placed each of the eight planks adjacent to one another. She then repeats this pattern which produces another set of eight planks that are adjacent to one another. The second set of eight planks are then moved so that the short (i.e., width) sides of this group are made contiguous with the short sides of the initial group of eight planks. We can say that the group of 16 touching planks serve as a foundation for a larger structure that is intended to be built (see Figure 6.14).

It is important to recognize the significance of the foundation when examining young and older children's VCPO constructions and also when comparing them to the blueprint of professional architects and engineers. As architects and engineers have always affirmed, the strength and durability of a structure lies in its foundation. Clearly, the main purpose of the foundation is to hold the structure above it and make sure it does not topple and remains erect. On the other hand, a poorly constructed foundation—or even a lack of a foundation—can be dangerous to the occupants of the structure. With more and more high-rise structures being built, it is essential that they possess strong foundations (Macaulay, 2000; Salvadori, 1990). Thus, it is extremely important to evaluate the quality of construction of a structure with regard to foundation.

What is the purpose of having a solid foundation? A foundation is important for a structure in at least three ways. First, the foundation is essential because it supports the load of the entire building, bridge, tower, or related construction. All structures have loads. So, in order to support those loads, foundations serve the purpose of ensuring that loads have no problem in terms of occupancy or movement within or across the structure. Second, a solid and strong foundation keeps the building or other structure erect while the forces of nature—strong winds, earth tremors, and the like—are displayed in full force. Well-built foundations keep the occupants and loads of a building or bridge safe during adverse situations such as earthquakes, floods, or strong winds. And third, a strong foundation is essential because it is built in such a way that it keeps the ground moisture from seeping in and ruining the structure.

According to professional architects and engineers, a foundation must be able to withstand both dead loads and live loads. As indicated earlier, the dead load refers to the weight of the entire structure. The structure is the dead load because it remains constant. In contrast, the live load refers to the weight of the people

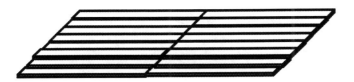

FIGURE 6.14 Anna's plank foundation

162 Thinking Like Architects/Engineers

and any objects that they take with them inside or on the structure. In buildings, these objects could be furniture or appliances. On bridges, these objects could be cars, bicycles, trucks, buses, or motorcycles. The foundation, then, must be firm and able to channel the weight of the entire building or other structure to the ground.

In the same manner, both young and older children's VCPO constructions are stronger when they have firm and strong foundations. This is certainly the case with Anna's structure. After creating her foundation, Anna attempts to create sides or borders along her foundation by placing planks along two of the edges of the foundation. In attempting to create a boundary along the entire length of one of the edges of the foundation, Anna falls a bit short. Two of the planks that serve as boundaries do not stretch the entire length of the edge; there is a small section that is not bounded. In order to cover the edge completely, Anna moves the two planks serving as boundaries ever so slightly to the right (See Figure 6.15).

What happens next is even more fascinating. Anna starts to build with more complexity by placing planks, laying flat, on the side edges. But she does so in such a way that each plank is situated on top of another plank in cantilever style—that is, each plank is placed not directly on top of another plank, but ever so slightly off, such that the other end of each plank juts out, thus creating the cantilever quality (see Figure 6.16). In total, there are seven planks on the left-hand side that serve as part of the cantilevered component of the structure.

Anna continues her construction by making a planked wall on the rear side of the structure. After that is completed, she seemed to want her structure to have a sense of symmetric balance. To achieve this, Anna decided to replicate the cantilevered component that she constructed on the left-hand side, and place the replicated set of seven planks on the right-hand side, thus, from an aesthetic standpoint, creating a balanced atmosphere (see Figure 6.17).

But the sense of balance is a bit short-lived in that Anna creates an asymmetry in the inner space of the structure. Shortly after she set the replicated group of cantilevered planks on the right-hand side, Anna started to stack planks in groups of six. She made six sets of a group of six planks and arranged them by placing two sets adjacent and somewhat flush to the left-hand side. She continued to place another two sets in an adjacent manner slightly to the right of the other two.

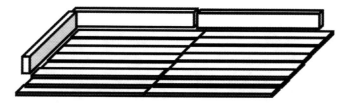

FIGURE 6.15 Border construction using planks

Thinking Like Architects/Engineers   163

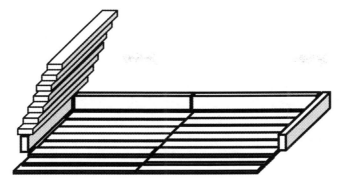

FIGURE 6.16 Anna's use of planks to construct cantilevers

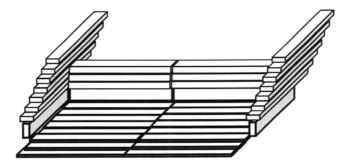

FIGURE 6.17 Anna's cantilevered structure in progress

As the construction unfolded, it seemed as if Anna wanted to use these four sets of stacks as a platform for a higher, more elaborate, level. As she constructed the higher level, she decided to place two groups of three planks in a flat position on top of the stacked sets. Anna then placed four planks fairly equidistant from each other on top of the two groups of three planks, but these four planks were placed in a way that the narrow side of each plank was facing down. Next, she placed one plank, wide side facing down, on top of the four planks in a perpendicular manner. To finish, she placed the final two sets of six-grouped stacks closer to the right-hand side of the structure (see Figure 6.18). In the final stages of her construction, Anna's structure had a great deal of resemblance to a Frank Lloyd Wright model of one of his home designs.

The structure that Anna constructed clearly reveals more precision in placement of VCPOs than that of most preschool aged children. Her mind seemed immersed in the project to the extent that she demonstrated motivation in completing the structure. The progression from creating the flat foundation to the construction of the borders, and then to the building of the cantilevered sides showed that Anna's structure followed most of the basic tenets of

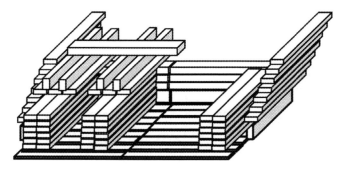

FIGURE 6.18 Anna's nearly completed structure

architectural and engineering thinking. Moreover, her structure upholds the principle of equilibrium, which is, perhaps, the most important concept of all in engineering mechanics. First formulated by the Flemish mathematician, Simon Stevin in 1586, the most well-known form of equilibrium is Isaac Newton's first law of motion, which states that an object at rest remains at rest unless acted on by an unbalanced force. In short, equilibrium is a condition in which all forces acting on a body are in balance. Anna's structure shows how the forces on her structure are in balance. The sheer creativity of Anna's construction and the balance of the cantilevers demonstrates the importance of considering children's VCPO constructions when developing school STEAM curricula.

Conclusion

In this chapter, we investigated the research literature that deals with engineering and block and brick play. It was concluded that this literature is sorely overdue. Early STEM initiatives in the 1990s and 2000s advocated for more emphasis on science, technology, engineering, and mathematics. But technology and engineering education in the schools were meager at best. Moreover, research in STEM seemed to focus much more on the development of mathematical and scientific thinking and not so much, if at all, on engineering thinking. And as for the development of architectural thinking, to my knowledge, with the exception of using naturalistic observation methodology to observe and listen to preschool children during constructive free play, there is little, if any, work devoted to this area. We also examined the development of block and brick play from infancy to the period before Kindergarten. Based on examination of researchers who have studied the developmental progression of events that take place along the trajectory of block construction, I have developed a generalizable model that summarizes the course that toddlers and young children take—from placing side by side, to piling, to stacking, to the building of rows and piles, and, eventually, to the development of the cognition of enclosure, which serves as the starting point for the development of levels of complexity in structure.

And finally, we investigated young children's VCPO constructions through the lens of professional architects and engineers and some of the basic principles that undergird architecture and engineering. My hope is that by placing the development of individual block, brick, or plank constructions side by side with the basic architectural and engineering principles explained carefully by Mario Salvadori, the reader will be more convinced that young children's constructions are by no means trivial activities; on the contrary, children who engage in constructive free play experience scientific principles first hand when part of a structure collapses and needs to be rebuilt, or when a VCPO constructed building is unable to fit toy cars and the child needs to readjust the structure in order for toy cars to go in. In the next chapter, we will examine the Space-Architecture Coding system (henceforth, SPARC, formerly SPAGAR) that has been developed in order to measure the types of spatial, architectural, and engineering thinking activities in which the young child plays an active role in the everyday context.

References

Adams, R., Evangelou, D., English, L., Figueiredo, A. D., Mousoulides, N., Pawley, A. L., & Wilson, D. M. (2011). Multiple perspectives on engaging future engineers. *Journal of Engineering Education*, 100(1), 48–88.

Bailey, M. (1933). A scale of block constructions for young children. *Child Development*, 4 (2), 121–139.

Bairaktarova, D., Evangelou, D., Bagiati, A., & Brophy, S. (2011). Early engineering in young children's exploratory play with tangible materials. *Children Youth and Environments*, 21(2), 212–235.

Balsters, J. H., Whelan, C. D., Robertson, I. H., & Ramnani, N. (2013). Cerebellum and cognition: evidence for the encoding of higher order rules. *Cerebral Cortex*, 23(6), 1433–1443.

Bloom, B., & Krathwohl, D. (1956) *Taxonomy of educational objectives: Handbook I, The cognitive domain*. New York: David McKay & Company.

Bodnar, C. A., Anastasio, D., Enszer, J. A., & Burkey, D. D. (2016). Engineers at play: Games as teaching tools for undergraduate engineering students. *Journal of Engineering Education*, 105(1), 147–200.

Brosterman, N. (1997). *Inventing Kindergarten*. New York: Harry N. Abrams, Inc., Publishers.

Casey, B. M., Pezaris, E. E., & Bassi, J. (2012). Adolescent boys' and girls' block constructions differ in structural balance: A block-building characteristic related to math achievement. *Learning and Individual Differences*, 22, 25–36.

Erikson, E. H. (1951) Sex differences in the play configurations of preadolescents. *The American Journal of Orthopsychiatry*, 21, 667–692.

Erikson, E. H. (1963). *Childhood and society* (2nd ed.). New York: Norton.

Evangelou, D. (2010). Why STEM now? Guest editorial: Child development perspectives in engineering education. *Early Childhood Research and Practice*, 12(2), 1–4.

Fleer, M. (2018). Conceptual Playworlds: The role of imagination in play and learning. *Early Years*. doi:10.1080/09575146.2018.1549024.

Fleer, M. (2020). Engineering PlayWorld—a model of practice to support children to collectively design, imagine and think using engineering concepts. *Research in Science Education*, 1–16. https://doi.org/10.1007/s11165-020-09970-6.

Gadzikowski, A. (2021). *Young architects at play: STEM activities for young children*. St. Paul, MN: Redleaf Press.

Gerber, A., Berkowitz, M., Emo, B., Kurath, S., Hölscher, C., & Stern, E. (2019). Does space matter?: A cross-disciplinary investigation upon spatial abilities of architects. In C. Leopold, C. Robeller, & U. Weber (Eds.), *Research culture in architecture* (pp. 289–300). Basel, Switzerland: Birkhäuser Verlag.

Ginoulhiac, M. (2018, July 13). *Architectural toys: The construction of an education*. 8th International Toy Research Association World Conference, International Toy Research Association (ITRA), Paris.

Ginsburg, H. P., & Ertle, B. B. (2016). Giving away early mathematics: Big Math for Little Kids encounters the complex world of early education. In K. Durkin & H. R. Schaffer (Eds.), *Wiley handbook of developmental psychology in practice: Implementation and impact* (pp. 222–263). Oxford: Wiley.

Ginsburg, H. P., Inoue, N., & Seo, K. H. (1999). Young children doing mathematics: Observations of everyday activities. In J. V. Copley (Ed.), *Mathematics in the early years* (pp. 88–99). Reston, VA: National Council of Teachers of Mathematics.

Ginsburg, H. P., Lin, C. L., Ness, D., & Seo, K. H. (2003). Young American and Chinese children's everyday mathematical activity. *Mathematical Thinking and Learning*, 5(4), 235–258.

Ginsburg, H. P., Pappas, S., & Seo, K. H. (2001). Everyday mathematical knowledge: Asking young children what is developmentally appropriate. In S. L. Golbeck (Ed.), *Psychological perspectives on early childhood education: Reframing dilemmas in research and practice* (pp. 181–219). Mahwah, NJ: Lawrence Erlbaum Associates.

Gold, Z. S., & Elicker, J. (2020). Engineering peer play: A new perspective on science, technology, engineering, and mathematics (STEM) early childhood education. In A. Ridgeway, G. Quiñones, & L. Li (Eds.), *Peer play and development in early childhood: International research narratives*. New York, NY: Springer.

Gold, Z. S., Elicker, J., Choi, J. Y., Anderson, T., & Brophy, S. P. (2015). Preschoolers' engineering play behaviors: Differences in gender and play context. *Children, Youth and Environments*, 25(3), 1–21.

Gold, Z. S., Elicker, J., Kellerman, A. M., Christ, S., Mishra, A. A., & Howe, N. (2021). Engineering play, mathematics, and spatial skills in children with and without disabilities. *Early Education and Development*, 32(1), 49–65.

Gregory, M. K., Whiren, A. (2003). The effect of verbal scaffolding on the complexity of preschool children's block constructions. In D. Lytle (Ed.), *Play and educational theory and practice* (pp. 118–133). Westport, CT: Praeger.

Hedegaard, M. (2007). The development of children's conceptual relation to the world, with focus on concept formation in preschool children's activity. In H. Daniels, M. Cole, & J. V. Wertsch (Eds.), *The Cambridge companion to Vygotsky* (pp. 246–275). New York: Cambridge University Press.

Hedegaard M. (2008). The educational experiment. In M. Hedegaard, & M. Fleer (Eds.), *Studying children: A cultural historical perspective* (pp. 181–201). New York, NY: Open University Press.

Hedegaard, M. (2014). The significance of demands and motives across practices in children's learning and development: An analysis of learning in home and school. *Learning, Culture and Social Interaction*, 3(3), 188–194.

Hirsch, E. S. (1996). *The block book*. Washington, DC: National Association for the Education of Young Children.

Kato, D., & Morita, M. (2009). Form, content, and gender differences in Lego® block creations by Japanese adolescents. *Art Therapy*, 26(4), 181–186.

Kothmann, B. (2019). Exploration: Play in engineering education. In A. James & C. Nerantzi (Eds.), *The power of play in higher education* (pp. 131–140). New York: Palgrave Macmillan.

Lange, A. (2018). *The design of childhood: How the material world shapes independent kids*. New York: Bloomsbury.

Leiner, H. C., Leiner, A. L., & Dow, R. S. (1986). Does the cerebellum contribute to mental skills? *Behavioral Neuroscience*, 100, 443–454.

Lincoln, Y. S., & Guba, E. G. (1985). *Naturalistic inquiry*. Beverly Hills, CA: Sage.

Locke, J. (1989 [1695]). *Some thoughts concerning education* (3rd ed.). London: Oxford University Press.

Macaulay, D. (2000). *Building big*. Boston, MA: Houghton Mifflin.

Milburn, T. F., Lonigan, C. J., DeFlorio, L., & Klein, A. (2019). Dimensionality of preschoolers' informal mathematical abilities. *Early Childhood Research Quarterly*, 47, 487–495.

Ness, D. (2001). The development of spatial thinking, emergent geometric concepts and architectural principles in the everyday context. Doctoral dissertation, Columbia University, New York.

Ness, D., & Farenga, S. J. (2007). *Knowledge under construction: The importance of play in developing children's spatial and geometric thinking*. Lanham, MD: Rowman & Littlefield Publishers.

Ness, D., & Farenga, S. J. (2016). Blocks, bricks, and planks: Relationships between affordance and visuo-spatial constructive play objects. *American Journal of Play*, 8(2), 201–227.

Ness, D., Farenga, S. J., & Garofalo, S. G. (2017). *Spatial intelligence: Why it matters from birth through the lifespan*. New York: Routledge.

Park, Y., Brösamle, M., & Hölscher, C. (2020). The function of gesture in architectural-design-related spatial ability. In J. Škilters, N. S. Newcombe, & , D. Uttal (Eds.), *Spatial Cognition XII: German Conference on Spatial Cognition* (pp. 309–321). Berlin: Springer.

Piaget, J., & Inhelder, B. (1963). *The child's conception of space* (F. J. Langdon & J. L. Lunzer, Trans.). London: Routledge & Kegan Paul.

Provenzo, E. F., & Brett, A. (1983). *The complete block book*. Syracuse, NY: Syracuse University Press.

Reifel, S. (1981). An exploration of block play as symbolic representation. Doctoral dissertation, University of California, Los Angeles.

Reifel, S. (1984). Block construction: Children's developmental landmarks in representation of space. *Young Children*, 40(1), 61–67.

Reifel, S., & Greenfield, P. M. (1982). Structural development in a symbolic medium: The representational use of block constructions. In G. Forman (Ed.), *Action and thought: From sensorimotor schemes to symbolic operations* (pp. 203–232). New York, NY: Academic Press.

Reifel, S., & Greenfield, P. M. (1983). Part-whole relations: Some structural features of children's representational block play. *Child Care Quarterly*, 12(1), 144–151.

Salvadori, M. (1964). *Structure in architecture*. Englewood Cliffs, NJ: Prentice-Hall.

Salvadori, M. (1980). *Why buildings stand up: The strength of architecture*. New York: Norton.

Salvadori, M. (1990). *The art of construction: Projects and principles for beginning engineers and architects*. Chicago, IL: Chicago Review Press.

Schunn, C. D., & Silk, E. M. (2011). Learning theories for engineering and technology education. In M. Barak & M. Hacker (Eds.), *Fostering human development through engineering and technology education* (pp. 3–18). Rotterdam, the Netherlands: Sense Publishers.

Stiles, J., & Stern, C. (2001). Developmental change in spatial cognitive processing: Complexity effects and block construction performance in preschool children. *Journal of Cognition and Development*, 2(2), 157–187. doi:10.1207/S15327647JCD0202_3.

Swan, C. (2014, November 26). The perils of modern Lego. Chris Swan's Weblog. https://blog.thestateofme.com/2013/01/01/the-perils-of-modern-lego.

Tian, M., Luo, T., & Cheung, H. (2020). The development and measurement of block construction in early childhood: A review. *Journal of Psychoeducational Assessment*, 38(6), 767–782.

Trawick-Smith, J., Swaminathan, S., Baton, B., Danieluk, C., Marsh, S., & Szarwacki, M. (2017). Block play and mathematics learning in preschool: The effects of building complexity, peer and teacher interactions in the block area, and replica play materials. *Journal of Early Childhood Research*, 15(4), 433–448.

Vandervert, L. (2017). Vygotsky meets neuroscience: The cerebellum and the rise of culture through play. *American Journal of Play*, 9(2), 202–227.

Vygotsky, L. S. (1986 [1934]). *Thought and language* (A. Kozulin, Trans.). Cambridge, MA: MIT Press.

Zinguer, T. (2015). *Architecture in play: Intimations of modernism in architectural toys*. Charlottesville, VA: University of Virginia Press.

7
CODING STEAM DURING CONSTRUCTIVE FREE PLAY

Now that we have a conceptual model of what children can do with VCPOs, it is possible to classify the types of VCPO activities children engage in. The main objective of the present chapter, then, is to consider and examine the Spatial Architectural Coding (SPARC) system (formerly SPAGAR; see Ness & Farenga, 2007). Researchers, practitioners, and even parents will find SPARC useful. Researchers will be able to use SPARC as a means of developing knowledge concerning young children's spatial development in particular domains. Practitioners will have the opportunity to implement SPARC as a way to understand their young students' propensities in emergent STEAM disciplines.

Recent research in spatial cognition has demonstrated that spatial thinking skill is both an essential process in student success in science, technology, engineering, arts (and architecture), and mathematics (STEAM) subjects (Ness, Farenga & Garofalo, 2017; Uttal & Cohen, 2012; Uttal, Miller & Newcombe, 2013) and overall success in the workforce (Kell & Lubinski, 2013; Khine, 2017). Given its strong relationship with the STEAM disciplines, spatial thinking skill is seen as a crosscutting domain that traverses and overlaps several intellectual fields of inquiry (Ness & Farenga, 2016; Newcombe, Uttal & Sauter, 2013).

But, what should be implemented in terms of spatial tasks, if any, to foster young children's spatial propensities? Should early childhood professionals avoid tasks altogether, and simply get children to engage in play? The consensus among early childhood practitioners is that some forms of guided practice or outright teaching is necessary in order to develop their emergent STEAM related knowledge. In this regard, should preschool children be limited to the typical mathematical or science related content, which usually consists of counting to ten or higher, learning basic geometric shapes, the notion of balance and symmetry, or the basic knowledge of classification?

DOI: 10.4324/9781003097815-8

For preschool children, guided instruction or outright teaching greatly undermines their potential in demonstrating not only their mathematical or scientific propensities but also evidence of their potentially powerful spatial thinking (Ginsburg, Pappas & Seo, 2001). There is strong evidence that young children have the potential to engage in a much more robust, dynamic curriculum than the typical "teaching" environments to which they are often exposed. Moreover, research has shown that preschoolers and Kindergarten children benefit greatly from active engagement in a conceptual STEAM curriculum (Andersson & Gullberg, 2014; Ginsburg, Inoue & Seo, 1999; Sarama & Clements, 2009). Equally as important as an active and dynamic STEAM content curriculum is a strong foundation in the crosscutting process of spatial thinking as this has been shown to be an essential skill in most STEAM related areas (Jee et al., 2014).

In this chapter, we will examine the content and role of spatial thinking in young children's free play as it relates to STEAM education. Indeed, as we have stressed throughout this book, an important conduit for examining the emergence of spatial cognition in children is constructive free play, namely, as they engage in activities involving blocks, bricks, planks, and related constructive play materials. The purpose of this chapter, then, is to examine and describe key findings associated with young children's emergent spatial skills, which indicate that during their constructive free play time young children engage in numerous types of spatial tasks, many of which have a high level of complexity, which is defined by the type of spatial task involved and the time engaged in that specific task (Trawick-Smith et al., 2017).

The various types of STEAM related spatial thinking categories identified herein have, for the most part, been unnoticed by educational practitioners for at least two reasons. First, unlike content skills (such as mathematics or language arts) and other process skills (such as problem solving and communication) spatial thinking has historically been a process that was ignored in the preschool and K-12 curriculum (Atit, Miller, Newcombe & Uttal, 2018). With the possible exception of the second edition of *Geography for Life: National Geography Standards*, the National Council for Geographic Education (NCGE), which revised its standards to emphasize the need to include spatial thinking as an essential topic in the geography curriculum (NCGE, 2012), the Next Generation Science Standards as well as the Common Core Standards in mathematics seem to have sidestepped the topic of spatial thinking skills. And second, given the complex nature of several spatial skill categories, practitioners and curriculum writers often consider it too early or "developmentally inappropriate" to teach these skills when in fact they have been shown to be evident in children's constructive free play (Ness & Farenga, 2007; Pritulsky et al., 2020).

Definition, Background, and Questions

Spatial thinking is a seminal skill that serves as a prerequisite in numerous STEAM related areas of inquiry—geology, biology, chemistry, physics, geography, engineering, architecture, geometry, and algebra are just a few of the many examples (Hsi, Linn & Bell, 1997; McGarvey, Luo, Hawes & Spatial Reasoning Study Group, 2018; NRC, 2006; Newcombe & Shipley, 2015; Uttal & Cohen, 2012; Uttal, et. al., 2013; Uttal, Miller, & Newcombe, 2013). Newcombe (2010) defines spatial thinking as an ability that "concerns the locations of objects, their shapes, their relations to each other, and the paths they take as they move" (p. 30). My colleagues and I have extended Newcombe's definition by adding that spatial thinking is "one's ability to perceive, recognize, or conceptualize physical or intellectual constructs in terms of their position or location in both static and dynamic systems" (Ness, Farenga & Garofalo, 2017, p. 10). What these two definitions have in common is the idea that spatial thinking involves one's interpretation and representation of space and constructs within it as well as its significance in STEAM disciplines. Examples of spatial thinking skill sets include, but are not limited to, conceptualizing space, using tools of representation, reasoning and proving, problem finding, problem solving, visualizing relationships, analyzing static and dynamic systems of objects, observing how objects behave in their environment, recognizing the relationship between two- and three-dimensional constructs, and differentiating between Euclidean space and other geometric models.

Spatial thinking and the development of complex spatial structures in the everyday context of constructive free play is common during the preschool years. Based on prior investigations of spatial cognition in the everyday context, no significant differences were found among preschool children in enriched environments with regard to time engaged in STEM activities related to block building activities in terms of age, gender, and socio-economic status (Ginsburg, Lin, Ness & Seo, 2003; Ness, 2001; Ness & Farenga, 2007).

While psychological research in STEAM concepts has become increasingly robust in the past two decades, it still remains incomplete in a number of respects. First, the growing corpus of research on spatial thinking treats the subject more in terms of a cognitive area of inquiry rather than as a crosscutting process skill. Second, resulting from these shortcomings is the paucity of discussion about spatial thinking skills in national and international STEAM standards. Third, while the literature on spatial cognition is growing, the research involves primarily investigations in which the researchers present children with predetermined tasks to complete and observe children's attempts to complete them. In short, as I have indicated in different parts of this book, the researchers of studies in spatial cognition, not the children, determine the tasks. Although the predominantly traditional model of investigation yields interesting results in the development of spatial thinking, it limits what can be observed in terms of what children do on their own and without researcher intervention.

In assessing students' engagement and the levels of complexity of structure, we have developed the Space-Architecture Coding system (henceforth, SPARC, formerly SPAGAR) which measures an individual's spatial, architectural, and engineering thinking in the everyday context (Ness, 2001; Ness & Farenga, 2007). In Table 7.1, I have included both the former SPAGAR and the revised

TABLE 7.1 The SPAGAR and SPARC coding systems

SPAGAR (2007)		SPARC (2021)	
Symmetric Relations		*Symmetric Relations*	
1	Line Symmetry	1	Reflections
2	Plane Symmetry	2	Translations
3	Rotational Symmetry	3	Rotations
4	Patterning	4	Patterning
Figural Relations		*Figural Relations*	
5	Figure Identification	5	Figural Identification
6	Shape Matching	6	Shape Matching
Direction/Location		*Direction/Location*	
7	Direction/Location	7	Navigating
Architectural Principles		8	Proportional Reasoning
8	Enclosure	*Engineering/Architectural Principles*	
9	Foundation	9	Stacking
10	Trabeated Construction	10	Enclosure
11	Posting	11	Proto-Cantilevered Construction
12	Engineering	12	Foundation
13	Proportional Reasoning	13	Posting
		14	Trabeated Construction
		15	Truss Construction
		16	Curvature Construction
		17	Complex Cantilevered Construction

SPARC coding systems so that readers will have the opportunity to appreciate the development of the categorization of attributes that may not have been noticed during the formulation stages of the SPAGAR system, but were eventually identified through several years of additional analytical inquiry of young children engaged in VCPO free play. In general, I found that children in the early years were actively engaged in more creative learning activities using three-dimensional representations, which reinforce emergent STEAM concepts. Accordingly, research has demonstrated that early exposure to STEAM activities and concepts not only helps to improve elementary students' dispositions and conceptual knowledge in STEAM (Bagiati, Yoon, Evangelou & Ngambeki, 2010; Bybee & Fuchs, 2006) but also provides opportunities for them to gain rich experiences using crosscutting process skills such as spatial thinking, problem solving, and problem posing, which serve as essential components in the overwhelming majority of STEAM experiences (Kell & Lubinski, 2013; Ness & Farenga, 2007; Sinton, Bednarz, Gersmehl, Kolvoord & Uttal, 2013; Stieff & Uttal, 2015; Uttal & Cohen, 2012).

Despite insight in studies on preschoolers' mathematical thinking, a number of issues remain understudied in the research. First, there has always been, and still remains, a greater emphasis on preschool children's arithmetic development or number concepts than on their understanding of space and form. Second, most studies use specifically-assigned tasks to examine mathematical performance. Few, if any, studies have examined preschoolers' informal mathematical thinking in the everyday context.

Third, even fewer studies have investigated the role of socio-economic (SES) status in children's mathematical thinking (Ginsburg, Pappas & Seo, 2001). Finally, based on observations of children during free play, preschoolers demonstrate evidence of basic architectural principles during their involvement in LEGO or block play. But in addition to the sorely understudied area of young children's spatial and STEAM related thinking in the everyday context, research investigating the underlying architectural principles which are manifest during preschool children's free play are almost entirely lacking.

To summarize, then, the basic problem is this: There is still a great deal to be learned about spatial and geometric thinking. Despite a number of contributions in the area (e.g. Clements, 1999), research in spatial and geometric thinking is limited in at least one important respect. It tells us very little, if anything at all, about children's spontaneous interest in, or their everyday knowledge of, space and geometry. Furthermore, there is extremely limited research that deals with the relationships between space, geometry, and architectural principles evident in preschool children's everyday activity.

For the remainder of this chapter, we will explore and identify young children's everyday spatial and geometric thinking during free play. We will also investigate underlying architectural or engineering principles inherent in preschool children's LEGO or block construction. To guide us in these investigations, I have posed the following questions:

1. What types of spatial and geometric thinking do four- and five-year-old children employ during free play?
2. What architectural principles underlie the constructions of four- and five-year-old children?
3. Which aspects of spatial, geometrical, and architectural thinking are most prominent during four- and five-year-old's free play?
4. What physical, social, environmental, or cultural conditions bring about spontaneous everyday spatial, geometric, and architectural activity?

In answering these questions, a series of approaches were used to investigate the emergent spatial abilities of several groups of preschool children. Naturalistic observation was employed as a method of examining the everyday constructive activities of four- and five-year-old children.

SPAGAR codes, which preceded SPARC, were developed using both a top-down and bottom-up approach. That is, the development of these codes evolved from examining the literature on spatial and geometric thinking and identifying specific characteristics of mathematical conceptualizations used by mathematicians themselves. At the same time, observation and analysis of video segments, in addition to hermeneutical debate—numerous discussions and considerations with other experts in diverse fields who are involved in naturalistic observation methodology—served as a type of bottom-up approach which led to the development of the codes described below. The procedure is similar to that of Ginsburg and his colleagues (Ginsburg et al., 1999, Ginsburg et al., 2001), who developed six mathematical category codes (namely, Classification, Magnitude, Enumeration, Dynamics, Pattern and Shape, and Spatial Relations) in a similar manner. With respect to this chapter, investigation was underway that reconsidered each of the 13 codes of SPAGAR (Ness, 2001; Ness & Farenga, 2007). We continue by initiating a discussion about how the initial 13 codes have been identified and examined through digital video analyses of four- to six-year-old children's block, LEGO, and plank play. This is followed by a discussion of how further analysis that was undertaken as a result of this project transformed and added to any inconsistencies, which may have been initially evident in the original coding scheme. Through this project, further analysis led to the discovery of four additional codes and the modification of three former codes—thus reaching 17 codes in total.

To begin, the 13 SPAGAR codes are now defined. Further, if a particular spatial or architectural domain contains codes, each code is defined after the domain under which it is listed. So, for example, after the Symmetric Relations domain is defined, the definitions of the three codes related to symmetry will follow—namely, Line Symmetry, Plane Symmetry, and Rotational Symmetry. The first seven codes—Line Symmetry, Plane Symmetry, Rotational Symmetry, Patterning, Figure Identification, Shape Matching, and Direction/Location—fall under Spatial and Geometric Relations, while the remaining six codes—Enclosure, Foundation, Trabeated Construction, Posting, Engineering, and Proportional Reasoning—fall under Architectural Principles.

Symmetric Relations

Various descriptions of symmetry differ considerably, and in some cases, diverge in meaning altogether. In the most general sense, the domain of Symmetric Relations is defined here as the arrangement of objects such that whatever form that these objects take on one side of an axis is mirrored on the other. This situation is an example of what is frequently referred to as bilateral symmetry. According to Hargittai and Hargittai (1994), the more generalized term for this kind of symmetry is point-group symmetry: that is, one side of a construction is a reflection or replica of the other side. In this sense, Symmetric Relations also involves balance; as described by O'Gorman (1998), balance provides both a sense of unity (in terms of aesthetics) and Firmitas, or structure. That is, it is common to associate balanced structures with symmetric ones—the notion of one side of a structure as a mirror image of the other (symmetry) is balanced by its very nature. In addition, as an architectural principle, balance and symmetry are two important attributes of a strong and stable structure. However, Symmetric Relations can take numerous other forms as well. We can see them in many examples in the everyday world. Some of the forms of symmetry that are not associated with the typical mirror image, or bilateral, definition are rotational symmetries (e.g., windmill, yin-yang), symmetries that involve repetition (see Patterning below), and even those that involve proportionate objects or figures, which are magnified by the same number.

So, given the expansiveness of symmetric relations, what kinds of symmetries do four- and five-year-old children exhibit during free play? The idea of symmetry is clearly illustrated in children's LEGO or block building, or when they use drawing tools. Through extensive observation, I have identified four types of symmetry in preschool children's free play activity: line symmetry, plane symmetry, rotational symmetry, and patterning. With *line symmetry*, involving structures in two dimensions, an object is placed (or centered) equidistant from the sides or "ends" of a larger object or structure. Centering, a form of line symmetry, refers to the placement of an object so that a structure demonstrates a symmetric appearance. It involves the aesthetics of symmetry and perhaps shows less complexity. Examples of *plane symmetry* involve structures in three dimensions, whereby one side of the structure is a mirror image of the other. *Rotational symmetry* occurs in children's constructions when an object of the structure looks as if it can be rotated around its axis, and it appears in the same position two or more times. One example of rotational symmetry would be the occurrence of a child drawing a pinwheel, a windmill, or creating a rotational object out of LEGOs or blocks.

Patterning, the fourth SPAGAR code, is defined as a type of symmetry in which the placement of a group of objects arranged in a way that demonstrates a subject-imposed, rule-governed activity or consistent relationship. The child arranges objects according to a rule, thus creating an intrinsically or extrinsically derived pattern. In addition, "space-group symmetry"—or the repetition of similar objects in line or row form—is associated with this spatial characteristic. As Hargittai and Hargittai (1994) suggest:

> Space-group symmetries are created by simple repetition of a basic motif, and describe the most economical growth and expansion patterns. Border decorations are examples of one-dimensional space-group symmetry in which a pattern can be generated through translational symmetry by repeating a motif

at equal intervals. Repetition can be achieved by a shift in direction, or it may be done by reflection, rotation or glide-reflection. Helices and spirals display one-dimensional space-group symmetries although, as a spiral staircase, they may extend to three dimensions.

(p. 81)

In accordance with Hargittai and Hargittai's findings, the forms of symmetry that I have observed among young children's spontaneous, everyday activities during free play are, for the most part, unforced and not strictly rigorous in mathematical terms.

Geometric Relations

There are two types of geometric relations in the SPAGAR coding system: Figure Identification and Shape Matching. *Figure Identification,* the fifth SPAGAR code, concerns the identification of figures, patterns, or shapes in either two or three dimensions, or awareness of their properties (e.g. circle, square, cube, and pyramid). Unlike Shape Matching (described next), with Figure Identification, the child has most likely already assimilated the structure or geometric form which has been identified. Two examples from the videotaped segments should help explain the general meaning of Figure Identification. A good deal of Figure Identification is derived from verbal evidence provided by the child.

In one segment, for example, Alejandro asks Karl for the "circle thing" in order to build a make-believe garage. Alejandro and Karl plan to use four "circle things"—that is, cylindrical blocks—in order to establish a foundation for their garage. In another segment, Les and Samantha, two three-year-old children (not part of the videotaped segments analyzed for this text), construct a large rectangle on the classroom floor out of different length rectilinear blocks. They refer to the final construction as a "big square"; although opposite sides appear parallel and create 90-degree corners, not all sides are equal in length. Nevertheless, Les and Samantha's reference to the constructed figure as a "square" demonstrates the children's command of different shapes and how the square-like features of their construction seem to stand out.

Shape Matching, the sixth SPAGAR code, concerns the use of geometric properties—size, shape, or contour—to complete rule-governed activities, such as puzzles and other similar play objects. Unlike Figure Identification, Shape Matching involves accommodation in that the child must adapt to certain geometric properties that may be imposed by the object in order to solve the task at hand.

In one videotaped segment, two children arranging puzzle pieces of two separate puzzles decide to compete to see who is quicker at putting puzzle pieces together. One child challenges the other to a race to see who can complete each individual puzzle first. It should be evident that this scenario demonstrates two children's involvement in the Shape Matching activity. Thus, the children need to adapt to the rule-governed characteristics of the two puzzles in terms of the different sizes, shapes, and contours of each of the pieces.

Direction/Location

Direction/Location, the seventh SPAGAR code, involves words, gestures, or actions relating to navigation, place, or location (e.g. over, under, behind, on top of, left, right; the building of track under a bridge). It demonstrates deliberate evidence of making navigation explicit, or a situation in which a child uses prepositions of navigation or other symbolic means in expressing geographical location. For example, one child is experimenting with a LEGO wheel and the color spectrum when the LEGO wheel spins. The LEGO wheel is constructed from a circular hub and individual rectangular LEGO pieces, each having a distinct color, attached to the side of the hub. A second child approaches the first and asks where the hubs are located. The first child verbally directs the second to the appropriate location using works like "Go right …" then "straight ahead …," followed by "into the kitchen … in the cabinet and below the counter …" In this case, navigation was clearly made explicit.

Six Architecture/Engineering Codes

The six architectural/engineering codes in the SPAGAR coding system are: Enclosure; three codes under the heading of "Supports"—Foundation, Trabeated Construction, and Posting; Engineering; and Proportional Reasoning. Children demonstrate *Enclosure*, the eighth SPAGAR code, when they create an arrangement of interlocking, touching, or continuous objects, thus forming an inner space. Enclosure can involve two-dimensional inner space, three-dimensional inner space, or structures that may be partially built to enclose (like an amphitheater model), but serve the function of covering or enclosing one or more objects.

Early studies on block play and the motives for building enclosures as opposed to other structural types tended to focus on sex differences (Erikson, 1951; Farrell, 1957; Liss, 1981). One of these studies relates to Erik Erikson's observations of young children's constructions when comparing boys with girls. In *Childhood and Society*, Erikson (1963) suggests that young girls tend to construct blocks, for the most part, as enclosures, or in an open-air fashion, whereas boys may be more inclined to construct in ways which demonstrate compactness and verticality. As we indicated in the previous chapter, this finding was corroborated by more recent research. Although this tendency among boys and girls in digital video analyses was noticeable, I have also observed boys engaged in more or less horizontal, open-space construction and some girls engaged in more compact, vertical constructions.

Within the domain of architecture/engineering are three codes that are categorized as Supports. The category of Supports is defined as a systematic arrangement of objects forming a base of a potentially large structure. The child's intention is to use the base to support a structure above it. Three types of Supports construction are evident in children's free play: Foundation, Trabeated Construction, and Posting. *Foundation*, the ninth SPAGAR code, refers to a systematic construction of objects forming the base of a potentially large structure. The intention is to create a strong base so that the structure on it remains erect. Foundation is evident when a child constructs a base for a larger structure without using post and beam (perpendicular) construction. *Trabeated Construction*, the tenth SPAGAR code, involves the use of blocks, planks, or similar objects as posts and beams to support additional levels or "floors" of a structure. Trabeated Construction is observed when a child demonstrates ideas about perpendicularity as a means of supporting a larger structure. These constructions occur, for example, when a child places four cylindrical or cubical blocks so that they are equidistant (posts), and then places long blocks horizontally (lintels) to give the appearance of post-and-lintel construction. In ensuring content validity, one of the architects who participated in our observations described Trabeated Construction as one of the most stable forms of foundation. *Posting*, the eleventh SPAGAR code, is the use of objects to support bridges, roadways, or track. Posting involves the arrangement of objects having vertical support or column-and-lintel construction. Children demonstrate posting when they build bridges, roadways, or train track from play blocks, particularly when certain blocks are used as suspensions for longer pieces of block.

Engineering, the twelfth code, describes a child demonstrating a sense of accuracy when arranging objects, or a child's skillful or artful synthesis or manipulation of objects. Engineering can involve informal or formal measurement or estimation, or the accuracy used in a construction. This can be based on length of objects or openings of enclosed structures for fitting objects. Engineering, which seems to engender the notion of precision, can also involve the drawing of figures.

Proportional Reasoning, the thirteenth SPAGAR code, occurs when the child demonstrates knowledge of the ratio of a smaller model (e.g. "toy car") to a larger one (e.g. "garage" constructed out of blocks) as being equal to the ratio between a life-size (smaller) object (e.g. car) and a larger life-size object (i.e. garage). It refers to a child's cognizance of a smaller model with respect to its placement in or near a larger one (e.g. the placement of a LEGO car inside a larger LEGO garage). Proportional Reasoning, then, deals with mathematical intuitions concerning space, without the use of a written number, when referring to the spatial, geometric, and architectural activity of four- and five-year-old children.

Current Modification to SPARC

Two specific areas of focus with respect to modification of SPAGAR concern the symmetry codes and at least two architecture/engineering codes. In rethinking the symmetry codes through hermeneutical discourse (Packer, 1989), I widened the notion of the individual's evidence of symmetry and delved deeper into specific transformations the child or older individual engages in. Accordingly, I identified specific transformations in addition to reflection (i.e., symmetry)—in particular, rotations and translations. With respect to reflection, the renaming of the *Line Symmetry* and *Plane Symmetry* codes and merging them into one code named *Reflections* was deliberated for modification. With respect to rotations, I modified the rotational symmetry code to encompass greater latitude in meaning by renaming the code *Rotations*. While Rotational Symmetry (see above) is described as occurring in children's constructions when it appears that an object in the structure can be rotated around its axis, the notion of rotation can involve greater flexibility in that it does not necessarily always involve reflection. A new code discovered under Symmetric Relations is *Translations*, which describes situations in which the child, who engages in constructive free play, demonstrates similar positioning of an object or group of objects, which are moved from one location to another.

In the architecture/engineering domain, I identified additional spatial behaviors associated with the *Engineering* code. To begin with, I considered the support codes—*Foundation, Trabeated Construction,* and *Posting*—to be more basic than the *Engineering* code and not as complex. I then considered the term "Engineering," as a code, to be too broad in terms of what might be involved in VCPO constructions and emergent spatial behaviors. Accordingly, sub-areas of *Engineering* that are under consideration as separate spatial behaviors are *Cantilever Construction*, whereby a structure contains blocks or bricks that exceed the vertical center of gravity. Another new engineering code under consideration is *Truss Construction,* which involves the making of triangles with VCPOs for supporting higher levels. A third code under investigation is *Curvature Construction,* whereby the individual designs and develops curvilinear structures from rectangular, cuboidal blocks or planks.

Thus, as a result of this study, modifications to the SPAGAR coding instrument yielded four general codes—Symmetric Relations, Figural Relations, Direction/Location, and Architectural/Engineering Relations—and the following sub-codes under consideration as a result of further analysis through hermeneutical debate: Reflections, Translations, Rotations, Patterning, Figural Identification, Shape Matching, Navigating, Proportional Reasoning, Stacking, Enclosure, Proto-Cantilevered Construction, Foundation, Posting, Trabeated Construction, Truss Construction, Curvature Construction, and Complex Cantilevered Construction—17 codes in total (two additional codes from the initial set of SPAGAR codes described above). Further analytical and hermeneutical research will help sort out and resolve any remaining inconsistencies in the revised SPARC coding instrument (see Figure 7.1).

Category		Subcategories	Levels of Complexity				
			1	2	3	4	5
Spatial Relations							
Symmetric Relations	\multicolumn{2}{l	}{The arrangement of smaller objects or the drawing of a completed figure in which both halves of the completed (or semi-completed) arrangement or figure are each other's mirror images. An object is placed (or centered) equidistant from the sides or "ends" of a larger object or structure.}					
	1) Reflections							
	2) Translations							
	3) Rotations							
	4) Patterning							
Figural Relations	\multicolumn{2}{l	}{"Figural Relations" includes Figure Identification and Shape Matching. They are complementary and inversely related in that the former has to do with objects that may be present in children's mental schema (e.g., squares and triangles), while the latter deals with the child's adjustment to newly introduced geometric properties.}					
	5) Figure Identification							
	6) Shape Matching							
Direction/ Location	\multicolumn{2}{l	}{Direction/Location: Words or actions—making navigation, place or location explicit (e.g. over-under-behind-on top of—left-right; the building of track under a bridge).}					
	7) Navigating							
	8) Proportional Reasoning							
Engineering/Architectural Principles							
Engineering/ Architectural Principles	\multicolumn{2}{l	}{This involves children's use of six general ideas that are found in both their constructions and those of architects and civil engineers.}					
	9) Stacking							
	10) Enclosure							
	11) Proto-Cantilevered Construction							
	12) Foundation							
	13) Posting							
	14) Trabeated Construction							
	15) Truss Construction							
	16) Curvature Construction							
	17) Complex Cantilevered Construction							

FIGURE 7.1 Spatial Architectural Coding (SPARC) system (formerly, the Spatial-Geometric-Architectural (SPAGAR) Categories)

So, in sum, SPARC consists of four general codes and 17 subcodes, and was developed and subsequently modified by the researchers with both a top-down and bottom-up approach (Ness, 2001; Ness, Farenga & Garofalo, 2017). The development of these codes evolved from examining the literature on spatial and geometric thinking and identifying specific characteristics of STEM conceptualizations. Observation and analysis of digital video segments of children's speech and actions provided additional data, thus contributing further to the validity and development of the coding system (Bakeman & Gottman, 1997). The content validity for the codes was additionally established by a panel of experts in the fields of architecture, science, mathematics, cognitive psychology, and linguistics. Subsequent researchers have identified other discoveries using the SPAGAR coding system (Ness, 2001). Ginsburg, Lin, Ness, and Seo (2003) found that preschool aged children exhibit strong proclivities toward activities involving patterns, shapes, and engineering and architectural relations from a cross-national perspective.

Much research referring to SPAGAR has been conducted since Ness and Farenga's (2007) further development and adjustment of the SPAGAR coding system. Johnson, Sevimli-Celik, and Al-Mansour (2013) recognized SPAGAR in terms of its importance and effectiveness with regard to child initiated and adult guided play. Coplan (2011) and Ferrara, Hirsh-Pasek, Newcombe, Golinkoff, and Lam (2011) linked the implementation of SPAGAR with the manner in which block play has consistently been considered an activity that is intrinsically associated with spatial thinking skills. Oda (2011) referred to SPAGAR to demonstrate the dichotomy between external and internal spatial representations as it relates to cognition in GIS spatial concept knowledge. In addition, Van Nes (2009) utilized SPAGAR in assessing children's spatial structuring ability and emergent number sense.

References

Andersson, K., & Gullberg, A. (2014). What is science in preschool and what do teachers have to know to empower children? *Cultural Studies of Science Education*, 9(2), 275–296.

Atit, K., Miller, D. I., Newcombe, N. S., & Uttal, D. H. (2018). Teachers' spatial skills across disciplines and education levels: Exploring nationally representative data. *Archives of Scientific Psychology*, 6(1), 130–137.

Bagiati, A., Yoon, S. Y., Evangelou, D., & Ngambeki, I. (2010). Engineering curricula in early education: Describing the landscape of open resources. *Early Childhood Research and Practice*, 12(2), 2–13.

Bakeman, R., & Gottman, J. M. (1997). *Observing interaction: An introduction to sequential analysis*. New York: Cambridge University Press.

Bybee, R. W., & Fuchs, B. (2006). Preparing the 21st century workforce: A new reform in science and technology education. *Journal of Research in Science Teaching*, 43(4), 349–352.

Clements, D. H. (1999). Geometric and spatial thinking in young children. In J. Copley (ed.), *Mathematics in the early years* (pp. 66–79). Reston, VA: NCTM Press.

Coplan, R. J. (2011). Not just "playing alone": Exploring multiple forms of nonsocial play in childhood. In A. D. Pellegrini (Ed.), *The Oxford handbook of the development of play* (pp. 185–201). New York: Oxford University Press.
Erikson, E. H. (1963). *Childhood and society* (2nd ed.). New York: Norton.
Erikson, E. H. (1951). Sex differences in the play configurations of preadolescents. *The American Journal of Orthopsychiatry*, 21, 667–692.
Farrell, M. (1957). Sex differences in block play in early childhood education. *The Journal of Educational Research*, 51(4), 279–284.
Ferrara, K., Hirsh-Pasek, K., Newcombe, N. S., Golinkoff, R. M., & Lam, W. S. (2011). Block talk: Spatial language during block play. *Mind, Brain, and Education*, 5(3), 143–151.
Ginsburg, H. P., Inoue, N., & Seo, K. H. (1999). Young children doing mathematics: Observations of everyday activities." In J. V. Copley (Ed.), *Mathematics in the early years* (pp. 88–99). Reston, VA: National Council of Teachers of Mathematics.
Ginsburg, H. P., Lin, C. L., Ness, D., & Seo, K. H. (2003). Young American and Chinese children's everyday mathematical activity. *Mathematical Thinking and Learning*, 5(4), 235–258.
Ginsburg, H. P., Pappas, S., & Seo, K. H. (2001). Everyday mathematical knowledge: Asking young children what is developmentally appropriate. In S. L. Golbeck (Ed.), *Psychological perspectives on early childhood education: Reframing dilemmas in research and practice* (pp. 181–219). Mahwah, NJ: Lawrence Erlbaum Associates.
Hargittai, I., & Hargittai, M. (1994). *Symmetry: A unifying concept*. Bolinas, CA: Shelter Publications, Inc.
Hsi, S., Linn, M. C., & Bell, J. E. (1997). The role of spatial reasoning in engineering and the design of spatial instruction. *Journal of Engineering Education*, 86(2), 151–158.
Jee, B. D., Gentner, D., Uttal, D. H., Sageman, B., Forbus, K., Manduca, C. A., Ormand, C. J., Shipley. T. F., & Tikoff, B. (2014). Drawing on experience: How domain knowledge is reflected in sketches of scientific structures and processes. *Research in Science Education*, 44(6), 859–883.
Johnson, J. E., Sevimli-Celik, S., & Al-Mansour, M. (2013). Play in early childhood education. This is a chapter. In O. N. Saracho & B. Spodek (Eds.), *Handbook of research on the education of young children* (pp. 265–274). New York, NY: Routledge.
Kell, H. J., & Lubinski, D. (2013). Spatial ability: A neglected talent in educational and occupational settings. *Roeper Review*, 35(4), 219–230.
Khine, M. S. (2017). Spatial cognition: Key to STEM success. In M. S. Khine (Ed.), *Visual-spatial ability in STEM education* (pp. 3–8). Berlin: Springer.
Liss, M. B. (1981). Patterns of toy play: An analysis of sex differences. *Sex Roles*, 7(11), 1143–1150.
McGarvey, L., Luo, L., Hawes, Z., & Spatial Reasoning Study Group (2018). Spatial skills framework for young engineers. In L. D. English, & T. Moore (Eds.), *Early engineering learning, early mathematics learning and development* (pp. 53–82). Singapore: Springer.
National Council for Geographic Education (NCGE). (2012). *Geography for life: National Geography Standards* (2nd ed.). Washington, DC: NGCE.
National Research Council (2006). *Learning to think spatially: GIS as a support system in the K-12 curriculum*. Washington, DC: National Academies Press.
Ness, D. (2001). The development of spatial thinking, emergent geometric concepts and architectural principles in the everyday context. Unpublished doctoral dissertation, Columbia University, New York.

Ness, D., & Farenga, S. J. (2007). *Knowledge under construction: The importance of play in developing children's spatial and geometric thinking*. Lanham, MD: Rowman & Littlefield Publishers.

Ness, D., & Farenga, S. J. (2016). Blocks, bricks, and planks: Relationships between affordance and visuo-spatial constructive play objects. *American Journal of Play*, 8(2), 201–227.

Ness, D., Farenga, S. J., & Garofalo, S. G. (2017). *Spatial intelligence: Why it matters from birth through the lifespan*. New York: Routledge.

Newcombe, N. S. (2010). Picture this: Increasing math and science learning by improving spatial thinking. *American Educator*, 34(2), 29–35.

Newcombe, N. S., & Shipley, T. F. (2015). Thinking about spatial thinking: New typology, new assessments. In J. S. Gero (Ed.), *Studying visual and spatial reasoning for design creativity* (pp. 179–192). New York, NY: Springer.

Newcombe, N. S., Uttal, D. H., & Sauter, M. (2013). Spatial development. In P. D. Zelazo (Ed.), *Oxford handbook of developmental psychology* (pp. 564–590). New York, NY: Oxford University Press.

Oda, K. (2011). College students' GIS spatial concept knowledge assessed by concept maps. Unpublished doctoral dissertation, Texas A&M University, College Station, Texas.

O'Gorman, J. F. (1998). *ABC of architecture*. Philadelphia, PA: University of Pennsylvania Press.

Packer, M. J. (1989). *Entering the circle: Hermeneutic investigation in psychology*. Albany, NY: SUNY Press.

Pritulsky, C., Morano, C., Odean, R., Bower, C., Hirsh-Pasek, K., & Michnick Golinkoff, R. (2020). Spatial thinking: Why it belongs in the preschool classroom. *Translational Issues in Psychological Science*, 6(3), 271–282.

Sarama, J., & Clements, D. H. (2009). *Early childhood mathematics education research: Learning trajectories for young children*. New York: Routledge.

Sinton, D. S., Bednarz, S., Gersmehl, P., Kolvoord, R., & Uttal, D. (2013). *The people's guide to spatial thinking*. Washington, DC: National Council for Geographic Education.

Stieff, M., & Uttal, D. (2015). How much can spatial training improve STEM achievement? *Educational Psychology Review*, 27(4), 607–615.

Trawick-Smith, J., Swaminathan, S., Baton, B., Danieluk, C., Marsh, S., & Szarwacki, M. (2017). Block play and mathematics learning in preschool: The effects of building complexity, peer and teacher interactions in the block area, and replica play materials. *Journal of Early Childhood Research*, 15(4), 433–448.

Uttal, D. H., & Cohen, C. A. (2012). Spatial thinking and STEM education: When, why and how? In B. Ross (Ed.), *Psychology of learning and motivation*, Vol. 57. New York, NY: Academic Press.

Uttal, D. H., Meadow, N. G., Tipton, E., Hand, L. L., Alden, A. R., Warren, C., Newcombe, N. S. (2013). The malleability of spatial skills: A meta-analysis of training studies. *Psychological Bulletin*, 139(2), 352–402. doi:10.1037/a0028446.

Uttal, D. H., Miller, D. I., Newcombe, N. S. (2013). Exploring and enhancing spatial thinking: Links to achievement in science, technology, engineering, and mathematics? *Current Directions in Psychological Science*, 22(5), 367–373.

van Nes, F. (2009). Young children's spatial structuring ability and emerging number sense Doctoral dissertation, Freudenthal Institute for Science and Mathematics Education, Universiteit Utrecht. Available from ProQuest Dissertations and Theses database (UMI No. 817613174).

8

PROMOTING STEAM PLAY WITH VCPOS

What Children Can Tell Us

It wasn't until 1954 that a team of scientists at General Electric in Schenectady, New York succeeded in making the very first synthetic diamonds. "Project Superpressure," as it was called, was an amazing collaborative effort. It demonstrated the "can do" attitude of the post-World War II era, and General Electric announced that the company was going to make diamonds. But the company stated that even if the venture was unsuccessful in making diamonds, something interesting was going to happen because high temperatures and high pressures, up to that time, were an unexplored area of chemistry (Hazen, 1999). And the company did indeed find interesting things. It is important to note that both graphite and diamond are both crystalline forms of the element carbon, and that if graphite is subjected to extreme amounts of heat and pressure, diamonds can form. The way General Electric went about this huge STEAM undertaking was to first assemble a team of scientists and engineers. They had materials engineers, they had chemists, they had physicists—STEAM experts who approached different aspects of the diamond making problem. The company had experts in electrical heating, so that carbon, the key element in diamonds, can be subjected to extremely high temperatures. Also, the company had experts in materials science and engineering for the development of super hard materials that would make it possible to make pistons that would smash into the graphite (a carbon crystalline) and subject it to higher and higher pressures.

It took several years of trials but eventually in December 1954 the first synthetic diamonds were manufactured by the team of STEAM experts at General Electric. And, in fact, within a few months the Company was producing a large number of diamonds in a commercial process. Today, diamond synthesis is a world-wide enterprise of vast proportions. Every year, more than 100 tons of synthetic diamonds are manufactured in plants throughout the world. This means

DOI: 10.4324/9781003097815-9

that number of diamonds manufactured each year is greater than all the natural gemstone diamonds that have been mined since ancient times. Many people might not consciously recognize the uses for synthetic diamonds in their everyday life. But these diamonds have changed the things that society can do and the way we live. For example, a person who wears eyeglasses can go to an optician to have a pair of eyeglasses repaired or get a new pair of eyeglasses and come out of the store a short time later, maybe an hour, with the new or fixed eyeglasses. The short time spent in the optician's store is a result of synthetic diamond technology. Currently, synthetic diamonds are so inexpensive that any small business can afford to have a synthetic diamond grinding tool to speed up the process of service and decrease waiting times. In construction, diamond saws, which are produced with synthetic diamond technology, are used with precision to remove the asphalt quietly without the use of jackhammers that make so much noise and tear up the surrounding roadways. Because cheap synthetic diamonds are now readily available, synthetic diamond equipment is used in many areas of business and industry.

There are a number of big ideas that come out of this development of synthetic diamonds. First, one important takeaway is that there has been a societal interest in, and even fascination with, diamonds since ancient times. It wasn't until 1797 when the English chemist, Smithson Tennant, realized that diamond was pure carbon and that, if heated to an extreme temperature without oxygen, it would turn into graphite, a crystalline form of carbon that is used for writing with pencils. After this discovery, chemists believed that the reverse would also be possible—that graphite, under extremely high temperatures and pressure, would become diamond. And so the impetus to produce diamonds was an obsession for chemists from the late 19th century onward, all of whom worked alone and failed to produce diamonds in their laboratories. Second, it showed that in addition to its use in jewelry, diamond had applicative power in that it could be utilized in industry, especially for cutting, and subsequently, scientists also found uses for diamond in high-tech fields. For example, high-tech companies use synthetic diamonds in the production of thermal conductors and semiconductors in the field of electronics. In other words, the push for diamond production was at once a functional endeavor and an aesthetic one. So since natural diamond was an extremely limited resource, there was a great incentive to produce synthetic diamond. And third, the success of reproducible synthetic diamond in 1954 demonstrates that this very undertaking was a team sport—that is, it truly attests to the fact that the production of synthetic diamond demanded the expertise of many STEAM professionals working collaboratively.

My point in introducing the development of synthetic diamond is to emphasize how important it is to recognize that STEAM related endeavors, which, at first may seem impossible, can actually come to fruition with ingenuity and creativity, and to note the underlying connection between STEAM professionals and young children during constructive free play. There are many parallels between young children at play and the STEAM professionals who discovered synthetic diamond. In many respects, the scientists and engineers who first produced diamonds were engaged in seemingly playful experiences as they tested and retested their attempts at diamond production. Also, through these playful experiences, these STEAM professionals at General Electric used their imagination in identifying alternative possibilities in the event a particular attempt failed. This point brings us back to the idea of play and making mistakes that we discussed in Chapters 2 and 6. Similarly, children use their imagination when they are engaged in constructive free play. A failed attempt for the child is when she builds a structure that buckles and then she finds alternative possibilities based on her experiences that will eventually prevent the structure from collapsing. As David Elkind (2007) so aptly states, "Like other human potentials, imagination and fantasy can only be fully developed through practice" (pp. 15–16). It is also worth noting that the STEAM professionals in the synthetic diamond example worked as a team. For instance, without the materials engineer, it would have been difficult for the team to produce pistons strong enough to ram the graphite. In the same manner, each child has her own experiences which contribute to the success of a structure in progress. The following excerpt highlights the role of collaborative, parallel, and competitive constructive free play of four- and five-year-old children using plastic play bricks.

> Katie comes over the block area and wants to take some "people" toys to play with. Fernando says, "No. This is our people!" Katie points out that they need to share. He finally picks out a minifigure and gives it to her. Katie then walked away seemingly satisfied. While this was going on, Gabe knocked his structure over, but said nothing and did not get upset. Ronny says, "Hey this is not bigger." Fernando replies "Yes it is!" They all resume working on their own structures, and Fernando says, "Let's do it more bigger …" as he works with Ronny and adds to his structure. Gabe says, "Huh?" Fernando repeats, "Let's do it more bigger …" and moves his structure over next to Gabe's. Gabe replies, "This is going to be very bigger than yours." Fernando goes to the block bin to retrieve more blocks and says, "Mine bigger …" as he adds some more to the top of his structure. Gabe continues to add to his, but again accidentally knocks his structure over as he tries to add a section to the top of his original structure [he does not get upset]. Fernando says, "You see? I told you … I did nothing …" Gabe says, "I will make it bigger than yours. Mine's going to be bigger than yours …" and repeats this one more time as he adds to his structure. Fernando replies, "Want to see mine? It's bigger …" they continue adding to the tops of their respective structures. Fernando picks up a block, and Gabe says, "Hey, I had that first!" Fernando replies, "No, Ronny had it first …"
>
> GABE: "Ronny had it first?"
> FERNANDO: "Yes."
> GABE: "Why you took it away from him?"

Fernando and Gabe go over to the bin to get more LEGOs. Ronny, who has been sitting next to the block bin for this whole segment, moves slightly across the floor toward Fernando's structure, which is standing about six inches away. Fernando steps over and says, "No, no Ronny … We're making robots." Ronny mumbles something about his, and Fernando says to Ronny, "Look, Ronny. Put yours next to mine …" as he actually adds it to the top of his own. By this point, he has to stand up so he can work on it. Ronny says "I want to make mine more bigger …" Fernando says, "Look Ronny. It's more bigger …" Ronny puts his hands on the tower as if he were going to take his part back so he could have his own, but Fernando convinces him to combine structures. He says, "No, no, Ronny! Look it. We are bigger." Fernando still adds more to the top. Fernando repeats, "Look. We are bigger!" Ronny is holding a LEGO, and it is unclear what he wants to do. Fernando takes the LEGO from Ronny and begins to add it to the structure himself, but accidentally breaks off a piece of the tower. Fernando says, "Uh oh …" Ronny attempts to gather the LEGOs up off the floor as Fernando plays around with the tower. Fernando takes part of the top off and asks Ronny to hold his structure. Ronny does not respond, so Fernando says, "That's okay …" and adds some more to the top.

This excerpt highlights the importance of young children's perseverance during constructive free play. In general, children who are given opportunities early in their lives to pretend play without adult interruption tend to self-regulate more than children who don't have these opportunities (Elias & Berk, 2002; Meyers & Berk, 2014). And more self-regulation leads to more perseverance and motivation when participating in a play task (Mrazek et al., 2018). An equally important finding of the above excerpt is that, like STEAM professionals, the children are learning what happens when a structure collapses and what to do to try to prevent this from happening in future constructions. From a mathematical perspective, the children are also engaged in informal measurement concepts. Fernando continues to be resolute in his objective to create something that is "more bigger" than the other children's structures. They all continue to work on their own structures, but it seems that Fernando is not one to enjoy playing alone, so he tries to enlist Gabe and create a mutual goal. Gabe, however, apparently still feeling competitive when he first noticed Fernando had created a taller structure, is committed to make a "bigger" structure than Fernando's. Gabe clearly prefers that they work on their own structures and he is focused on having a bigger structure than Fernando's. It is at this point that Fernando begins to become competitive with Gabe. Fernando is heading into direct competition with Gabe. To that end, when Ronny comes over with his structure to compare sizes, Fernando convinces him to combine both of their structures to make a really high single structure, as Fernando puts it, on top of his own. At this point, both Fernando and Gabe have to stand to work on their structures, yet they both continue undeterred as they work—and play—to be the one with the tallest structure. Ronny again retreats to become a secondary figure in the interaction as he begins to quietly work on the floor to create a new structure of his own.

In response to the above introduction, this final chapter aims to suggest ways in which researchers of early childhood and cognitive development, educational practitioners, and parents can increase their roles in providing play environments that support playful learning with VCPOs, perseverance during free play, young children's development in STEAM knowledge, and the freedom to fantasize and engage in imagination. Also, while I emphasize the parallels between young children's thinking and that of STEAM professionals, I would also underscore the important point that young children's conclusions about how the world works are intrinsically different from those of older children and adults.

How Young Children Learn STEAM

On many an occasion throughout the book, I emphasized the need for parents and practitioners to observe young children and make anecdotal records as they engage in free play, in our case, constructive free play. I mention this because it is extremely important to identify what is developmentally appropriate from the perspective of the child and not that of the adult. All too often, teachers of many different academic, artistic, and recreational disciplines as well as parents ask children to imitate what they are doing as if they think that their way is the "right" way and the children's way is "wrong." As Elkind (2007) points out, when a teacher, parent, or caregiver imposes their own version of how a child should play or what the child should do, they are, in a sense, failing to value the uniqueness and originality of what the child is doing and the child's own priorities when engaged in play.

Elkind (1998) identified three obstacles that practitioners must overcome before effective exposure to what we now call STEAM can occur. First, practitioners need to recognize the Piagetian concept that infants and young children do not think in the same way as adolescents and grown-ups do. Elkind introduces the idea that infants and young children are, in essence, new arrivals to a new country with totally different languages. Up to this point, children have preconceived notions about how the physical world works. Due to their lack of logical consistency from the adult's perspective, young children are committed to their own beliefs because they base these beliefs on their own experiences. Therefore, it is futile for the practitioner to use reflective or logical analysis to ascertain how children learn. Second, teachers and parents need to recognize the transductivity of young children's cognition. Rather than using inductive or deductive methods, transductive thinking occurs when young children relate object to object or event to event. Also, Elkind (1998) refers to Piaget and his theoretical perspective of young children's conceptions of the world when he argues that they display animism, purposivism, and phenomenalistic causality as attributes of transductive thinking. Third, as with cognition, young children's motivations are different from those of adults, and they have different priorities for the things that they wish to study or what is important to them. Young children need to first respond to fundamental environmental stimuli such as sensory learning, temporal sequencing, and spatial relationships.

Practitioners need to be aware of the developmental importance of Elkind's (1998) concerns to make meaningful use of observations and conclusions emanating from children's free play activities. My point in bringing up these obstacles is to emphasize that it is detrimental, if not harmful to children, for adults to attempt to hasten their rate of development. Rather, practitioners and parents need to recognize the diversity of children and meet the needs of each and every child. In this regard, it is perhaps most important to be aware of the cognitive propensities of young children, and how these propensities can be linked to what Vygotsky would call scientific (i.e., conventionally systematic) concepts. Doing so necessitates early childhood specialists engaging in what we discussed in the early chapters, namely, playful learning practices that respect children's prior experiences and backgrounds rather than employing a highly scripted and structured preschool STEAM curriculum.

All the examples that were provided in this book of young children at play are unmistakably related to what Perkins refers to as children's "understanding performances," which take place while the individual participates in an activity that transcends rote, mechanical procedures. Perkins provided an example of a teacher who was beginning to present the taxonomy of plants and animals to her young students. To introduce this topic, she asked her students to find a drawer full of odds and ends (e.g., pencils, paper clips, boxes of staples, etc.) and find ways to create a classification system for the drawer's contents. In Perkins' own words:

> By definition, understanding performances are activities that go beyond the rote and the routine. An understanding performance is always something of a stretch. The teacher who asked students to sort their junk drawers was calling for an understanding performance because they had never done such a thing before and had to think about it. Had they already done it five times, asking them to construct one more variant would not be much of an understanding performance.
>
> *(1998, p. 42)*

In light of our discussion of STEAM development, the processes and products that the children produce demonstrate that thinking, understanding, and experiences are associated. The preschool teacher or early elementary teacher, then, should provide young students with suggested activities that do not focus overwhelmingly on routine, but instead extend their knowledge in ways that make them understand and appreciate the novelties of what they are learning.

The teacher, in this case, observes and makes anecdotal records of what the child is doing and, in addition, understands the importance of providing activities that stretch knowledge that help in the development of STEAM concepts. An important part of implementing understanding performances is for the adult caregiver or teacher to observe children during free play and identify any STEAM related activity in which they are engaged. For example, during constructive free play with VCPOs, the teacher can use the SPARC coding system discussed in Chapter 7 to see if there are any recognizable examples of symmetric relations (e.g., reflections, rotations, translations, or patterning) in the children's constructions. In Chapter 5, I discussed the deleterious effects of having a fixed mindset in STEAM subjects and simultaneously serving as a teacher. As the Annenberg Foundation (2008) has shown, many educators at the early childhood level—as well as others in K-12 and beyond—feel uneasy when they try to approach STEAM topics such as the understanding of motion, buoyancy, magnetism, sound, and important concepts in mathematics. An educator's lack of conceptual knowledge in these areas will probably be unable to precisely evaluate the child's strengths and possible areas of improvement. But it is never too late to give up the unwarranted beliefs that relate to the fixed mindset. Moreover, evaluating the child's level of understanding involves formative assessment—such as observations of children's playful learning activities—not tests.

As discussed in Chapter 5, play forms the core of basic and complex forms of understanding. Protobehaviors are the observed subskills for basic process skills (Ness & Farenga, 2007). Parents and educational practitioners can identify these subskills by observing each child during playful learning. So, emergent mathematical, scientific, and engineering behaviors refer to subskills that signify mathematical, scientific, and engineering thinking. Constructive free play opens up possibilities for young children to actively participate in understanding performances when they act out protobehaviors such as manipulating VCPOs, recognizing and identifying patterns in their structures, identifying attributes of particular phenomena, such as color, texture, shape, and size, and making one-to-one correspondences. These are just a few examples of protobehaviors that serve as the basic components of STEAM process skills. In support of Perkins' (1998) construct of understanding performances, the young child's recognition and identification of the attributes of particular objects lead to more advanced behaviors—such as classifying, communicating, ordering, and sequencing—in later grades, but only when the parent or educator provides a conducive environment that supports this new understanding. These basic process skills can eventually be combined to form more complex process skills, such as manipulating and identifying variables, hypothesizing, and logical reasoning. Table 8.1 lists the basic process skills and complex process skills that emanate from playful learning.

The work of Perkins (1998) emanates from earlier developmental psychologists such as Lewin (1935), who maintained that young children are bound by situational limitations. According to Lewin, the nature of the objects with which

TABLE 8.1 Alignment of protobehaviors with basic process skills and basic process skills with complex process skills

Sample Protobehaviors	Sample Basic Process Skills
Manipulating objects in the physical environment	Exploring
Recognizing and identifying patterns	Observing
Identifying attributes of particular phenomena, such as color, texture, shape, size, letters, numbers	
Grouping based on attributes, such as color, texture, shape, size	Classifying
Building language concepts	Communicating
Developing an understanding of verbal or written symbolism	
Being aware of the spatial orientation of objects (high, low/right, left/next to)	Locating
Knowing the number words	Counting
Making 1–1 correspondences	
Recognizing objects in quantity or magnitude	Measuring
Recognizing large, small/near, far	

Sample Basic Process Skills	**Sample Complex Process Skills**
Communicating	Manipulating and identifying variables
Observing	
Predicting	
Classifying	
Communicating	Hypothesizing
Observing	
Predicting	
Classifying	
Communicating	Proving and reasoning (in mathematics and engineering)
Sequencing	
Measuring	
Drawing	
Communicating	Interpreting data
Classifying	
Measuring	
Observing	Comparing and contrasting
Classifying	
Measuring	
Locating	

children play serve as motivational devices that promote understanding, but this understanding can only occur when the child develops facts and conceptual knowledge about the object. When a child encounters an object like a block or brick, she may determine its properties, such as length, width, height, and weight. This particular example offers the child an understanding performance if she is encountering the object for the first time. The child will learn to identify the object with three-dimensional properties. Lewin's thesis parallels that of Gibson's theory of affordances in that when learning for the first or second time about an object, an understanding of its physical properties and possibly functionality will help the child identify the limited number of ways in which the object can be used, and thus, will influence the learning experience and the extent to which the child understands the object's purpose.

With a Vygotskyan perspective, Bruner (1966) argues in favor of the need for the educational practitioner to identify the important characteristics that impact the solution of a problem, and to make those characteristics more vivid for the child. Early childhood practitioners need to impart knowledge that demonstrates the characteristics of a problem germane to the solution. With reference to the theory of concept formation (Vygotsky, 1933/1966), early childhood practitioners who are cognizant of the young child's effortless emergent STEAM proclivities may be able to present the child with a larger framework that allows the gap between her spontaneous, everyday knowledge and formal knowledge to be bridged which will be indispensable in later grades.

An important part of making emergent STEAM content connections is providing the child with the opportunity during free play to be involved in reflection as a way to interpret real-life, three-dimensional representations in different arrangements. The teacher can do this by getting the child to interpret the representations verbally, either in speech or writing, or through two-dimensional illustrations. In preparation for STEAM in the elementary school years, the early childhood practitioner should familiarize children with a variety of perspectives on a given concept. As Stephen Farenga and I have contended (Ness & Farenga, 2007), many children involved in VCPO play may not have been exposed to the properties of the three-dimensional objects, like the unit block, brick, or plank in a way that allows them to draw conclusions through direct observation. Children without these experiences will likely be unable to conclude that the actual three-dimensional VCPO can be represented in many ways; in other words, that spatial representation is a dynamic, not static, ability that takes practice. Given the dynamism of representing objects in space, practitioners can implement verbal discourse, writing, and diagramming as possible ways to expose children to different representations of the same object. In diagramming, for example, a three-dimensional VCPO piece can be represented two-dimensionally, whereby specific symbolic referents, such as dotted lines, refer to the object's depth, or third dimension.

The big idea here is that young children should be brought into contact with these other types of discourse, which will serve to mediate between their out-of-school (or out-of-preschool) experiences and what Vygotsky would refer to as "scientific," or conventionally systematic concepts that are formally introduced in school.

Correspondence Systems in STEAM

In this section, I provide examples of STEAM concepts that young children demonstrate during free play that I would suggest early childhood educators might want to consider for each child's STEAM development. I have found these STEAM concepts to be apparent while children are actively involved in free play activities. While one of the more critical tasks of the educator is to provide ways for children to bridge the gap between spontaneous actions and scientific concepts, it is important to stress that the implementation of a formal preschool STEAM curriculum that underscores formal procedures should not be embraced. It is important, however, that the early childhood teacher facilitates each child's intellectual curiosities in the areas of STEAM. Doing so will require the teacher to dispense with the fixed mindset in STEAM subjects and develop more openness in appreciating and presenting basic STEAM concepts.

The early childhood educator's delivery of a stimulating environment will help foster a rich child-centered environment in which young children's motivation serves as a catalyst for inquisitiveness and scientific inquiry (Piaget, 1972). Accordingly, I have identified STEAM topics that have been based on young children's questions when participating in VCPO constructions. I suggest components of STEAM related correspondence systems that the early childhood specialist should convey to young children in a way that encourages their intellectual curiosities. Of course, in early childhood, many children may not understand all the content to which they are exposed. What the teacher should consider is to use these experiences that foster intellectual curiosity in a way that encourages children's intellectual development for future discourse and discovery.

Introducing STEAM Concepts and Process Skills

During VCPO play, some of the mathematical concepts that are apparent include, but are not limited to, the following: symmetry, location, classification, number concepts, mapping, measurement concepts (e.g., area, capacity, length, width, height), Euclidean geometric concepts (e.g., parallelism, perpendicularity, congruence, and similarity), and projective space. Process skills in STEAM are included as action verbs to show that STEAM inquiry is a never-ending process and not merely a product. These process skills encompass the "doing" of STEAM. Process skills in mathematical thinking include, but are not limited to, the following: problem solving, problem posing, measuring, communicating, conjecturing, proving, representing objects or ideas in different ways, locating objects or places, classifying or ordering, making comparisons that involve magnitude and comparison, and operating on numerical quantities. The following is an example of a preschool- or Kindergarten based activity which connects proto-mathematical behaviors with basic and complex process skills discussed in Table 8.1. This activity, similar to Perkins' (1998) "junk drawer" example, can occur during a daily clean-up time.

- Placing the same color LEGOs back in their bins
- Matching shapes, putting the same shapes in the same places
- Identifying the shapes of blocks when cleaning up

These spontaneous activities that serve as examples of process skills in emergent STEAM are sorting, grouping, and classifying. The groups of classifications form the foundation for identifying and recognizing patterns, and the symmetries that are identified through the repetition of patterns form relationships, which take time to develop. One's awareness of the repetition of patterns and relationships can lead to the development of the differences between correlation and causation and also the development of algebraic thinking—cognitively complex tasks that are demonstrative of higher order thinking, which is at the heart of executive functioning.

Just as there are emergent mathematical concepts, there are also emergent science concepts and physical and motor skills that are evident during block play. These concepts include, but are not limited to, the following: forces (e.g., gravity, friction), physical properties of objects, matter, mass, size, shape recognition, balance, discrimination between materials, notions of horizontal and vertical, visualizing objects from different perspectives, conservation of weight, area, and volume, representational models for investigating problems and relationships, and understanding how form and structure of materials relate to their function. Similarly, teachers should be aware of science process skills that emerge: participating in trial and error, problem solving, problem posing, inductive thinking, making predictions, building models, making observations, gathering data, manipulating tools and materials, measuring properties of materials, and classifying objects.

In their connection with STEAM, emergent science activities provide an opportunity for young children to test their theories. During play, young children are frequently experimenting (e.g., dropping, shaping, pushing, pulling, constructing) using empirical means to develop an understanding of the environments in which they live. These empirical experiences often occur at the same time as language experiences (e.g., naming something new with an invented word, identifying challenging tasks, or sharing outcomes with parents, teachers, or peers). The integration of language occurs naturally as a result of the stimulus provided by these experiences. These informal experiences provide opportunities for children to explore and express what was learned in their own language.

Children may have intuitive ideas about many laws of the physical world, and come to school with these ideas. While some of their concepts are accurate, others need to be adjusted and clarified with them. I have provided the following examples of common out-of-school, spontaneous activities that early childhood practitioners can use to introduce young children to emergent science concepts.

- Based on experience at the swing, the child realizes that the harder one pushes, the higher the swing goes. A similar activity can take place indoors when a child pushes a block or brick across the table and relates the amount of time it takes to get to the other side with the strength of the push.
- Have children experiment with medium-sized rubber balls, and have them test and retest what happens when the ball bounces. The intention is to have the child learn that the more strength one applies to the ball, the higher it will bounce.
- As early as infancy, the young child drops something from a table. In this case, the child experiences the direction the object goes. Each time this event happens, the child looks down toward the floor. The teacher can connect this concept with basic ideas about balance and gravity when the child is engaging in constructive VCPO play, and their structure collapses.
- A young child can experiment with various angles and heights when using a ramp or incline to determine the distance that objects can travel when released. When this is done a sufficient number of times the child begins to develop an understanding of the relationship between the angle of the incline and the distance the car or ball travels. When I was at the LEGOLAND California theme park with my son, who was six years old at the time, we played with the inclined ramp to determine how the LEGO-constructed car would need to be assembled—in terms of weight and structure—in order to produce the fastest car. This was a truly fascinating experience for both son and father.

During VCPO play, some of the emergent engineering concepts that are apparent seem to have a significant overlap with those in mathematics and science. Additional concepts that were not considered above include, but are not limited to, the following: tension, compression, elasticity, brittleness, plasticity, buckling, materials, post and beam, truss, cantilever, arch, column, load, structure, support, and forces—many of the terms we defined in Chapter 1. Process skills in emergent engineering thinking include most of those found in the mathematics and science examples. Some additional process skills that are found in engineering include the following: identifying stability and change, identifying causality, scaling and proportioning, and thinking spatially—most of which are included in Appendix G of the Next Generation Science Standards (NGSS Lead States, 2013).

Based on the above activities, it is also possible for the early childhood practitioner to introduce the idea of variables. Given that preschool children think differently from older children and adults, one way that the variable concept can be introduced is by identifying specific structural problems in VCPO play or by modeling specific activities, like the ones above, which demonstrate cause-and-effect situations. In these instances, it would be important for the educator or parent to connect the emergent or intuitive ideas that young children have with direct models of activities that demonstrate causality.

Recognizing Inquiry in Preschool

In Appendix A, I include inquiry indicators, similar to those in Ness and Farenga (2007) that serve as a guide to help cultivate developmentally appropriate STEAM practices for young children. This guide will help early childhood educators identify emergent STEAM concepts and processes in children of diverse backgrounds and experiences. The development and revisions of this guide were the result of observations of young children who were observed while they were involved in constructive free play activities. In the case studies throughout this book, we observed that children have a natural inclination toward inquiry based dispositions in STEAM activities. Ash and Kluger-Bell (1999) identified inquiry indicators for K-5 classrooms. In adopting their format for teaching early childhood STEAM, we have based the inquiry indicators in Appendix A on three questions (Ness & Farenga, 2007): How are the children learning?; How are the teachers supporting children in their learning?; and How does the environment support progressive STEAM development? The objective of the inquiry indicators is to provide teachers with the capability to identify what is important in the activities of young children doing STEAM inquiry and what the environment of an inquiry based early childhood classroom might look like. They are made available to teachers to help them guide their young students' learning experiences and to assist with formative assessment strategies. I strongly suggest that the practitioner modifies the indicator checklists in order to accommodate the culture and unique environment of their classroom.

In stark contrast to many early childhood programs that stress formal learning environments that pose a great deal of risk and potential harm to young children's cognitive development, the educational goals that are outlined in Appendix A are designed to complement and provide support for the sustainability of constructive free play activities and more playtime in preschools and elementary schools overall.

In a plethora of early childhood environments throughout the country, parents, teachers, and administrators are being pressured by policymakers to start formal instruction earlier and earlier. As Hirsh-Pasek, Golinkoff, Berk, and Singer (2009) make abundantly clear, this formal instruction drastically decreases the play time that used to be afforded to both young and older children, and, instead, play has been replaced with skill and drill practice and high-stakes testing. Much of this is because there are many people who are ill-informed and getting mixed signals. Countless parents are concerned that when their children enter

Kindergarten they will not possess adequate literacy skills for achievement in language and STEAM. Consequently, parents spend a good deal of money sending their children to private educational centers that provide "educational readiness" tasks for four- and five-year-olds before they enter Kindergarten.

Therefore, it is of utmost importance to counter the mandates that have taken play out of learning. Accordingly, the guide that I have provided in Appendix A is tailored to any parent or practitioner who works with young children to help recognize and support their emergent STEAM proclivities during free play. Early childhood settings must be open and friendly environments for STEAM inquiry. Children come to the preschool or early elementary grades with challenging and highly theoretical questions about the objects in their everyday environments as well as naturally-occurring events. While this book's theme is STEAM thinking through play, there are some basic priciples about how children learn that are essential for every early childhood specialist. Young children's classrooms should include environments that embrace the early childhood concept of playful learning, where children learn through active exploration, select their own activities in learning stations that support fantasy and imagination, are given time for self-expression, and are given opportunities to engage in problem solving, problem posing, and experimentation.

Additional Materials for Researchers and Practitioners

In addition to Inquiry Indicators for Early Childhood STEAM (see Appendix A), I have also created and developed two scales that can be used by both researchers and practitioners for the purpose of further study regarding the relationship between VCPO free play and STEAM development. The first scale, the Constructive Materials Play Attitude Scale (CoMPAS) (see Appendix B) will provide opportunities for researchers to further examine the role of constructive play and its impact on young children's STEAM thinking. CoMPAS is useful for many research purposes. Researchers interested in gender studies can use CoMPAS for the purpose of identifying gender roles as they relate to VCPO use as well as perceptions as to whether boys or girls would be more inclined to play with blocks, bricks, planks, or model construction systems. In addition to gender, CoMPAS can be used to measure possible SES differences as they relate to VCPO free play and STEAM cognition.

In addition to CoMPAS, the second research tool that I created for the purpose of studying young children's engagement in STEAM free play with VCPOs is the Constructive Play Materials Inventory – Parents (CPMI-P) (see Appendix C). This research tool can be used to identify parents' perceptions of their children's constructive free play time with VCPOs. This scale adds another layer to the study of young children's engagement in STEAM play with VCPOs by identifying the extent to which parents encourage constructive free play time for their children. It also can be used as a device to identify parents' beliefs and attitudes related to their children's use of specific VCPOs as well as how different VCPOs are used based on gender. In addition to general information about children, the CPMI-P tool is organized around five general areas: 1) children's frequency of VCPO activity; 2) self-regulation and time engaged in playing with VCPOs; 3) the role of parents' perceptions of brick play—given that, in Chapter 4, we learned of the high affordance of bricks; 4) social relationships and VCPO play; and 5) type of VCPOs and its potential influence on STEAM learning.

References

Annenberg Foundation (2008). *Minds of our own: Lessons from thin air*. Washington, DC: Annenberg Foundation. Retrieved from: www.learner.org/resources/series26.html#jump1.

Ash, D., & Kluger-Bell, B. (1999). Identifying inquiry in the K-5 classroom. *Foundations*, Vol. 2 (pp. 79–85). Washington, DC: National Science Foundation.

Bruner, J. (1966). *Toward a theory of instruction*. Cambridge, MA: Harvard University Press.

Elias, C. L., & Berk, L. E. (2002). Self-regulation in young children: Is there a role for sociodramatic play? *Early Childhood Research Quarterly*, 17(2), 216–238.

Elkind, D. (1998). *Educating young children in math, science, and technology*. Paper presented at the Forum on Early Childhood Science, Mathematics, and Technology Education, Washington, DC, February 6.

Elkind, D. (2007). *The power of play: How spontaneous, imaginative activities lead to happier, healthier children*. Cambridge, MA: Da Capo Lifelong Books.

Hazen, R. M. (1999). *The diamond makers*. Cambridge: Cambridge University Press.

Hirsh-Pasek, K., Golinkoff, R. M., Berk, L. E., & Singer, D. (2009). *A mandate for playful learning in preschool: Presenting the evidence*. Oxford: Oxford University Press.

Lewin, K. (1935). *A dynamic theory of personality*. New York: McGraw-Hill.

Meyers, A. B., & Berk, L. E. (2014). Make-believe play and self-regulation. In L. Brooker, M. Blaise, & E. Edwards (Eds.), *The Sage handbook of play and learning in early childhood* (pp. 43–55). Thousand Oaks, CA: Sage.

Mrazek, A. J., Ihm, E. D., Molden, D. C., Mrazek, M. D., Zedelius, C. M., & Schooler, J. W. (2018). Expanding minds: Growth mindsets of self-regulation and the influences on effort and perseverance. *Journal of Experimental Social Psychology*, 79, 164–180.

Ness, D., & Farenga, S. J. (2007). *Knowledge under construction: The importance of play in developing children's spatial and geometric thinking*. Lanham, MD: Rowman & Littlefield Publishers.

Next Generation Science Standards (NGSS) Lead States. (2013). *Next Generation Science Standards: For states, by states*. Washington, DC: The National Academies Press.

Perkins, D. (1998). What is understanding? In M. S. Wiske (Ed.), *Teaching for understanding: Linking research with practice* (pp. 39–58). San Francisco: Jossey-Bass.

Piaget, J. (1972). *Science of education and the psychology of the child* (rev. ed.). New York: Viking.

Vygotsky, L. (1933/1966). Play and its role in the psychological development of the child. In M. Cole, V. John-Steiner, S. Scribner, & E. Souberman (Eds.), *Mind in society: The development of higher psychological processes* (pp. 92–104). Cambridge, MA: Harvard University Press.

APPENDIX A: INQUIRY INDICATORS FOR EARLY CHILDHOOD STEAM

How are the Children Learning?

The observer can determine if the child demonstrates the relevant behavior. These indicators serve as evidence of the child's cognitive abilities in STEAM in terms of content, process, and product.

Children view themselves as active participants in the process of learning.

Children's Behaviors	Evident	Not Evident	Samples of the Behavior
• They are engaged in STEAM related activities.			
• They engage in the activities for almost of the entire time engaged in free play.			
• They collaborate and work cooperatively with their peers.			
• They modify ideas, take risks, and question or challenge ideas.			
• They listen to differing points of view.			

Children accept an "invitation to learn" and readily engage in the exploration process.

Children's Behaviors	Evident	Not Evident	Samples of the Behavior
• They make observations and ask questions.			
• They challenge their ideas through experimentation and testing.			

DOI: 10.4324/9781003097815-10

Children plan and carry out investigations.

Children's Behaviors	Evident	Not Evident	Samples of the Behavior
• They design a fair test as a way to try out their ideas.			
• They verify, extend, or discard ideas.			
• They conduct investigations by observing, measuring, and recording data.			

Children communicate using a variety of methods.

Children's Behaviors	Evident	Not Evident	Samples of the Behavior
• They express ideas verbally, in writing, drawing, or through modeling (e.g., block play)			
• They listen, speak, and write about STEAM related activities with parents, teachers, and peers.			
• They use the language of the processes of STEAM.			

Children propose explanations and solutions and build a store of concepts.

Children's Behaviors	Evident	Not Evident	Samples of the Behavior
• They offer explanations before, during, and after the activity is completed.			
• They classify information (what does and doesn't work).			
• They are willing to revise explanations based on observations and results.			

Children raise questions.

Children's Behaviors	Evident	Not Evident	Samples of the Behavior
• They ask questions—verbally or through actions.			
• They redefine questions to test ideas.			

Children use observations.

Children's Behaviors	Evident	Not Evident	Samples of the Behavior
• They see details, seek patterns, detect sequences and events; they notice changes, similarities, and differences.			
• They identify patterns based on previously held ideas.			
• They draw conclusions based on observations.			

How are the teachers supporting children in their learning?

Teachers model behaviors and skills.

Teachers' Behaviors	Evident	Not Evident	Samples of the Behavior
• They show children how to use new tools or materials.			
• They guide children in working independently.			
• They encourage children to question, test, and revise ideas.			

Teachers support content learning.

Teachers' Behaviors	Evident	Not Evident	Samples of the Behavior
• They help children form tentative explanations while moving toward content understanding.			
• They make tools and materials available to children that support STEAM ideas appropriate to content learning.			
• They use appropriate content terminology, as well as STEAM language.			

Teachers use multiple means of formative assessment.

Teachers' Behaviors	Evident	Not Evident	Samples of the Behavior
• They use multiple formative assessment strategies.			
• They use multiple summative assessment strategies.			
• They interact with parents to determine the child's level of out-of-school STEAM related activities.			
• They help children go to the next stage of learning with appropriate clues and prompts. (They are aware of the child's zone of proximal development.)			

Teachers act as facilitators.

Teachers' Behaviors	Evident	Not Evident	Samples of the Behavior
• They use open-ended questions that initiate investigation, observation, and thinking.			
• They listen to children's ideas, comments, and questions in order to help them develop their skills and thought processes.			

How does the Environment Support Progressive STEAM Development?

Children work in an appropriate and supportive physical environment.

Environmental Conditions	Evident	Not Evident	Description of Conditions
• The room is set up to support small-group interaction and investigation in STEAM.			
• Lists of children's questions are prominent and available for all to see.			

Environmental Conditions	Evident	Not Evident	Description of Conditions
• A variety of general supplies are available, both at desks and in easily accessed cabinets.			
• A variety of STEAM materials specific to the area being explored are easily accessible.			
• Children's work is displayed in a variety of ways in order to reflect their investigations.			

Children work in an appropriate and supportive emotional environment.

Environmental Conditions	Evident	Not Evident	Description of Conditions
• Their thinking is solicited and honored.			
• They express ideas and opinions.			
• They interact with one another and with the teacher.			
• They share information and ideas with each other—as individuals or in groups.			

Children work in a variety of configurations to encourage communication.

Environmental Conditions	Evident	Not Evident	Description of Conditions
• Work may be done individually, in pairs, small or large groups, or in whole-class situations.			
• Children respond to feedback.			

APPENDIX B: CONSTRUCTIVE MATERIALS PLAY ATTITUDE SCALE—COMPAS

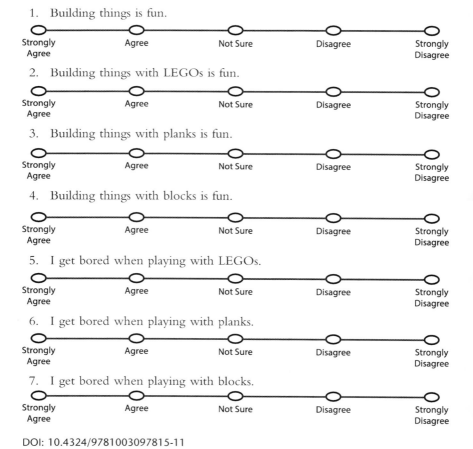

1. Building things is fun.

   Strongly Agree — Agree — Not Sure — Disagree — Strongly Disagree

2. Building things with LEGOs is fun.

   Strongly Agree — Agree — Not Sure — Disagree — Strongly Disagree

3. Building things with planks is fun.

   Strongly Agree — Agree — Not Sure — Disagree — Strongly Disagree

4. Building things with blocks is fun.

   Strongly Agree — Agree — Not Sure — Disagree — Strongly Disagree

5. I get bored when playing with LEGOs.

   Strongly Agree — Agree — Not Sure — Disagree — Strongly Disagree

6. I get bored when playing with planks.

   Strongly Agree — Agree — Not Sure — Disagree — Strongly Disagree

7. I get bored when playing with blocks.

   Strongly Agree — Agree — Not Sure — Disagree — Strongly Disagree

8. School should have more time given to building with blocks, LEGOs, and planks.

| Strongly Agree | Agree | Not Sure | Disagree | Strongly Disagree |

9. I would like to be a scientist after I leave school.

| Strongly Agree | Agree | Not Sure | Disagree | Strongly Disagree |

10. I would like to be an architect after I leave school.

| Strongly Agree | Agree | Not Sure | Disagree | Strongly Disagree |

11. Building things will help me with my school work.

| Strongly Agree | Agree | Not Sure | Disagree | Strongly Disagree |

12. I would like to build things when I leave school.

| Strongly Agree | Agree | Not Sure | Disagree | Strongly Disagree |

13. Science lessons bore me.

| Strongly Agree | Agree | Not Sure | Disagree | Strongly Disagree |

14. A job doing a lot of math would not be interesting.

| Strongly Agree | Agree | Not Sure | Disagree | Strongly Disagree |

15. I prefer to make my own structures.

| Strongly Agree | Agree | Not Sure | Disagree | Strongly Disagree |

16. Using building materials at school is a waste of time.

| Strongly Agree | Agree | Not Sure | Disagree | Strongly Disagree |

17. I prefer to follow someone else's directions when I build things.

| Strongly Agree | Agree | Not Sure | Disagree | Strongly Disagree |

18. Even when things come with directions to follow, I still like to build my own things.

| Strongly Agree | Agree | Not Sure | Disagree | Strongly Disagree |

206 Appendix B

19. I like to build with a friend.

   Strongly Agree — Agree — Not Sure — Disagree — Strongly Disagree

20. When I build, I like to create my own structures.

   Strongly Agree — Agree — Not Sure — Disagree — Strongly Disagree

21. I find it hard to think of my own designs or structures to build.

   Strongly Agree — Agree — Not Sure — Disagree — Strongly Disagree

22. Each time I play with construction materials, I build the same thing.

   Strongly Agree — Agree — Not Sure — Disagree — Strongly Disagree

23. I think playing with construction materials is an activity for boys.

   Strongly Agree — Agree — Not Sure — Disagree — Strongly Disagree

24. I think playing with construction materials is a girl's activity.

   Strongly Agree — Agree — Not Sure — Disagree — Strongly Disagree

25. Building with blocks, LEGOs, or planks is good practice for being a scientist.

   Strongly Agree — Agree — Not Sure — Disagree — Strongly Disagree

26. Building with blocks, LEGOs, or planks is good practice for being good in math.

   Strongly Agree — Agree — Not Sure — Disagree — Strongly Disagree

27. Working in the block corner is an interesting way to spend the day.

   Strongly Agree — Agree — Not Sure — Disagree — Strongly Disagree

28. I spend a lot of time playing with blocks at home.

   Strongly Agree — Agree — Not Sure — Disagree — Strongly Disagree

29. I spend a lot of time playing with LEGOs at home.

| Strongly Agree | Agree | Not Sure | Disagree | Strongly Disagree |

30. I spend a lot of time playing with planks at home.

| Strongly Agree | Agree | Not Sure | Disagree | Strongly Disagree |

APPENDIX C: CONSTRUCTIVE PLAY MATERIALS INVENTORY— PARENTS (CPMI-P)

General Information

1. Child's **Age:** My child is _____ years and _____ months old.
2. Circle **One Response:** My child is   1) male   2) female
3. School **Level:** In terms of school level, my child is
   Not attending school   In preschool   Kindergarten–Grade 2   Grades 3–5   Grades 6–8   Grades 9–12
4. Knowledge **of Play Materials I:** During free play, how would you describe "blocks"? (You may tick more than one option)

   ☐ Wooden cubes with letters and numbers on them
   ☐ Three-dimensional (i.e., 3-D) wooden pieces that have different shapes
   ☐ Any 3-D play piece
   ☐ Other
   ☐ Not sure

5. Knowledge **of Play Materials II:** During free play, how would you describe "LEGOs"? (You may check more than one option)

   ☐ Plastic pieces with the same shape that snap together
   ☐ Plastic pieces with different shapes that snap together
   ☐ Different plastic pieces with people figures that snap together
   ☐ Other
   ☐ Not sure

6. **Knowledge of Play Materials III:** During free play, how would you describe "planks"? (You may tick more than one option)
   - ☐ Small, rectangular pieces
   - ☐ Pieces that come in different shapes
   - ☐ A long piece of wood
   - ☐ Other
   - ☐ Not sure

Frequency of Activity

Directions: Circle the number (0 to 4) that best answers the questions asked in the survey.

How often:

1. Does your child play with blocks?

About Once A Day	About Once A Week	About Once A Month	About Once A Year	Never
4	3	2	1	0

2. Does your child play with LEGOs?

About Once A Day	About Once A Week	About Once A Month	About Once A Year	Never
4	3	2	1	0

3. Does your child play with planks?

About Once A Day	About Once A Week	About Once A Month	About Once A Year	Never
4	3	2	1	0

4. Do you take your child to a science museum?

About Once A Day	About Once A Week	About Once A Month	About Once A Year	Never
4	3	2	1	0

5. Do you help your child engage in construction play activities involving blocks, LEGOs, or planks?

About Once A Day	About Once A Week	About Once A Month	About Once A Year	Never
4	3	2	1	0

6. Does your child play with other children when engaged in construction play activities involving blocks, LEGOs, or planks?

About Once A Day	About Once A Week	About Once A Month	About Once A Year	Never
4	3	2	1	0

7. Do you talk with your child about math?

About Once A Day	About Once A Week	About Once A Month	About Once A Year	Never
4	3	2	1	0

8. Do you talk with your child about science?

About Once A Day	About Once A Week	About Once A Month	About Once A Year	Never
4	3	2	1	0

9. Do you talk with your child about architecture?

About Once A Day	About Once A Week	About Once A Month	About Once A Year	Never
4	3	2	1	0

10. Do you talk with your child about engineering?

About Once A Day	About Once A Week	About Once A Month	About Once A Year	Never
4	3	2	1	0

11. Do you talk with your child about computer-related technology?

About Once A Day	About Once A Week	About Once A Month	About Once A Year	Never
4	3	2	1	0

12. How often does your child

About Once A Day	About Once A Week	About Once A Month	About Once A Year	Never
4	3	2	1	0

Self-Regulation

When playing with blocks or planks, my child:

1. Is engaged with building for

1 to 5 minutes	6 to 15 minutes	16 to 30 minutes	31 to 60 minutes	More than 60 minutes
4	3	2	1	0

2. Concentrates on the foundation of the structure for

1 to 5 minutes	6 to 15 minutes	16 to 30 minutes	31 to 60 minutes	More than 60 minutes
4	3	2	1	0

3. Plays alone for

1 to 5 minutes	6 to 15 minutes	16 to 30 minutes	31 to 60 minutes	More than 60 minutes
4	3	2	1	0

4. Plays with others for

1 to 5 minutes	6 to 15 minutes	16 to 30 minutes	31 to 60 minutes	More than 60 minutes
4	3	2	1	0

5. Plays with me for

1 to 5 minutes	6 to 15 minutes	16 to 30 minutes	31 to 60 minutes	More than 60 minutes
4	3	2	1	0

When playing with LEGOs, my child:

6. Is engaged with building for

1 to 5 minutes	6 to 15 minutes	16 to 30 minutes	31 to 60 minutes	More than 60 minutes
4	3	2	1	0

7. Focuses on the foundation of the structure for

1 to 5 minutes	6 to 15 minutes	16 to 30 minutes	31 to 60 minutes	More than 60 minutes
4	3	2	1	0

8. Spends the following amount of time reading the instructions

1 to 5 minutes	6 to 15 minutes	16 to 30 minutes	31 to 60 minutes	More than 60 minutes
4	3	2	1	0

9. Plays alone for

1 to 5 minutes	6 to 15 minutes	16 to 30 minutes	31 to 60 minutes	More than 60 minutes
4	3	2	1	0

10. Plays with others for

1 to 5 minutes	6 to 15 minutes	16 to 30 minutes	31 to 60 minutes	More than 60 minutes
4	3	2	1	0

11. Plays with me for

1 to 5 minutes	6 to 15 minutes	16 to 30 minutes	31 to 60 minutes	More than 60 minutes
4	3	2	1	0

12. Spends the following amount of time constructing without the use of instructions

1 to 5 minutes	6 to 15 minutes	16 to 30 minutes	31 to 60 minutes	More than 60 minutes
4	3	2	1	0

Social Relationships

How often does your child play with constructive play materials (i.e., LEGOs, blocks, planks)

1. With mixed group?

Almost Never	Once in a While	Sometimes	Frequently	All the Time
4	3	2	1	0

2. With group of same gender?

Almost Never	Once in a While	Sometimes	Frequently	All the Time
4	3	2	1	0

3. With group of the opposite gender?

Almost Never	Once in a While	Sometimes	Frequently	All the Time
4	3	2	1	0

4. By competing with others?

Almost Never	Once in a While	Sometimes	Frequently	All the Time
4	3	2	1	0

5. By working collaboratively to build the same structure?

Almost Never	Once in a While	Sometimes	Frequently	All the Time
4	3	2	1	0

6. By working with others but constructing his/her own structure?

Almost Never	Once in a While	Sometimes	Frequently	All the Time
4	3	2	1	0

7. Independently?

Almost Never	Once in a While	Sometimes	Frequently	All the Time
4	3	2	1	0

8. With a sibling?

Almost Never	Once in a While	Sometimes	Frequently	All the Time
4	3	2	1	0

9. With a parent?

Almost Never	Once in a While	Sometimes	Frequently	All the Time
4	3	2	1	0

10. With a caretaker other than parent?

Almost Never	Once in a While	Sometimes	Frequently	All the Time
4	3	2	1	0

11. With a teacher?

Almost Never	Once in a While	Sometimes	Frequently	All the Time
4	3	2	1	0

12. With a teacher and other children?

Almost Never	Once in a While	Sometimes	Frequently	All the Time
4	3	2	1	0

Type of Material

1. My child has fun building with LEGOs.

Strongly Agree	Agree	Not Applicable	Disagree	Strongly Disagree
4	3	2	1	0

2. My child has fun building with blocks.

Strongly Agree	Agree	Not Applicable	Disagree	Strongly Disagree
4	3	2	1	0

3. My child has fun building with planks.

Strongly Agree	Agree	Not Applicable	Disagree	Strongly Disagree
4	3	2	1	0

4. My child's school should have more time given to building with blocks, LEGOs, and planks.

Strongly Agree	Agree	Not Applicable	Disagree	Strongly Disagree
4	3	2	1	0

5. My child is interested in science.

Strongly Agree	Agree	Not Applicable	Disagree	Strongly Disagree
4	3	2	1	0

6. My child is interested in architecture or engineering.

Strongly Agree	Agree	Not Applicable	Disagree	Strongly Disagree
4	3	2	1	0

7. Building things with blocks, LEGOs, or planks will help my child with school work.

Strongly Agree	Agree	Not Applicable	Disagree	Strongly Disagree
4	3	2	1	0

8. Science lessons bore my child.

Strongly Agree	Agree	Not Applicable	Disagree	Strongly Disagree
4	3	2	1	0

9. A job doing a lot of math would not be interesting for my child.

Strongly Agree	Agree	Not Applicable	Disagree	Strongly Disagree
4	3	2	1	0

10. Using building materials such as LEGOs, blocks, or planks at school is a waste of time.

Strongly Agree	Agree	Not Applicable	Disagree	Strongly Disagree
4	3	2	1	0

11. My child believes that using LEGOs, blocks, or planks is for babies.

Strongly Agree	Agree	Not Applicable	Disagree	Strongly Disagree
4	3	2	1	0

12. I prefer to follow someone else's directions when I build things.

Strongly Agree	Agree	Not Applicable	Disagree	Strongly Disagree
4	3	2	1	0

13. Even when LEGOs or blocks come with directions to follow, my child still likes to build her/his own things.

| Strongly Agree 4 | Agree 3 | Not Applicable 2 | Disagree 1 | Strongly Disagree 0 |

14. My child likes to play with blocks, LEGOs, or planks with a friend.

| Strongly Agree 4 | Agree 3 | Not Applicable 2 | Disagree 1 | Strongly Disagree 0 |

15. My child likes to create structures with LEGOs or blocks independently, even if the materials come with directions.

| Strongly Agree 4 | Agree 3 | Not Applicable 2 | Disagree 1 | Strongly Disagree 0 |

16. My child finds it hard to think of designs or structures to build without the use of directions.

| Strongly Agree 4 | Agree 3 | Not Applicable 2 | Disagree 1 | Strongly Disagree 0 |

17. Each time playing with construction materials, my child builds the same thing.

| Strongly Agree 4 | Agree 3 | Not Applicable 2 | Disagree 1 | Strongly Disagree 0 |

18. I think playing with construction materials is a girl's activity.

| Strongly Agree 4 | Agree 3 | Not Applicable 2 | Disagree 1 | Strongly Disagree 0 |

19. I think playing with construction materials is an activity for boys.

| Strongly Agree 4 | Agree 3 | Not Applicable 2 | Disagree 1 | Strongly Disagree 0 |

20. Building with blocks, LEGOs, or planks is good practice for being a scientist.

| Strongly Agree 4 | Agree 3 | Not Applicable 2 | Disagree 1 | Strongly Disagree 0 |

21. Building with blocks, LEGOs, or planks is good practice for being good in math.

Strongly Agree	Agree	Not Applicable	Disagree	Strongly Disagree
4	3	2	1	0

22. Working in the block corner is an interesting way to spend the day.

Strongly Agree	Agree	Not Applicable	Disagree	Strongly Disagree
4	3	2	1	0

23. My child spends a lot of time playing with blocks at home.

Strongly Agree	Agree	Not Applicable	Disagree	Strongly Disagree
4	3	2	1	0

24. My child spends a lot of time playing with LEGOs at home.

Strongly Agree	Agree	Not Applicable	Disagree	Strongly Disagree
4	3	2	1	0

25. My child spends a lot of time playing with planks at home.

Strongly Agree	Agree	Not Applicable	Disagree	Strongly Disagree
4	3	2	1	0

INDEX

Note: page references in *italics* refer to illustrations; those in **bold** refer to tables.

Abhau, M. 22
abstractions 98–100, *99*, 104; empirical 98, 99–100, *99*, 104; pseudo-empirical *99*, 100; reflective 98, 99–100, *99*, 104
accommodation 37–38, 39
Acquired Immune Deficiency Syndrome (AIDS) 85
adolescents 24, 54, 66, 142, 159–160, 188
aerodynamics 120, 124
affordance 3, 49, 55, 73, 90, 96–105, 107, 108, 110–111, 121, 141, 142, 192, 198
Ahearn, W. H. 79
Airfix 74
Al-Mansour, M. 181
algebra 170–171, 194
Ammann, Othmar 88
Anastasio, D. 138
anchor stone blocks 57, 62–63, 142
Anderson, T. 136–137
Andrus, B. 104
animal play 37, 45
Annenberg Project 115, 122–123, 124, 190
arches 7, 60, 144, 155, 195
architecture 1, 2, 4, 10, 12, 21, 22, 25, 39, 42, 44, 57, 61, 62, 70, 84, 109, 128, 138, 142, 146, 149, 153; architectural principles 9, 10–11, 135, 165, **172**, 173, 174, 175, **180**; architectural thinking 1, 2, 3, 13–14, 21–23, 24–25, 30, 62, 106, 138–143, 164, 171, 173; architectural toys 142–143; coding system 3, 155, 165, 171–181, **172**, **180**
Ariely, D. 108–109
Aristotle 36
arts in STEAM 4, 12
Ash, D. 196
assimilation 37–38, 39
astronomy 28, 129–130
Ausini 75
Australia 47
autism 79

Baer, Steve 84
Bagiati, A. 136
Bailey, M. 60
Baillargeon, Renee 48
Bairaktarova, D. 136
balance 98–100, **120**, 128, 147–148, 160, 162, 164, 169, 175, 194, 195
balconies 17, 153
Balfanz, R. 55–56
BanBao 75
Bar-El, D. 104
baric perceptions 64, 65, 66
Bassi, J. 160
beams 16–17, *16*, 18, 63, 144, 146, 147, *147*, 151–153, *152*, 155, 157, 159, 178, 195
beetle-in-the-box analogy 122
Bela 85

Index

Bengtsson, Ivar 67–68
Berk, L. E. 25, 30, 102, 123, 196
Bertrand, Victor and Rita 78–79
Big Elephant 86
biology 27, 41, 48, 170–171
blocks 1, 2–3, 7, 49–50, 54–68, 78–79, 98–100, *99*, 110, 123, 136–137, 139, 143–148, *147*, 153–159, *154*, *158*, 178–179, 181; double blocks 7, 8, 16, 17, 60; and gender 60–61, 160, 177; half unit blocks 7, 8; quadruple blocks 1, 7, 7, 8, 10, 14, 60, 147, *147*, 152, 153, 155, 156, 157, 158, 159
Bloom, B. 141
Boaler, J. 43, 127
Bodnar, C. A. 138
Bonnard, Pierre 89
Born, Max 62
Bradley, R. 90–91
Bransford, J. D. 115
Brett, A. 61, 143
bricks 2–3, 18–20, **21**, 28–29, 44, 49–50, 54–55, 71–86, 90, 96, 98–99, 104–111, 141, 153, 160, 198; *see also* LEGO
Brio 67–68
Brophy, S. 136–137
Brösamle, M. 142–143
Brosterman, N. 57, 61, 143
Brown, A. L. 115
Bruner, J. 192
Bühler, K. 45
Burkey, D. D. 138

Cada Bricks 75–76
cantilevers 15, *16*, 17, 128, 146, *148*, 149, 152–153, *153*, 160, 162, 163–164, *163*, **172**, 179, **180**, 195
carbon 151, 184, 185
carbon dioxide 122
cartography 2, 6–8, 10, 13, 16, 23–25, 26, 30
cartotecture 2, 25, 26, 27, 30
Casey, B. M. 160
Cattell, Raymond 60
causality 188–189, 195, 196
cause-and-effect 124, 126, 128, 196
centering 175, **180**
chemistry 28, 29, 85, 106, 170, 184–185
Chen, C. 110
Cheung, H. 146
China 47, 73, 75–77, 80, 81, 90
Choderow, N. J. 30
Choi, J. Y. 136–137

Christ, S. 137–138
Christensen, P. 13
Chu, Steven 88
City and Country School, Greenwich Village 59
classification 10, 99, 116, 169, 174, 189, **191**, 193, 194
Cobi 71, 76
Cocking, R. R. 115
cognitive development 3, 4, 48, 50, 54, 55, 60, 70, 72, 78, 91, 99, 101, 102, 103, 104–106, 109, 111, 115, 135, 141, 142, 143; and affordance 49, 73, 101; and social skills 26, 30; *see also* creativity; imagination; intuition
cognitive intrigue 102, 118
COGO 76–77
Cole, M. 46
collaborative/cooperative play 3, 18–19, 42, 44, 105, 137, 186
columns 14, 15, 16, *16*, 17, 18, 148, *148*, 152, 158, *158*, 159, 178, 195; *see also* posting
Common Core Standards 123, 170
communicating 190, **191**, 193–194
comparison/magnitude 10, 174, **191**, 193–194
competitive play 41, 42, 186–188
compression 17–18, 22–23, *23*, 55–56, 139–140, 144, 146, 154, 157, 195
concepts 122–123, *125*; development 119, 123–124, 137, 157, 172; formation 100, 130, 139, 192; scientific (systematic concepts) 139, 140, 157, 189, 192–193, 194; spontaneous 54, 124, 136, 139–140, 155–156, 157, 192
constructive free play 2–3, 4, 26, 35–50, 54–55, 88, 116, 117, 135, 142, 151, 164, 165, 169–181, 185–186, 190, 196, 197
Constructive Materials Play Attitude Scale (CoMPAS) 197, 204–207
Constructive Play Materials Inventory – Parents (CPMI-P) 197–198, 208–216
contesting 41
continuity **21**, 44, 144
Conway, John 85
cooperative/collaborative play 3, 18–19, 42, 44, 105, 137, 186
Copeland, R. 22
Coplan, R. J. 181
Cornell, Eric Allin 29
correlation 194
correspondence systems 193

Index 219

countable objects 49
Counting **191**
Courtney, R. 37
Crandall family 57
creative destruction 106–107, 141–142
creativity 4, 12, 45–46, 55, 59, 101–102, 103–104, 116, 117–118, 135, 137, 160, 172; and blocks 70, 141; and bricks 70, 141; instructions limit 29, 101–111; and planks 70, 141; promoting 28, 62, 66, 75, 78, 117; themed VCPOs limit 19, 61, 68, 102–103, 104–108, 110–111, 141; *see also* imagination
Crook, Laurence 97
cross-cultural perspectives 41, 42, 43–44, 72, 114, 181
crossbeams 152, 157
cubes 56–57, 59, 64, 65–66, 71, 72, 75, 83
Curvature Construction **172**, 179, **180**
cylinders 6, 7, 60, 64, 65, 66

Darwin, Charles 37, 41
deconstruction ("creative destruction") 106–107, 141–142
Decool 86
deflection 152–153, *153*, 154
dialectic 39–40
diamonds 184–186
Dickson, C. A. 79
digitalization 12, 66, 108
direction 25, 129, **172**, 174, 177, 179, **180**, 195
disabilities 137–138
Double Simplex 85
Duo Le Pin 86
Dweck, C. 127
dynamics 10, 174
Dyrssen, C. 22

earthquakes 63, 150–151, 158, 161
Eberle, Scott 42
ecological perspective 60, 72, 97
Edison, Thomas 62
Egan, K. 117
Einstein, Albert 62, 129
Elias, C. L. 102
Elicker, J. 136–138
Elkind, David 186, 188–189
Elkonin, Daniil B. 45
emotional development 3, 26, 45, 46, 60, 90, 91, 141, 203
empirical abstractions 98, 99–100, *99*, 104

enclosure **21**, 44, 60, 116, 144, *145*, 153–154, 164–165, **172**, 174, 177, 179, **180**
engineering 14, 18, 42, 57, 62, 70, 86–88, 90, 105, 109, 119, 126, 128, 135–168, 169, 170–171, 178, **191**, 195; coding system 171, **172**, 174, 177–178, 179, **180**; engineering principles 12, 47, 87, 90, 135, **172**, 173, 177–178, **180**; engineering thinking 3, 10–12, 18–21, **21**, 47, 106, 135–168, 171, 190, 195
Enlightenment 36
Enszer, J. A. 138
enumeration 10, 116, 174
environment 202–203
epistemology 2, 38, 44, 138
equilibrium 164
Erector 87–89, 142
Erikson, E. H. 60, 160, 177
Eschner, K. 88
Euclid 171, 193
eudaimonia 36
Euler, Leonhard 83
Evangelou, D. 136
evolutionary perspective 37, 40, 41, 46

fantasy 37, 43, 45–46, 116–117, 186, 197
Farenga, S. J. 54, 102–103, 124, 129, 181, 192, 196
Ferguson, Harry 74
Ferholt, B. 45
Ferrara, K. 181
Feynman, Richard 2, 43, 118–121, 122, 123–124, 130
Figural Relations **172**, 179, **180**
Figure Identification **172**, 174, 176, 179, **180**
figures/minifigures 28, 29, 49, 72, 75, 78, 82, 86, 100–101, 105, 107, 136
Finland 46–47
Fleer, Marilyn 47, 48–49, 129, 137
forces 118, **120**, 149–150, 157, 164, 194, 195; *see also individual forces*
Forman, G. 42–43, 61
foundations 7, 146–151, *147*, *148*, *149*, 160, 161–162, *161*, **172**, 174, 177, 179, **180**
Fragkiadaki, G. 48
free play 10, 26, 30; *see also* constructive free play
Freud, Sigmund 36–37, 45
Froebel, Friedrich 28, 42, 55–57, 58, 60, 61, 62–63, 139, 142
furniture production 84, 109–110

Gabbra people 43–44
Gadzikowski, Ann 141–142
Galidor (LEGO theme) 107–108
Gallistel, Charles 47, 48
garage, model 1, 18–20, **21**, 44, 116, 159, 176, 178
Gaskins, S. 43
Geertz, C. 10
Gelman, Rochel 47, 48
gender 55, 60–61, 72, 79, 88–90, 136, 143, 160, 177, 197–198
General Electric 184, 186
geography 24, 71, 170
geometry 21–22, 24, 28, 30, 55–56, 57, 58, 59–60, 66, 83, 84–85, **120**, 126, 137–138, 170–171, 173–174, 176–177, **180**, 193
geoscience 28–29
Germany 57, 76, 78, 80, 90
Gibson, James 96, 97, 192
Gifts, Froebelian 28, 42, 55–57, 58, 60, 61, 62–63, 139, 142
Gilbert, Alfred Carlton 87, 88, 89
Ginoulhiac, M. 142
Ginsburg, H. P. 10, 72, 110, 116, 146, 174, 181
Glenn, William 87
Gold, Z. S. 136–138
Golinkoff, R. M. 25, 30, 123, 181, 196
Gordon, J. E. 14
Gould, Stephen Jay 41
graphite 184, 185, 186
gratification 37, 40
gravity 22, 50, 55, 56, 69, 70, 100, **120**, 128, 160, 194, 195
Greenberger, G. 22
Greenfield, P. M. 144
Grey, Michael Joaquin 140
Groos, Karl 37, 40, 45
Gropius, Walter 62
grouping **191**, 194
growth mindset 43, 126–128, 129
Guanella, F. M. 61
Guba, E. G. 10
GUDI 77

Haight, W. 43
Hakkarainen, Pentti 46, 47
Hakken to Boken project 46
haptic (touch) perceptions 64, 65, 139
Hargittai, I. and M. 174–176
Hasbro 77–78
Hedegaard, M. 137

Hegel, Georg 39–40
Henricks, Thomas 42
Hewitt, K. 61
high-stakes play 103
high-stakes testing 26, 103, 104, 115, 117, 119, 135, 196
Hildebrandt, Paul 84
Hill, Patty Smith 58–59
Hillis, Danny 66, 160
Hirsch, E. S. 61, 143
Hirsh-Pasek, K. 25, 26, 30, 123, 181, 196
Hölscher, C. 142–143
horizontal construction 144, 145, 148, 151–152, 177
Hornby 74
Hornby, Frank 86–87
Howe, N. 137–138
Huizinga, Johan 37
Hulson, E. L. 60
Hunt, T. E. 110
Hussain, S. 73
hypothesizing 26, 156, 190, **191**, 194

Ibi Kindergarten, Japan 46
IKEA effect 108–110
imagination 4, 19, 26, 36, 42, 44, 45, 46, 66, 103, 104–105, 108, 109, 129, 137, 186, 188
Inhelder, B. 117
inquiry indicators 196–198, 199–203, **200–201**
instructions: absence of 35, 69, 70, 74, 98, 101, 142; with LEGO and LEGO clone toys 29, 71, 76, 91, 104–111; limit creativity and intellectual development 29, 91, 101–111
intuition 26, 36, 135, 178, 194–195, 196

Jack Stone (LEGO theme) 107–108
Japan 46, 47, 63, 73, 90, 160
Jenga Building, New York 17, 153
Jie Star 77
Johnson, B. 102–103
Johnson, D. D. 102–103
Johnson, J. E. 181
Jones, Anna Lloyd 28
Jones, I. 73
Joyce, B. A. 129

K-12 curriculum 126, 170, 190
Kamii, C. 116
Kapla planks 69–70, 159, 160–164, *161*, *162*, *163*, *164*

Kato, D. 160
Kato, Y. 116
Kazi/GBL 76, 77
Kellerman, A. M. 137–138
Ketterle, Wolfgang 29–30, 104
Keva Company 69, 70–71
Kiddicraft 72
Kilpatrick, William 58
Kindergarten 25, 28, 46, 56, 57, 58–59, 61, 142, 170, 194, 196–197
kites 119–120, **120**
Kluger-Bell, B. 196
Ko, P. 73
Kodomo project 46
Koffka, Kurt 97
Kooijman, Ellen 28–29
Kothmann, B. 138
Kove, Nicholas 74
Krafft, K. C. 102
Krathwohl, D. 141
Kre-O 71, 77–78, 80
Kristiansen, Ole Kirk 71
Kroto, Harold 88, 105

Laboratory of Comparative Human Cognition 46–47
Lam, W. S. 181
Lancy, D. F. 43
Lange, Alexandra 138–139, 140
language development 20, 24, 44, 54, 61, 73, 79, 107, 121–123, **191**, 194
LaQ 73
Lauwaert, M. 71–72
LaVelle 88–89
Le Corbusier 57
LEGO 2, 12, 14–15, 17, 28–29, 49–50, 54–55, 71–73, 91, 100–101, 104–111, 116, 128, 141, 143, 175, 177, 187, 194, 195; LEGO clones 72, 73–83, 85–86, 91, 104–111
Lele 86
Lepin 86
Lewin, K. 100, 190–192
Lilienthal, Otto and Gustav 62
Lin, C. L. 181
Lincoln, Abraham 63
lincoln logs 63
Lincoln, Y. S. 10
Lindh, J. 73
Lindqvist, Gunilla 44–45, 46, 47
line symmetry **172**, 174, 175, 179
lintels 17, 68, 69, 86–87, 151, 153, 154–155, *154*, *155*, 157–159, *158*, 178

Lithuania 47
Little Laundress set 88–89
load 14, 15, 16, 17, 18, 22, 150, 151–154, *153*, 158, 161–162, 195
location 1–2, 4, 20, **21**, 25, 44, 171, **172**, 174, 177, 179, **180**, **191**, 193
Locke, John 139
LOZ 78
Luo, T. 146

MacDonald, R. P. 79
macrosymbolic toys 49
magnitude/comparison 10, 174, **191**, 193–194
makerspaces 12, 70, 71
mapping 1, 2, 13, 21, 23–25, 30, 193
Martineau, M. 79
Marx, Karl 39–40
Maslyk, J. 128
Massachusetts Institute of Technology (MIT) 66
mathematical thinking 21–22, 79, 106, 110, 116, 126–130, 137, 156, 173, 190, 193–194
Mazdeh, S. 90
McLoyd, V. 101
measurement 10–11, 20, **21**, 44, 57, 155, 156, 186–188, **191**, 193
Meccano 27, 63, 86–89, 105, 142, 160
MegaBloks 49–50, 54–55, 71, 73, 78–79, 98
Menon, D. 128–129
metal-based construction sets 50, 54–55, 86–88, 142
Miharu Kindergarten, Japan 46
Minds of Our Own? 115
mindsets 43, 88, 126–128, 129, 190, 193
Minecraft 85, 86, 104, 105, 140
Mis Ladrillos 79
Mishra, A. A. 137–138
mistakes 43, 64, 126–127, 186
Miyakawa, Y. 116
Mochon, D. 108–109
Monash University, Melbourne 47
Montessori blocks 64–66
Montessori, Maria 58, 64
Morita, M. 160
motivation 4, 30, 100, 101, 111, 116, 129, 130, 137, 163, 187, 189, 190–192
motor skills 38, 56, 60, 64, 78, 160, 194
Msall, C. 104
museums 12, 69, 70–71, 84

National Aeronautic and Space Administration (NASA) 85, 119
National Assessment of Educational Progress 114
National Council for Geographic Education (NCGE) 170
National Research Council (NRC) 124, 126
natural sciences 26, 27, 28, 55, 85
Naudeau, S. 42–43
navigation 23–24, **172**, 177, 179, **180**
Ness, D. 102–103, 124, 143, 181, 196
Newcombe, N. S. 171, 181
Newton, Isaac 100, 128, 164
Next Generation Science Standards (NGSS) 126, 127, 170, 195
Norton, M. I. 108–109
number concepts 173, 193

Obama administration 4
object relation theory 27, 30
observation: by children 125, 129–130, **191**, 192, 194; of children in free play 10, 39, 59, 66, 121, 124, 155–156, 173–174, 189, 190
Oda, K. 181
O'Gorman, J. F. 175
Onion, Rebecca 89
ontology 2, 38, 44, 96–97, 138
Oppenheimer, J. Robert 62
order **21**, 44, 64, 65, 144
over-structuring 102, 117–118
Oxford Bricks 79–80, 82

Page, Hilary 71–72
Pajeau, Charles 66
parents 26, 90–91, 107–108, 109, 117, 124, 126, 129–130, 188–189, 190, 196–198
Park, Y. 142–143
Parkinson, J. 105
pattern 10, 28, 42, 72, 116, 118–119, 126, 129–130, **172**, 174, 175–176, 179, **180**, 190, **191**, 194
Pelletier, Marc 84
Penrose, Roger 85
Perkins, D. 119–120, 189, 190, 194
Perl, Martin 88
perpendicularity 178, 193
perseverance 4, 8, 187, 188
persistence 8, 27, 30
Pezaris, E. E. 160
Phillips, William 88
photosynthesis 122–123

physical sciences 26, 30, 69, 118
physics 16–17, 28, 70, 85, 119, 130, 139–140, 170–171
Piaget, Jean 37–39, 40, 45, 60, 61, 65, 98–99, 100, 115, 117, 141, 143, 144, 188–189
pidgins 44
piles 145, *145*, 164–165
plane symmetry **172**, 174, 175, 179
planks 3, 49–50, 54–55, 68–71, 98–99, 101, 141, 159–164, *161*, *162*, *163*, *164*
play 2, 25–26, 35–53; collaborative/cooperative play 3, 18–19, 42, 44, 105, 137, 186; cross-cultural 41, 43; social constructive play 137; sociodramatic play 41, 116, 117; solitary play 3, 42; *see also* constructive free play
Playworlds 2, 44–49, 129, 137
Plenge, Georg 62
POGO 86
point-group symmetry 174–175
Poland 76
Pollman, M. J. 61
polyhedra 28, 83, 84, 85
Ponte, I. 42–43
"Possum in the House" 48
post-and-lintel construction 17, 68–69, 151, 153, 154–155, *154*, *155*, 157–159, *158*, 178
posting 10, 14, 144, 146, **172**, 174, 177, 178, 179, **180**, 195
Pottman, H. 68–69
Pratt, Caroline 58–60
prisms 57, 60, 66, 83
problem posing 43, 115, 116, 127–128, 171–173, 193–194
problem solving 43, 64, 101, 115, 128, 137, 171–173, 193–194
process skills 115, 118–120, **120**, 124, *125*, 127, 129, 170, 172–173, 190, **191**, 193–196
Programme for International Student Assessment (PISA) study 114
"Project Superpressure" 184
proportional reasoning **172**, 174, 177, 178, 179, **180**
Proto-Cantilevered Construction **172**, 179, **180**
protobehaviors 124–125, *125*, 190, **191**
Prout, A. 13
Provenzo, E. F. 61, 143
proximity **21**, 44, 144
pseudo-empirical abstractions *99*, 100

Pursell, Carroll 89
Pythagorean theorem 67, **120**

Qman Enlighten Bricks 80
qualitative thinking 115–116
quantitative thinking 10, 49, 115–116
questions 1–2, 42–43, 118, 121, 128, 130
Quigg, Chris 85

Rai, P. 48
Rasti 79, 80
reflections **172**, 176, 179, **180**, 190
reflective abstractions 98, 99–100, 99, 104
Reich, H. L. 60
Reifel, S. 61, 143–144, 146
Reuben Hollis Fleet Science Center 70
Richardson, C. and M. 110
Richter, Friedrich Adolf 57, 62
Rittle-Johnson 116
Robertson, D. 107–108
rods 59, 64, 65, 67, 84
Roe, Anne 26–28, 30
Roeper, A. 118
roller coaster, model 7–11, 7, 9, 11, 13, 14–16, 24–25
rotational symmetry **172**, 174, 175, 179
rotations 149, **172**, 179, **180**, 190
Rowe, M. B. 119
rows 144, 145, 145
Russon, James 74

Sadler, T. D. 128–129
Salomon, G. 119–120
Salonius-Pasternak, D. 42–43
Salvadori, M. 147, 148, 150–151, 152, 153–154, 157, 159, 165
Savalli, C. 105
Scarlett, W. G. 42–43
Schiller, Friedrich 36
Science for All Americans 114
scientific concepts (systematic concepts) 139, 140, 157, 189, 192–193, 194
Scientific Playworlds 48, 49, 129
self-efficacy 121, 128–129
self-regulation 68, 103, 117–118, 121, 187, 198, 210–211
sensori-motor skills 38, 39, 40, 64–66
Seo, K. H. 181
sequencing 189, 190, **191**
seriation 65, 99
Sevimli-Celik, S. 181
Sewell, William 87

Shape Matching **172**, 174, 176–177, 179, **180**
Sheng Yuan 86
Shukur, G. 73
Silver, E. A. 128
Singer, D. 25, 30, 123, 196
Sluban 75, 81
snap bricks 18, 44, 49–50, 71, 73, 91
social constructive play 137
social skills 26, 30
socio-economic status (SES) 10, 41, 72, 79, 88, 101, 114–115, 143, 171, 173, 197
sociodramatic play 41, 116, 117
solitary play 3, 42
South Korea 77–78, 79–80, 90
Space-Architecture Coding System (SPARC) coding system 155, 165, 169–183, **172**, **180**, 190
space-group symmetry 175–176
SPAGAR Coding System 3, 171–172, **172**, 174–181, **180**
spatial thinking 3, 13, 56, 79, 83, 97–98, 101, 104–105, 110, 126, 129, 137–138, 143, 144, 165, 169–181; definition 4, 171
sponges 22–23, 23
spontaneous concepts 54, 124, 136, 139–140, 155–156, 157, 192
spools 66–67
squares 58, 81, 83, 84, 155, 176, **180**
stability 15, 98, **120**, 147–149, 148, 149, 150–151, 195
stacking 4, 28, 68, 70, 164–165, **172**, 179, **180**
Stannard, L. 73
Star Diamond 81
Star Wars 85, 86, 102–103, 105, 106, 108
STEAM (science, technology, engineering, arts, and mathematics) 4, 12, 114–116; coding STEAM related behaviors 143, 146, 169–181, **172**, **180**; and language 121–123, **191**, 194; negative attitudes about 127, 190; protobehaviors 124–125, 125, 190, **191**; STEAM professionals 26, 27–28, 87–88, 109–110, 116, 146–165, 184–186, 188; women in 28–29, 89–90
steel 23, 151, 152–153
STEM 4, 12, 48, 89–90, 114, 126, 127, 136, 137, 138, 141, 164
STEMosphere 71
stereometry 57
Stern, C. 110

Stevin, Simon 164
Stickle Bricks 81
Stiles, J. 110
structuralism 37–39
structure/structuring 13, 14–16, 181
Sullivan, J. 106
support (architectural) 7–9, 7, *9*, 10–11, 177, 178, 179, 195; *see also* foundations; posting
Sutherland, Ivan 62
Sutton-Smith, Brian 41–42, 91
Swan, C. 106–107, 141
Sweden 44, 47, 67–68
symmetry 61, 118, 152, 162, 169, **172**, 174–176, 179, **180**, 193; line symmetry **172**, 174, 175, 179; plane symmetry **172**, 174, 175, 179; point-group symmetry 174–175; rotational symmetry **172**, 174, 175, 179; space-group symmetry 175–176

tacit dialoguing 121, 128
Tacoma Narrows Bridge 150
Taipei, Taiwan 18, 19, 44
teamwork 3, 47, 184–186
technological thinking 3, 18, 30, 90, 126–130
Tennant, Smithson 185
tension 16, 17–18, 22, *23*, 55–56, 139–140, 144, 146, 157, 195
Tente 81–82
themed VCPOs limit creativity and cognitive development 19, 61, 68–69, 88, 91, 96, 102–103, 104–108, 110–111, 141
Thorndike, Edward L. 58, 60
three-dimensional: forms 28, 42, 56, 60, 66, 83, 85, 171, 175–176, 192; space **21**; *see also* Gifts, Froebelian
Tian, M. 146
Tinkertoys 63, 66–67, 84, 160
tool use 12, 39–40, 55
towers 10, 12, 14–15, 17, 18, 60, 63, 64–65, 78, 145, *145*, 149, 161, 187
trabeated construction 17, 144, 155, 158, **172**, 174, 177, 178, 179, **180**
transductivity 188–189
translations **172**, 175–176, 179, **180**, 190
Trawick-Smith, J. 105, 110
Trends in International Mathematics and Science Study (TIMSS) 114
triangles 58, 66, 67, 73, 81, 84, **120**, 121, 179, **180**

triangular prisms 57, 60, 66
trinomial cubes 64, 65–66
truss construction **172**, 179, **180**, 195
two-dimensional: forms 55–56, 83, 175, 176, 192; space **21**, 177

uncountable objects 49
Uttal, D. 104

valence 97
van der Bruggen, Tom 69
van Nes, F. 181
variables 103, 151, 190, **191**, 195–196
Verdine, B. N. 73, 79
vertical construction 15, 144, 145, 147, 148, 177
visuospatial constructive play objects (VCPOs), definitions 4, 49–50, 54–55
volume 20, **21**, 44, 64, 118, **120**, 194
Vygotsky, Lev 39–40, 44–45, 100, 115, 117, 124, 139, 140, 155–156, 157, 189, 192–193

walls 152, 153–154, 155, 157, 158, 159, 162
Wange 82
weight 22, 64, 66, **120**, 148–149, *149*, 161–162, 192, 194
Wieman, Carl 29
wind 15, 69, 148, 148–150, *149*, 154, 158, 161
Winner 82
Withagen, R. 97
Wittgenstein, Ludwig 122
Wolfgang, C. 73
Woma 82–83
Worsley, M. 104
Wright, Frank Lloyd 28, 57, 61, 63, 163
Wynn, Karen 48

Xinh 86
Xipoo 83
Xu, X. 110

Yang, T. 110

Zhang, X. 110
Zinguer, T. 142
Zome 83–85
ZOOB (Zoology, Ontology, Ontogeny, and Botany) system 140

Printed in the United States
by Baker & Taylor Publisher Services